WINE TALK

WINE TALK

BY

FRANK J. PRIAL

WINE COLUMNIST FOR

The New York Times

Times
BOOKS

Published by TIMES BOOKS, a division
of Quadrangle/The New York Times Book Co., Inc.
Three Park Avenue, New York, N.Y. 10016.

Published simultaneously in Canada by
Fitzhenry & Whiteside, Ltd., Toronto.

DESIGNED BY VINCENT TORRE

Library of Congress Cataloging in Publication Data

Prial, Frank J
    Wine talk.

    Columns from the New York Times.
    1. Wine and wine making. I. Title.
TP548.P739   641.2′2′08   78-58165
ISBN: 0-8129-0793-0

Manufactured in the United States of America

To Jeanne

ACKNOWLEDGMENTS

My thanks to the people of *The New York Times* who have worked with me on "Wine Talk": Charlotte Curtis, who was present at the birth; Joan Whitman and Annette Grant, the most patient of editors, and A. M. Rosenthal, the executive editor who started the whole thing and who has been strongly supportive ever since.

Also to the people in the wine world who have shared generously with me their knowledge and experience, among them: Alexis Bespaloff, Gerald Asher, both Peter Sichels, Alexis Lichine, and Abdallah Simon.

CONTENTS

Contents

Contents

INTRODUCTION

WHAT FASCINATES ME the most about the world of wine is the people who inhabit it. I suppose that ultimately that's true in any field of endeavor. You will meet many of the wine people I have encountered over the years in these pages and I think you will find them interesting too.

I must confess I have an ulterior motive in writing about the people who intrigue me in the world of wine. I want to get them down on paper because I fear we may not see their like again.

As wine becomes a bigger and more aggressive business, it becomes more and more the province of bankers and marketing men. Even now, the men in the boardrooms can be faintly patronizing about the crusty farmers who grow the grapes and make the wine as well as the often donnish experts who talk about obscure vintages, can tell a wine by its taste and aroma but who couldn't sell a case if their life depended on it. The businessmen call the rest of the wine crowd "cork-sniffers."

Fortunately—for them and for us—most of the wine people you will encounter in this book are both cork-sniffers and good business people: August Sebastiani, who almost single-handedly transformed an obscure winery in California's Sonoma Valley into one of the largest and most successful in the nation; Serena Sutcliffe, one of the first women Masters of Wine and a successful saleswoman and broker at the same time; and Alexis Lichine, who is probably the dean of cork-sniffers but who also practically created the system by which wine is distributed and sold in this country.

There are others—less prominent, perhaps, but equally interesting —such as Albert Ricciuti, a retired United States Army sergeant who returned to France twenty years after World War II, married a girl he had met briefly two decades earlier, and now runs a thriving champagne business. Then there is . . . but you can find them yourself.

There is no particular order to these essays and profiles. An attempt has been made to intersperse practical advice with lighter topics, to avoid bunching stories about France or Italy or California. But it is a book to dip into, to start in the middle or at the end. All these stories were fun to write. I hope you have as good a time reading them.

Frank J. Prial

WINE TALK

The Best Bottle

WHEN the talk turns to wine, I can usually hold my own. But there is one game of wine one-upmanship that is always difficult to play: that business about the best bottle.

It starts off innocently enough with a story about a trip or a dinner. "They served us the 1955 so-and-so and, really, it was the best bottle of wine I've ever had."

Someone else picks it up. "Oh, the '55? We had the '29 in Paris last year." And so it goes. Eventually, it's my turn. "I'll bet you've had some fantastic wines," someone prompts.

True. But which was the best? There have been some extraordinary wines. There was the 1870 Château Mouton Rothschild at a dinner at Mouton just last October—and there was the 1916 that preceded it and the 1921 Château d'Yquem that followed it, all at the same meal.

There were, a couple of years ago an Ay, in the Champagne region, two bottles of the 1914 Bollinger. They had a slight patina of age and an unforgettable mellowness, but were as fresh and lively as a 1970 bottle.

There was a 1943 Musigny, made from pre-*phylloxera* vines. There was that 1958 Cabernet Sauvignon in San Francisco a year or two back and the extraordinary 1935 Simi Zinfandel we had at the winery in Healdsburg just a few months ago.

Should I—could I—pick one of these as the best? It would mean leaving out a couple of memorable Trockenbeerenauslese, the rarest of all German wines, including a 1959 from the Bernkasteler Doktor Vineyard, opened in the cellars of Karl Lauerburg, one of the vineyard owners, in fall, 1976.

It would mean, too, omitting a superb 1945 Château Haut-Brion savored in Bordeaux five years ago, and it would require ignoring a great panoply of younger but already magnificent wines—such as a Bonnes-Mares from the vineyard of Comte de Voguë or a Chambolle-Musigny, Les Charmes, from the Grivelet vineyard, both wines from the 1966 vintage.

The easiest way out, of course, would be to pick one of these wines—any one—build it up a bit, say it was undoubtedly the greatest and let it go at that. But it wouldn't be the truth. The correct answer should be: none of the above.

Wine drinking is not a sterile, academic business of vineyard's names and vintages and esoteric trappings: proper glasses, optimum temperatures, and all that. Any professional can recall wines that showed poorly in tastings only to come into their own, with great style, at the lunch or dinner that followed the serious sniffing and sipping.

Caught up in a game of "best bottle," how could I admit that one of the most memorable of all for me was a jug of Almadén Mountain Chablis shared one warm Sunday afternoon, in 1954, with four other sailors on the Coast Guard cutter *McLane*.

We had come in from a wearing, pounding patrol and were tied up at our regular berth at Aberdeen, Washington on the coast southwest of Seattle. Most of the crew was on liberty but the cook had prepared a lovely batch of fried rabbit for those of us still on board.

It was our first decent meal in days. Not having the ship bucking under us was a treat in itself, but the combination of the warm spring breeze, the view of the river and the fir forests beyond, the rabbit, and that cold wine made for an afternoon few gourmet chefs could surpass.

The fact that that jug was illegal probably made the meal even more interesting. But we were in port and there was no one around. . . .

There is a bottle of wine that, with luck, I get to sample every year or so and, each time I do, I swear it is the pinnacle of the winemaking art. It isn't, of course, but don't argue. It is that bottle of the house Sancerre that begins every meal I enjoy at Chez Allard, still one of the all-time great bistros of Paris.

I have no idea where Allard gets his Sancerre. The label says simply that the wine is bottled for Allard, 41 rue St. André des Arts, and that it is of a very recent vintage.

Is it the best of all Sancerres? Would it triumph in a blind tasting, with all those white coats and clipboards and spittoons for the judges? Who knows? Who cares? It's a well-made wine. It is served young and fresh and cold and it is used to wash down some of the finest seafood in Paris in one of the friendliest restaurants in the world.

Of the famous bottles I mentioned, that 1943 Musigny stands out. So do the two 1914 Bollingers. The Musigny was a gift from Roger Chauveron when he closed up the Café Chauveron on East 53rd Street. Drinking it a year or so later it brought back memories of magical dinners at Chauveron at its peak as well as long afternoons spent in the deserted restaurant listening to Chauveron tell stories about the restaurant business in Paris in his boyhood, only a few of which ever found their way into the profile of him I later wrote.

The Bollinger? It was great Champagne, of course. But who could sip it looking out over the rolling vineyards leading down to the Marne without thinking of that fateful year in which it was made— 1914? That's the sort of thing that makes a bottle memorable.

That 1966 Bonnes-Mares was excellent, but I remember even more a tasting of Bonnes-Mares in Nuits-St.-Georges in December, 1975. I had driven down from Paris to spend a week in the Beaujolais country. I was irritated because the schedule left no time before leaving Paris to see a three-gallery show of pictures by an artist I greatly admire, Bernard Cathelin.

MISE AU DOMAINE

MOREY SAINT-DENIS
APPELLATION MOREY SAINT-DENIS CONTROLÉE

1970

DOMAINE DUJAC
S.C.E. SEYSSES PÈRE & FILS   PROPRIÉTAIRE A MOREY - ST. DENIS (COTE D'OR)

Driving back north, I had a choice of bypassing Burgundy and going straight through to Paris to see the Cathelin show, or of stopping off in Burgundy to visit Jacques Seysses, the young genius whose Domaine Dujac I knew was producing some of the finest wines in Burgundy.

I chose the Domaine Dujac and called Jacques from Villefranche. He promised to set up an interesting tasting. After searching in a cold, driving rain, I located the Seysses' home, upstairs over an old cellar in the center of Nuits-St.-Georges. To my astonishment, I found myself being welcomed into a magnificent modern home, where I was completely surrounded by paintings by Bernard Cathelin. "Oh," said Mr. Seysses, "but he was the best man at our wedding."

We tasted every Domaine Dujac Bonnes-Mares since the first in 1969. They are extremely fine wines but to drink them among the Cathelins made them even more extraordinary for me.

The finest bottle? Perhaps it was a huge *fiasco* of Chianti we had one day in a vast *trattoria* in Florence. It had been a long trip; there had been a number of dinners in private homes and in elegant restaurants. But nothing could compare with the bustle, the noise, the friendliness of that *trattoria*. The jug of wine came without having been requested. It was placed in the center of the table already one third empty. As we ate, we drank. When the meal was over, the waiter squinted at the bottle with a practiced eye and estimated how much we had drunk. It was added to our bill. It came to about $2. Not a great wine, but certainly a memorable bottle.

People often say: "I had this wonderful little wine at an outdoor place in Capri. It was marvelous. But when I finally located a bottle of it here, it tasted awful."

Of course, it could have been handled poorly on the long and bumpy trip from wherever it was made to where it was drunk. Some wines literally do not travel. Memories are different. Every time we look back on a trip to, say, Capri, the sky is brighter, the water bluer, the girls more beautiful, and the wine, well, the wine seems better, too.

Few other things are so dependent on place and time and mood for their impact as wine. Oh, it can be a solitary pleasure. Gulbenkian, the millionaire, once said a perfect dinner required two people: himself and a good maître d'hôtel. I myself recall staying on at a French country house after the crowd had left and eating lunch alone in the 12th century refectory. One day for lunch the housekeeper brought out a 1966 Château Pouget, a fourth growths Margaux, little known in this country. Dining alone at that place at that time, the Pouget seemed without question to be the best bottle of wine in the world.

Once Baron Philippe de Rothschild was asked about the best bottle he had ever tasted. "It was a Mouton, of course," he replied. Then, he sat back, smiled and looked off in the distance. "It was right here in this room," he began. "It was a brilliant evening. . . ." It was ten minutes before he got around to the wine and I forget now what vintage it was. The people and the talk made the wine what it was.

In truth, it really is almost impossible to single out a "best" bottle. But then, it would be wrong to be doctrinaire about the matter—which makes wine such a fascinating interest. That best bottle? Who knows? It may be the one we open tonight.

A Red-Wine Cellar

A FELLOW I KNOW in Ohio built himself a new house a few years back. Wanting the best, he acceded readily to a suggestion from his architect that he include a wine cellar—even though he was hardly a wine enthusiast. As soon as the cellar was finished, he filled it with bottles of wine—red and white.

Last time I checked, none of them had been drunk. It was there for show. It was as if the man had ordered six yards of books to fill some new shelves.

Wine appeals to all the senses: its color to the eyes, its bouquet to the nose, its taste to the palate. There is a theory that people clink glasses so that even the one remaining sense, hearing, can be included. But wine appeals to another urge—the collector's instinct. The idea of maintaining a wine cellar is irresistible, it seems, to anyone who has ever drunk a bottle or two. Apartment dwellers who have known only terraces most of their lives, speak lovingly of their "wine cellar."

The Ohio man with his impressive display—filled with what is by now probably undrinkable wine—is an extreme case. Although I'm told there are magnificent cellars in Texas and Southern California, assembled by speculators or dilettantes, that are never touched.

WINE TALK

Most wine lovers are happy knowing they have a few cases of something they like stashed in a hall closet or under the kitchen sink. More often than not, it is a wine to be drunk in the next year or so—more likely in the next couple of weeks. Some connoisseurs shrug off the idea of a wine cellar and refuse to "lay down" wine. A case of 1975 Bordeaux, they reason, costs, say, $120 now (1978). The wine will be ready to drink in a minimum of five years. Then the same wine, may cost $180. But storage has its hazards, unless it is an expensive temperature-controlled cellar.

But suppose the wine was poorly stored? Perhaps before it was purchased? One bad bottle could wipe out that nice little inflation hedge. Then, too, the $120 is tied up for five years. Even a savings account is a better investment. There is also the very strong possibility that the bottom will fall out of the market, as it regularly does. An unusually large number of people, some of them very knowledgeable in wine, took a bath on 1970, 1971, and 1972 Bordeaux, when the market collapsed in 1973 and 1974. Famous names such as Château Beychevelle 1970 dropped down below $4 a bottle retail, far less than the importers had paid for them at the height of the frenzy a few years earlier. It could happen again.

Having said all that, it is safe to assume that a lot of people still want to build themselves a wine collection. For them, then, what follows may be of service. To simplify things we will talk only about reds in this piece and no "cellar" will cost more than $500.

Wine drinkers love to talk about their "everyday" wine, implying, of course, the existence somewhere of some very special wines. Everyday wines once meant jug wines, sweet and boring. Most recently, taste and technology have decreed differently.

Tastes particularly have changed. Many Americans have developed their palates to the point where they can no longer accept sugary, shapeless jug red wine. To counter that trend, the wineries, especially in California, have produced new lines of wines that are relatively inexpensive but closer to the great wines of California and Europe than the old jug wines ever were.

In some cases these wines are second labels of famous vintners. Inglenook's Navalle line of wines is an example; so is Sebastiani's line of Mountain Varietals. Robert Mondavi's Table Red is another. One of my favorites is Fetzer Vineyard's Mendocino Premium Red, an increasingly popular item in good wine shops at about $2.25 a bottle. Let's put a case in our imaginary cellar: $27.

No cellar should be without Beaujolais, and the 1976 vintage in Beaujolais was one of the best. Burgundy firms such as Latour and

Jadot all have good Beaujolais, but do not hesitate to try lesser or unknown labels in the 1976 vintage, providing the price is right—under $4. A case then, at $3.50: $42.

Bundles are spent promoting certain name-brand regional Bordeaux wines: Mouton-Cadet, Grande Marque, and Pontet Latour are examples. These are simple, well-made wines blended for consistency, made in quantity, and backed by powerful marketing campaigns. They cut through the confusion of wine buying by offering an unvarying style and a label that eschews the confusion of a château-bottled product. For newcomers to this kind of wine—dry red Bordeaux—the brand-name regionals are a good choice. But not for our sample cellar.

In any given year, except the very worst in Bordeaux, there are at least a few good wines produced. More than a few actually—a lot. Some vintages are overshadowed by others: 1971 by 1970, 1967 by 1966, and now, to some extent, 1973 and 1974 by 1975.

There is a great demand for 1975 Bordeaux at the moment. In truth, the wine received inordinately high praise when the harvest was over. Dealers everywhere say that customers are demanding the 1975's and refusing earlier vintages. What a pity. The 1973's are perfect for drinking right now (1978); the 1974's just appearing on the market are lesser wines but most palatable, while the 1975's are still many years from their peak. To drink them now would be a tragedy —except for the very cheapest which have little or no staying power.

Accordingly, we will add to our little cellar a case of a good 1973 Bordeaux, in this case Château Prieuré-Lichine at about $70. This is a deep velvety wine with true Margaux elegance. Margaux is the *commune* in which the vineyards are located.

At the same time, succumbing to the 1975 rush, we will look around for something not entirely outlandish. This is the wine we will "lay down" for five years and hope for the best. My choice: Château Cos d'Estournel, one of the finest properties in the *commune* of St.-Estèphe. The Cos is a long-lived wine that should begin to pay dividends, if properly kept, around 1983. Cost for a case now, around $75.

To show that you are not just a Johnny-come-lately to wine, it is nice to be able to pull out an older bottle from time to time. Recently, wandering into a shop in New York, I came across the 1967 Château l'Angelus—a highly respected St.-Emilion—at $11 a magnum or $66 a case. As I said, 1967 was a year overshadowed by 1966, one of the great vintages. True, '67 was a far lesser product, but it has fooled quite a few people. There is not much 1967 around now but those that are, if they have been cared for, are fine wines. Let's just assume that we can all get that same l'Angelus, even though the merchant told me he had only eight cases. We'll add it to our cache.

It is a bit premature for the 1976 Burgundies and some of the years preceding 1976 were extremely chancy. One bottle can be good, the next terrible. We will go back in time to 1971, another fine year, and assume we can find a few good bottles still around. We'll choose three bottles of Chambertin-Clos de Bèze, from one of the truly great vineyards of the world, for which we will gladly pay $12 a bottle or $36. These, by the way, are to be consumed fairly soon, as should be the l'Angelus.

Rather than a Rhône Valley wine, we are going to choose a good Barolo, from the 1971 or 1970 vintages. Calissano, Bosca, and Borgogno, are well-known names. It is possible to find good Barolos for $4 a bottle or $48. They are among the least-known of the world's fine wines.

A fine Rioja from Spain is next on our list. These wines, made in the Bordeaux style are still incredible bargains. Get some now because the producers warn that in the new Spain, inflation is striving mightily to catch up with the rest of Western Europe. Marqués de Murrieta, Marqués de Riscal, Rioja Vega, and Bodegas Bilbainas are some prominent shippers. Sometimes these wines are available at under $3 or about $32 a case. Don't worry too much about vintage unless they seem suspiciously old. One case of Rioja, let's say $36.

Finally a few California wines. Californians would say we have left the best to last. No question. We start with a case of Stag's Leap Gamay Beaujolais. At $3.50, or $42 a case, this is one of the bargains in the premium wine category. Dark, rich, fruity, it is like no other Gamay anywhere. One case. For Cabernet Sauvignon, Sonoma Vineyards 1974 at under $4, or about $45 a case is right for us.

And, doubling up for the first time, some Sebastiani Vineyards Proprietor Vintage 1968 Cabernet, which is available in some good stores. This wine, almost 10 years old, sells for about $7. Two bottles brings us to exactly $501.

The only thing I'm sorry we left out was the 1973 Château Mouton Rothschild, the one with the great Picasso label to celebrate the year Mouton was made a first growth in Bordeaux. At about $15 a bottle, or $170 a case, it is a bit high for us here, but what a great addition to any cellar.

... And a White

A WHITE WINE CELLAR—is there such a thing? One certainly would think so, what with the current white wine craze all across the country. But that craze is limited, by and large, to newcomers to wine, most of whom are years away from establishing cellars of their own.

Experienced wine drinkers are usually red-wine drinkers with only occasional forays into the whites, for special meals and special occasions. Connoisseurs will gladly show you their old clarets and great Burgundies. Often they will completely overlook their white wines.

The exceptions are usually rare old Sauternes, the great wines of the Rhine and Mosel, and, for California enthusiasts, the powerful Chardonnays of vineyards such as Freemark Abbey and David Bruce.

Most white wines are uncomplicated, utilitarian wines that go well with fish. Beyond that, they hold little interest for the serious wine drinker. He keeps a case or two of Mâcon Blanc around; drinks it up fairly quickly and gets another. And that's it.

Still, there are some extraordinary surprises to be found in white-wine bottles. The range is quite remarkable, from the dry, fruity wines of Italy such as Verdicchio and Est! Est! Est! to the spicy Gewürztraminers of Alsace to the clean, white jug wines of California, there is enough to enrapture even the most dedicated red wine fan—at least once in a while.

As we did with the reds, we will put together an imaginary $500 cellar of whites with perhaps a few *rosés* added for a touch of color.

Let's start with a basic white wine. To my taste, this is one area where the Californians and the New Yorkers still have some distance to travel. They have, so far, been unable to come up with a basic white wine to compare with that simple Mâcon Blanc mentioned above. So for the foundations of our little collection, two cases of a Mâcon or Mâcon-Lugny, Lugny being an area within the Mâcon region of France, which is just south of Burgundy and just north of Beaujolais.

By law, these wines must be 100 percent Chardonnay. If they are young—and never buy them any other way—they should be crisp and fresh and brilliant in color and they should sell for $3.50 a bottle or less (1978). Now and then it is possible to find a good one for $2.50. Let's say $3 a bottle or $72 for our two cases.

If the price of these wines climbs much higher, and we keep hearing that it will, the relationship to the California wines will no longer apply. While the Californians do not do much with inexpensive wines, they are now making some extremely good Chardonnays in the $3.75 to $4.50 range. Sebastiani and Sonoma Vineyards both have Chardonnays in this range. Two different styles, but two good wines.

One note: resist whatever temptation you might have to buy Pouilly-Fuissé. Only an expert can tell most Pouilly-Fuissé from Mâcon Blanc, usually because there is no difference. Some of the very best Pouilly-Fuissés are richer than the Mâcons, but the price difference is ridiculous. Some Pouilly-Fuissés are going for $8 a bottle, simply because the wine has become fashionable in this country in recent years and demand for it is high.

The greatest of all white Burgundies is generally conceded to be Le Montrachet, of which someone once said it is "to be drunk on one's knees with head bared." Only about 1,000 cases are made even in a good year, so the price of this extraordinary wine is very high: $30 a bottle or more.

Still it would be a shame not to have some hint of what greatness in white wine is all about. Let's choose a few bottles from some of the nearby vineyards, specifically the Bâtard-Montrachet, an intense, powerful wine with great elegance and a subtle, smoky taste that is unforgettable. At about $17 a bottle, two bottles of this wine, from a shipper such as Joseph Drouhin, is all we can afford: $34.

As a substitute, we might consider a great Meursault, such as Les Perrières, a softer, rounder wine than the Montrachets, but still a superb Burgundy. Lesser-priced Meursaults often are indistinguishable from routine whites and the good ones are very expensive— about $12. So, as an alternative to the Bâtard, three Meursault Les Perrières for $36.

If any region of France has suffered from our gratuitous appropriation of their wine names, it is Chablis. "I'll have a glass of Chablis," is a common request in bars and restaurants, but what is served is not real Chablis but the California version that bears absolutely no resemblance.

True Chablis is a steely, dry wine with great flavor, a green-gold tinge, and a delicate bouquet. There are seven famous Chablis vineyards and the prices of their wines are not unreasonable. A 1974 Les Clos, for instance, sells for $5 or under $55 a case. We will take a case.

There are fine Italian whites, excellent whites from Bordeaux, particularly the Graves region, and, of course, dozens of fine whites from the Loire Valley. Ordinarily we would include some Sancerre or at least a Muscadet, but bad weather in spring, 1977 has driven the prices of these wines far too high. We will wait them out.

Just north and slightly east of Chablis, Alsace begins. Alsace with its magnificent food and almost unknown wines. The finest of the Alsatian wines is the Reisling, which is made in a dry style wholly unlike the wines of Germany. But the Alsatian Reisling has a bouquet and a finesse that are incomparable. They are also subtle, so we will buy some Gewürztraminer, a charming, totally unique wine that does not try to hide its appeal. Its spicy fragrance and taste are like nothing else in the wine world. Anyone who considers himself conversant with fine wine should know and enjoy Gewürztraminer. A good one from a shipper such as Dopff or Trimbach or Willm sells for about $4. Half a dozen of them: $24. Young ones, please; the youngest you can find.

And now on into Germany. There were two great vintages back to back in the Rhine and Mosel: 1975 and 1976. The 1975's are ready to drink so we will choose one of them, Ockfener Bockstein Kabinett. Ockfen, a wine town on the Saar River, a tributary of the Mosel, produces some of the best wines of that region of Germany, and Bockstein is probably the best vineyard in Ockfen. There are many owners. It is possible to find six or seven Ockfener Bocksteins of the same vintage in one good wine shop. Kabinett is the first of five grades into which the very best German wines are divided. Good bottles in this category should sell for about $4. So, a case for our hypothetical cellar: $48.

The 1976's in Germany were truly amazing wines. They were so rich in sugar that some winemakers despaired of making any inexpensive wines. We are going to add something very special to our collection—a bottle from the same vineyard, Ockfener Bockstein, but this one will be from the 1976 vintage and it will be a Beerenauslese, which means that it was made from individually picked, overripe grapes. A bottle from the Doctor Fischer vineyard will cost about $30. Save it for four years or more, for a very special occasion.

No good cellar these days can ignore California wines. The 1975 Sebastiani Chardonnay mentioned above sells for $3.99 a bottle or about $45 a case. This is a fresh, clean Chardonnay with no oak taste. August Sebastiani was surprised when it won an award at the Los Angeles County Fair in 1977 because he didn't think it was the best he could do. No matter, it is a lovely wine. We'll buy a case.

If you prefer a nice oaky flavor that comes from wood aging, try the 1975 Sonoma Vineyards Chardonnay that sells for about $50 a case. For a change of pace, many people prefer a dry Chenin Blanc, and one of the best is Chappellet Vineyard's 1976 that sells for about $5 a bottle or about $55 a case. Add one case at $55.

Finally, the icing on the cake, the *pièce de résistance* of any white wine collection: Champagne. These are good times for Champagne lovers, particularly in the New York area where competition has driven prices down, at least for a while. There are not-half-bad genuine Champagnes selling around New York for under $7 a bottle. We will be a bit more cautious and pick a case of Pommery et Greno nonvintage *brut* which will cost exactly $100. That just rounds out our $500 cellar.

We never did get around to *rosés* in this collection but then, who needs them? Most of them are not worth bothering about unless you happen to be in a part of the world where it is made. If you insist, however, the new California *rosés*, made from Cabernet Sauvignon, Pinot Noir, and Petite Sirah grapes can be very good. Recommended: Firestone Vineyard's Rosé of Cabernet at about $3.75 a bottle and Mirassou Vineyard's Petite Rosé at about the same price. Again, the younger the better.

Alsace—A Hidden Treasure

CROSS THE RHINE from Germany into France and, miraculously, sauerkraut becomes choucroute, wurst becomes saucisson, and the wine—well, the wine becomes one of the finest, and least-known in the world, the great white wine of Alsace.

Like choucroute and the local charcuterie, Alsatian wine does not hide its Germanic influences. The elegant Riesling grape is the same one used for the great wines of the Rhine and the Mosel. But there the resemblance stops. There is a touch of sweetness in the finest German wines; there is none in the best of Alsace. Fruit, yes; enormous fruit and bouquet, but no sugar. Alsatian wines are fermented completely dry.

Alsace—A Hidden Treasure

Tucked away behind the Vosges Mountains, some 275 miles due east of Paris, Alsace is a truly unique wine region. Not only are the grapes different—Riesling, Gewürztraminer, Sylvaner—so also are the bottles, tall, German-style, and the labels. In Alsace, the grape variety identifies the wine, much the way it does in California. One rarely buys a Cabernet in Bordeaux, at least not by that name. All Alsatian wines, with a few exceptions, are sold by grape variety.

Alsace has been called the martyred province of France. War after war has torn apart its old towns and devastated its agriculture. From 1870 to 1918, Alsace was part of Germany. Part of the province's difficulties in the world wine markets stem from that time. The Germans, conscious of the quality of their own wines, forced the growers of Alsace to produce cheap blending wines. The great Alsatian wine tradition was soon forgotten by the wine drinking world.

After World War I, the growers of such towns as Hunawihr, Riquewihr, and Bernheim ripped out the cheap vines that had been forced on them and began the long task of rebuilding. Then came World War II and more devastation. Once again, the Alsace growers rebuilt. Today, the wines they produce are, at their best, superb, and uniquely Alsatian.

Perhaps the best introduction to Alsatian wines is Gewürztraminer. Its qualities are there for anyone to enjoy. It is different without being particularly complex. *Gewürz* means spice and if any word best describes the character of Gewürztraminer it is spice. It can hold its own with the richest of Alsatian dishes, from the quiches and onion tartes to the choucroute garni and roast goose. For all its flowery bouquet, good Alsatian Gewürztraminer is a powerful wine, which incidentally, makes it a good apéritif.

The most popular of the Alsatian wines is Sylvaner, a delightful drink if it is consumed within a year after it is made. It really shouldn't be bottled, although a great deal of it is. Compared to a good Gewürztraminer, most ordinary Sylvaners are dull and uninteresting.

There are quite a few other grapes used in Alsace, including the Chasselas, a common grape in France, and the Knipperle. Both of them show up in the local wines sold in casks and in bottled wines called Zwicker or Edelzwicker which are blends of various grapes. *Edel* means noble, so Edelzwicker is supposed to be a blend of the best grapes.

Edelzwicker is sold in this country from time to time so it might be worth explaining what it is. It is usually made from the second, or more likely the third, pressing of the best grapes. A shipper will

During harvest in Alsace the grape pickers dump their harvest into the great wooden back baskets, which are in turn dumped into large, almost square, casks. The grapes are then taken to the press where each type of grape is pressed separately.

certainly use the first pressing for his own brand. After that, depending on the quality of the vintage, he will use the pressings or sell them off to be used in Edelzwicker.

Two other wines that can be seen in this country from time to time are the Tokay d'Alsace and the Muscat, both of which produce good solid wines with Alsatian characteristics, but little elegance.

The vineyards of Alsace, the best ones, occupy a small area rarely more than a mile wide, on the eastern slopes of the Vosges Mountains.

Grapes are grown in a strip some 60 miles long, but the best are in the area stretching north from Guebwiller to St. Hippolyte, a distance of about 25 miles.

Winemaking in Alsace is truly a cottage industry. Many of the *vignerons* own half an acre of vines or less and tend them in the evenings and on weekends when they are free from their jobs in the auto plants and mills. After all, Alsace is as much an industrial area as it is a wine-growing region.

Many growers have contracts with the huge cooperatives; others sell their grapes, or their wine if they go that far in the process, to the same family firms that their fathers and grandfathers sold to—Hugel, Dopff, Willm, Trimbach, and Schlumberger. Some still make wine in their own ancient vats and casks and sell it to the hordes of tourists that descend on Alsace each year from Germany, Switzerland, and all over France.

The finest Alsatian wines are made, just as they are in Germany, from the Riesling grape. Eventually, the most dedicated Alsatian wine fan tires of Gewürztraminer and asks for something subtler.

Hugh Johnson describes Alsatian Riesling best: "It offers," he says, "something more elusive, a balance of hard and gentle, flowery and strong, which leads you on and never surfeits." It is, like most great wines, an experience that changes from glass to glass, from bottle to bottle, and from sip to sip—always the same, but always something a bit different.

Because of the number of small growers, almost all wines from Alsace are blends, with a typical shipper or cooperative buying grapes or wines from a hundred farmers. There are some single vineyard wines, though, and a couple come to this country, including the Clos Ste. Hune of the Trimbach family, a Riesling, and the Clos Gaensbroennel of the Willms, a Gewürztraminer. These are wines for the true Alsace devotee. They are expensive, $9 and up, reflecting the care and pride that go into them.

Actually, Alsatian wines have long been good bargains. Even today, there are excellent Gewürztraminers and Rieslings for $4 and less, particularly from the cooperatives.

Like most white wines, Alsatian wines should be drunk fairly young. Well-kept, they can last four or five years, but it is wise to look for the youngest when shopping. There is no way to guarantee that an older bottle has not been lying next to a radiator for two years.

The best vintages in Alsace correspond more closely to those in Burgundy than they do to the Rheingau to the north. One exception: 1975 was an excellent year in Alsace, as it was in Germany, but not in

Burgundy. Given its northerly location, Alsace has been fortunate in its weather in recent years. The most recent crop, 1977, bids to be a fine vintage, if not up to the standards of 1976 which was exceptionally fine, just as it was in Germany and in Burgundy. Both 1974 and 1973 were good years in Alsace, too. Earlier than that, unless you know your supplier very well, it would be well to skip the wine as too old.

At the source, in Alsace, it's a different story. Last year at the Auberge de l'Ill, the great three-star restaurant in Illhaeusern, I shared a 1945 Gewürztraminer from Schlumberger with one of the owners. It was in perfect condition.

Hubert Trimbach, whose family has been making wine in Alsace for centuries, has a theory that the best wines, particularly the Rieslings, will keep for five years or so in his cellars, begin a gradual decline, then after another decade, come back with a different but equally fascinating character. One day, in his winery, he opened the bottles to prove his theory. He succeeded.

While they prefer their wines dry, the Alsatians try for super quality wines in the Auslese and Beerenauslese categories, as do the German vintners. These are wines made from grapes left on the vines to gather the last thin rays of the October (or November) sun, to make an intense concentrated wine of extraordinary flavor. Occasionally, these wines make it to our shores. Expect to pay considerably more for them.

The 1973 Vintage: Now or Never

DURING the last two weeks of September, 1973, I was in Tuscany. It was hot—oh, yes it was hot. It was dry, too, and the breeze crackled through the olive trees, turning up the silver underside of the leaves every minute or two. Great fall weather for Italian grapes.

Early on the morning of Sunday September 30th, I arrived at the

The 1973 Vintage: Now or Never

Gare St. Jean in Bordeaux after an all-night trip from Nice, to find rain-swept streets drying out under a warm autumn sun. Later in the day, I learned that I had missed almost two weeks of chilling rain, two weeks that had taken a serious toll of one of the biggest and best grape crops in Bordeaux in recent years. No one was quite sure what had happened, but no one was willing to predict that it would turn out well.

Anyone who has any reason to recall the summer of 1973 in Bordeaux knows that it began well, with no frost and continued to be what the University of Bordeaux probably would call a textbook growing season.

There were a few cool weeks in July. To be sure, temperatures that slow the development of the fruit are more prized in California than in France, but long, slow ripening is always favored, so long as the season doesn't extend into the risky rainy fall which is exactly what happened in 1973.

The crop was magnificent up until those last two weeks in September. Then, as if in response to some Biblical imperative, the rains came. Even so, growers who chose to wait out the weather often triumphed over it. The rain was followed by superb October weather —I remember it well—and some growers gave their grapes a chance to soak up an extra couple of weeks of sunshine. Thus, you had growers who panicked and picked early—in late September, during the rain, and pickers who gambled and picked in mid-October after the ensuing week or so of drying sun.

By all rights, *The New York Times* should provide a list of châteaus that picked during the rain, a week after it, two weeks after it, and of those that, like Lafite, picked during the second onslaught of rain in mid-October. Sorry, but the computer can't handle it.

What can be provided is a handful of tasting notes on a group of 1973 Bordeaux examined in 1977. The tasting—23 wines were involved, none of them first growths such as Latour and Margaux— recalled a similar investigation of the 1972 vintage several months earlier.

Not surprising to anyone who follows this sort of thing, the 1972's turned out better than the previous year's vintage, when the grapes really never had time to ripen. These days, a good winemaker defies the elements and 1972 was a year in which just that happened. Good, small wines were made.

The 1973's were something else again. The wines are fuller, rounder, richer, and more complex than the 1972's, with the exception, as a general rule, of the St.-Emilions and Pomerols which, in

1973 were exceedingly disappointing. The 1973's were, and are, far more expensive than the 1972's. Since neither is a great vintage, a case actually can be made that the less attractive, shorter-lived 1972's are better buys than the 1973's which are slightly better in quality but far more expensive to buy.

At a recent tasting of the 1973 Bordeaux, the Médocs came off best, with several Margaux proving to be very attractive wines. Châteaus Lascombes and Prieuré-Lichine were favored unanimously. This writer had some admiration for a Brane-Cantenac that most others in the tasting group found to be unpleasant.

Of the St.-Juliens, Château Beychevelle showed best but it simply was not in the class of the Margaux. Of two Pauillacs, Pichon-Longueville and Grand-Puy-Lacoste, I preferred the latter. It was a bit thin, but it had a lovely bouquet and some of the elegance that goes with the best Pauillacs.

Two St.-Estèphes, Châteaus Montrose and Phelan-Segur, both came off well. The Phelan, normally the lesser of the two, seemed the least advanced. The Montrose was a good, solid wine, with excellent color and body.

The St.-Emilions sampled were Châteaus Haut-Corbin, Beauséjour, Canon, and Ausone. Ausone, which can be one of the great treasures of French wine, obviously was a very big wine, but it had a tarry flavor to it and an off-smell—the kind of things that should not happen to wine of this class. The others showed little promise.

The Pomerols, which are produced right next door to the St.-Emilions, were Châteaus La Pointe and l'Evangile. After being open for three or four hours, the La Pointe began to exhibit some of the velvety texture usually associated with Pomerol but it was not a first-rate wine. The l'Evangile was a soft, unimpressive bottle. It was smooth but it really had very little style.

Two of the best wines in the tasting were from the Graves: Châteaus Pape Clément and Carbonnieux. The Pape Clément was the best of the two with good balance, deep color, and good, lasting flavor. There is a certain asperity to a good Graves and this bottle had it. The Carbonnieux was lighter in color and texture but it was a pleasant bottle, better than some better-known labels in the tasting.

There were no first growths in this particular batch, but there were two small wines, Château Caillavet, carrying a Premier Côtes de Bordeaux *appellation*, and Château Grand Village, a Bordeaux Supérieur. Tasted against the better, classified growths, both showed poorly. A second bottle of the Grand Village, tried by itself a day later was a fresh, light, fruity wine showing all the best characteristics of a young Bordeaux.

The prices of some of these wines were disturbing. Château Lascombes $7.49, Brane-Cantenac, $7.29, Beychevelle, $8.19 and Pichon-Longueville, $7.99. Château La Lagune, classified only as a Haut Médoc and, in this tasting at least, a very poor wine, $5.79. Two of the St.-Emilions, Beauséjour and Canon were $6.19 and $6.49, and the Ausone lists for anywhere from $12 to $18. Both Pomerols were over $6 and the Pape Clément was $7. Prieuré-Lichine was $5.99.

These are high prices for second-level properties from an indifferent year. Part of the explanation may lie in a release from Sotheby Parke Bernet in London about a wine auction on April 20, 1977. "The buoyant trend of the last few weeks continues," the release said, "and prices have increased again." Merchants and brokers in Bordeaux are holding back stocks, Sotheby's said, until the damage from the April frosts can be assessed and "It is once again a seller's market, with buyers keen to purchase the best vintages, now in relatively short supply."

If customers can be found to pay almost $9 including tax for second rank 1973's, what will the prices be on the good 1975's a couple of years from now?

The Storage Problem

SOMETIMES it seems as if people are more interested in storing wine than in buying or drinking it. Most of their fears are unfounded. Very few of us, even those who buy wines by the case, ever keep it long enough to have serious problems. Most sound wines can easily stand two or three years in a Manhattan apartment—provided a few simple rules are observed. Enthusiasts who plan to buy for investment, laying down, say, 1975's in anticipation of their improving in the bottle for drinking ten years hence, have a different situation. But let's forget them for a moment.

If you have been buying your Beaujolais by the bottle and have decided to get the 10 percent saving on a case purchase, or if you have discovered a little Bordeaux château that is not always in stock and want to buy a few cases to make sure you have it—then you are ready to store some wine.

It's very simple: find a closet that is relatively cool and make room among the old shoes for your cases of wine. The closet protects the wine from excess heat and from light. Heat is the biggest problem but it takes a long time for even the heat in a typical New York apartment to harm a good bottle of wine. Everyone has heard that 55 degrees is the ideal temperature for storing wine. This is true, particularly if you plan to keep your wine a decade or so. If your plans are shorter termed than that, relax and enjoy your wine.

Of course, our higher temperatures will affect wine. They will speed up its aging process. So, if you really want to keep some wine a long time, it would be wise to check it every so often. It is going to get old faster than the same wine kept in a professional cellar.

There are actually some inveterate city dwellers who have moved to the suburbs just to have a proper place to store expensive wines. Others keep a cellar in their summer homes. Still others find a friend with a wine cellar, or at least with a cellar in which wine can be stored.

Still others keep a closet air conditioned all year around. Some buy terribly expensive devices that look like refrigerators but are actually wine humidors and which can hold several hundred bottles. One reader moved to Florida, took a top-floor condominium in a high-rise oceanfront building, then had an insulated wine "cellar" built on the roof, right over his apartment. He reaches it by a circular staircase from the floor below. The temperature may be 100° outside; in his cave it is 55°.

That is, of course, a wealthy man's amusement. Most of us have to be content with the hall closet, which, by the way, also protects wine from light, another of its enemies. There is no harm in taking the bottles out to impress friends but for regular storage, they are better off in the dark. That is why most wine bottles are green—to cut off excess light and to filter out harmful rays of the sun.

Another enemy of wine in the city is vibration. Again, if you plan to drink up your collection in a year or two, have no fear. Over the long haul, however, vibration can break down a good wine. Another reader tells of waking up in the night when the square-wheeled IRT trains rattle under his Brooklyn brownstone. He lies there thinking of what the shaking is doing to his old Bordeaux.

Dedicated wine people take these things seriously. A Manhattan publicist, learning that a new office tower was about to go up across the street from his townhouse, was appalled at what the dynamite blasting for the foundation might do to his wines. He managed to get the contractor to move every one of his bottles to a warehouse. There they reposed in climate-controlled comfort until the skyscraper was finished. Then the contractor moved them all back home. Again, if you plan to drink your wines fairly soon, constant vibration probably will get to you before it does to your bottles.

Speaking of storing wine in a warehouse, yet another reader was kind enough to send along part of his correspondence with the Morgan & Brother Manhattan Storage Company. Morgan's rate for wine storage is 35 cents per case, per month with a $5 monthly minimum and a one-time handling charge of 35 cents per case ($5 minimum) when the wine comes into the warehouse. If you put your wine in the Morgan vault and then get lonely and want to visit it, the first time is free. After that, it will cost you $14 an hour with a 30-minute minimum. Temperature in the Morgan vaults on East 87th Street is kept between 55° and 60°.

Before you rush off to warehouse your Lafite-Rothschild, remember that storing ten cases will cost $60 a year or $600 over a ten-year period. Besides, the Morgan wine vault is usually full. You have to get on a waiting list to get space.

Assuming then that most wine stays at home there are a couple of other elementary points. Keep the bottles on their sides. Is there anyone besides the owners of about half the city's retail shops who does not know that yet? When a bottle is on its side, the wine is up against the cork. This keeps the cork wet and full so no air can get into the bottle. When a bottle stands up, the cork dries out and shrinks. Air gets into the bottle and turns the wine to vinegar.

If you have several cases, keep the whites and *rosés* on the bottom. They are more delicate than the reds and should be awarded the coolest spot in that closet.

As for wine racks, so long as you keep your bottles in a closet, there is no need to go overboard on a wine rack. Many people simply turn the cases on their sides and use them. Until a few years ago, most French wines came in sturdy wooden cases with dividers built in. Stacked up, they made perfect wine racks. The new cardboard cases are not as good, but they will do.

Ironically, there are times when the most elaborate precautions are to no avail. Those are the times when the wine reaches you already ruined, or well on its way. It is a sad fact that the handling of wine between the winery and the consumer is still abominably bad.

Many of the people who handle it have never had a good glass of wine in their lives. So they park their wine-laden trucks in the sun, leave containers of wine baking on docks or freezing in warehouses.

Retailers are often part of this chain of indifference. One reader reported being offered several bottles by a local retailer that had been fetched from the cellar. They were literally hot. The salesman assured her it did not matter.

Any bottle found to be bad when it comes from the shop should be returned. The trouble is, when the wine has been in storage, in a closet or anywhere else, for a few months, few retailers are going to agree that the wine was bad when he sold it to you.

Check for cloudiness in red wines and any discoloration in whites. Also check to see that the corks are properly set in place. Bulging corks can indicate that the wine may have expanded in the bottle, either from excess heat or from freezing. If air filled the space vacated by the partly pushed-out cork, there is a good chance that the wine is bad.

Port—The Englishman's Wine

"PORT," wrote George Saintsbury, "is the Englishman's wine. It strengthens while it gladdens as no other wine can do, and there is something about it which must have been created in pre-established harmony with the best English character."

Mr. Saintsbury wrote at a time when most Englishmen assumed that not only Port wine, but most of the world had been pre-established for their convenience. All that is gone now and even the French drink more Port than the English. But the Port tradition is English and that, hopefully, will never change.

We Americans are not Port drinkers—not of real Port, that is. In fact, we produce, mostly in California, more than six times the amount of Port made in the Douro region of Portugal, the world's only source of the genuine article. Consequently, most Americans, including many who consider themselves fairly knowledgeable about table wines, are woefully ignorant about Port.

True Port is a fortified wine which must be made from grapes grown in the Alto Douro region of northern Portugal, one of the wildest, most improbable places in the world to produce fine wine. Some of the vineyards are so remote that they can be reached only on foot or by donkey, even to this day.

Portuguese wines have been known in England since the time of Columbus, and even then, the shippers may have added a dollop of brandy to their casks to help preserve the wine on the sea. But the wine was not Port.

Strangely enough, the codfish was the basis of Portugal's wine trade. Portuguese fishermen, already working the Newfoundland Banks in the early 16th century, used red wine to buy the ship's stores they needed from the English. Then, after the Reformation, when Englishmen no longer felt constrained to eat fish on Fridays, the English fishing fleets sold their cod to the Portuguese (bacalhau is still a national dish). In exchange they took wine back to Britain.

In those times, the English merchants were already settled in Portugal, as they are today. But they were mostly in Viana do Castelo, further north than Oporto, where they dealt in a thin wine called red portugal, large quantities of which were sold to the British Navy. The British colony at Oporto dealt in cotton, wheat, and salted cod, which they exchanged for oil, fruit, and money.

The wines of Bordeaux were the Englishmen's favorites in the 16th and 17th centuries. Or they were until 1667, when Louis XIV raised all tariffs on imports. The British reacted by hiking duties on French wines. Later, when France banned English cloth, the British banned all French wines. The ban was lifted, then imposed again but, over the years, England was so often at war with France that claret was not only expensive, but very unpatriotic to drink.

Jacobites may have toasted "the king over the water," James II, but Loyalists hailed William III with bumpers of Port. All this created a shortage of Portuguese wine and sent the shippers in Portugal scurrying about the countryside looking for wine. What they found was the wine of the Douro, even then far superior to the thin stuff they had been sending home from Viana.

By 1700 some of the English founders of the legendary Port houses were already settled in Oporto, or, more accurately, in Vila Nova de Gaia, the city across the Douro from Oporto where the great wine lodges are located. The founders of Croft's were there. So were the Warres and Job Bearsley, who started what was to become Taylors.

What is more, they already had established the extraordinary relationship with the Portuguese Government that was to last down to the present day, though in much modified form. They were immune to most Portuguese taxes and laws; they selected their own judges and consuls; and they created, in essence, a small copy of England on the coast of Portugal. With one curious exception. Many of the English merchants were attended by black servants—English-speaking slaves from America. Apparently they preferred the American Blacks who spoke their language to the readily available but incomprehensible Portuguese.

The 19th century was, as Sarah Bradford has described it in her book *The Englishman's Wine*, the golden age of Port. The English upper class had always been Port fans, but the custom spread down through the middle class as well and most British families even of modest means, usually consumed their bottle of Port each day.

This was also the time of the first vogue for vintage Port. Port, like Champagne, is a blend. Master tasters in each firm blend dozens of wines and various vintages to achieve that firm's style. In particularly great years, though, the wine is set aside and bottled as the wine of that year. A great vintage Port is aged two years in wood and then up to 20 years in bottle and is, understandably, most expensive.

The dreaded *phylloxera* first attacked the vineyards of the Douro in 1868 and was not vanquished until almost two decades later when all the vines had been replaced with American rootstock. There are still Port connoisseurs around who say that the vintage Ports of the last pre-*phylloxera* years, the early and mid-1860's, which were first drunk in the 1880's, were the greatest of all Ports.

By Edwardian times, Port had attained the reputation of being the national drink of England and was even more popular in the years after World War I. But even then, as Mrs. Bradford put it, "The shadow of the dry martini already lay across the wine trade." Mrs. Bradford singles out another culprit for the gradual demise of Port as a stable in an English gentleman's life: the automobile. "The motor car," she wrote, "has largely obviated the necessity for strenuous exercise and as a result we cannot stomach the Olympian quantities of food and drink indulged in by our more strenuous ancestors. After a hard day's riding or hunting," she went on, "and a brisk walk to church, the Victorians would gladly sit down to an array of courses and bottles on a scale that would make the mid-20th century executive, deskbound and motor-borne, blanch and reach for the Alka-Seltzer."

There have been revivals of interest in Port during the late 1930's and again just after World War II. Recently, there has been a modest increase in interest in Port here in the United States. But these revivals have involved the more expensive wines and not the inexpensive ruby Port that was the backbone of the industry for several centuries. Fortunately, the French interest in inexpensive Port, to be drunk as an apéritif, and, surprisingly, a new interest in the wine of Portugal itself, have sustained the business.

For the benefit of newcomers to Port, there are several categories worth noting:

Vintage (the wine of a great year). There are usually three vintage years every decade. Each shipper decides when he will make a vintage year.

Late-bottled vintage. Aged in wood three or four times as long as vintage, but kept in glass a shorter time.

Crusted. Good Port but lesser than vintage, also bottled early then stored for ten years or more in bottles.

Tawny. Aged in wood until it loses its red color. Lighter in texture than the vintage Ports.

Ruby. Aged comparatively briefly, the least expensive of Ports.

Some great vintage years of the century include: 1912, 1927, 1935, 1945, 1955, and 1960. Recently, a 1927 Taylor was selling in Beverly Hills for $95, a 1945 for $75, and a 1955 Graham for $48. The best buys in old Ports are at Christie's auctions in London.

Read Carefully Before Drinking

A COLLEAGUE invited a wine buff to dinner. The guest picked up one of the bottles selected for the meal and read: *appellation contrôlée.*

"I would never have bought it," he told his dismayed host. "*Appellation contrôlée* means that all the growers in the area pooled their wines into a blend."

Château Figeac announces in large letters that it is a St.-Emilion wine, then backs up that claim by disclosing that it is entitled to the St.-Emilion *appellation*.

This would be news to the people at Château Lafite-Rothschild, whose label also reads *appellation contrôlée*. And it would surprise the people at the Domaine de la Romanée-Conti, who also have *appellation contrôlée* on their bottle.

Unfortunately, many people simply are unaware of what information can be gleaned from the label of a wine bottle. The following may help a bit.

Appellation contrôlée on a French wine label is, first of all, a guarantee that the wine comes from wherever the label says it comes from. Secondly, it is a guarantee that the wine meets the standards of quality usually associated with that place.

As a general rule, the smaller the place covered by the *appellation*, the better the wine. A wine for which the controlled *appellation* is Bordeaux is invariably a lesser wine than one for which the *appellation* is Pauillac, as in the case of Lafite, or Margaux, as in the case of Lascombes.

The Heitz Cellar label illustrated here indicates that the wine was made from grapes from various parts of the state of California. Most of Mr. Heitz's wines bear the appellation Napa Valley, which is where his winery is located. One Heitz wine, his famous Martha's Vineyard Cabernet Sauvignon, goes farther than just Napa to zero in on the specific vineyard from which the grapes in the wine came.

A Bordeaux A.C. means only that the wine in the bottle comes from grapes grown in the vast Bordeaux region—which takes in some good grapes and some, well, mediocre ones. A Pauillac or a Margaux A.C. means that the wine comes from grapes grown entirely within that particular *commune,* in these cases, two of the finest in the world.

Château Figeac announces in large letters that it is a St.-Emilion wine, then backs up that claim by disclosing that it is entitled to the St.-Emilion *appellation.* Château Trotanoy notes on its label that it is a Pomerol wine but puts the *Appellation Pomerol Contrôlée* line at the very top of the label.

American wines have controlled appellations, too, and as our wine business grows more sophisticated, so do our appellations. Appellations in this country are just as widespread as they are in France although the boundaries are not as finely drawn.

```
APPELLATION POMEROL CONTROLÉE




CHÂTEAU TROTANOY
POMEROL
1972
SOCIÉTÉ CIVILE DU CHATEAU TROTANOY
PROPRIÉTAIRE A POMEROL (GIRONDE)


MIS EN BOUTEILLES AU CHATEAU
```

RED BORDEAUX' WINE
CONTENTS : 1 PT. 8 FL. OZ.   ALCOHOL : 12% BY VOLUME
Shipped by : Jean-Pierre MOUEIX, Négociants à LIBOURNE - France
IMPORTED BY :
AUSTIN, NICHOLS & CO, INC., NEW YORK.
PRODUCE OF FRANCE

Château Trotanoy notes on its label that it is a Pomerol wine but puts the *Appellation Pomerol Contrôlée* line at the very top of the label.

The largest appellation is "American." It is used on some New York State wines that are blended with wines from California. The best California wines will zero in on a community or even a grower to give the most accurate appellation possible. Thus the Freemark Abbey winery will label some of its Cabernet Sauvignon "Bosche," for the man from whose vineyard all the grapes in the wine were purchased.

The Heitz Cellar label illustrated indicates that the wine was made from grapes from various parts of the state of California. Most of Mr. Heitz's wines bear the appellation Napa Valley, which is where his winery is located. One Heitz wine, his famous Martha's Vineyard Cabernet Sauvignon, goes farther than just Napa to zero in on the specific vineyard from which the grapes in the wine came.

The Federal Government would like to pin down all the California appellations. If they ever get around to it, it will be a Herculean task. The fact is, no one is really certain where the Napa Valley begins or ends. Some wineries use the appellation Northern California. What

Walter S. Taylor, founder of Bully Hill Vineyards, at his winery in Hammondsport, New York.

does that mean? Others use North Coast. North of what? San Diego? Still, the French worked it all out and, if they can agree on anything so emotional and complex, so can we.

More than 100 years ago, the different châteaus of the Médoc, the most famous part of the Bordeaux wine region, were classified in terms of quality. Lafite, for example, was named a first growth, Beychevelle a fourth. The wines of St.-Emilion were classified in 1955. Only three categories were used: first great growths, great growths,

[31]

and principal growths. Two of the 12 first great growths are considered first among equals: Château Ausone and Château Cheval Blanc. Château Figeac's label, illustrated here, indicates that it is one of the other ten.

Pomerol, a lovely area of Bordeaux tucked in next to St.-Emilion, never has been classified, although Château Pétrus is considered its greatest property, and Trotanoy, whose label is shown here, is said to be one of the ten or so most important after Pétrus.

Both French labels indicate the vintage, 1972. The Heitz label has no vintage date, which means that the wine probably is a blend of two or more vintages. Sometimes, California vintners will label a bottle "Lot 73–74" to indicate what years are in the blend.

Both the Figeac and the Trotanoy labels indicate that the wine was bottled at the château (*mis en bouteilles au château*). For many years, it was the custom of the wine merchants to buy the wine in casks from châteaus, then bottle it in their own cellars in Libourne (for Pomerol and St.-Emilion) and Bordeaux (for the Graves and Médoc). Lesser wines, particularly the ones with a simple Bordeaux *appellation* are still made this way.

The equivalent in California is the notation on a bottle that says "produced and bottled in our cellar." Note that in the case of the Heitz Zinfandel, the line reads "perfected and bottled in our cellar." This means that Heitz bought the wine elsewhere, then blended it in his own cellar.

The Figeau label shows that the château is owned by the Manoncourt family and shipped by Nathaniel Johnston & Fils in Bordeaux. This means that the firm of Nathaniel Johnston, one of Bordeaux's oldest, buys the wine, already bottled from the Manoncourts, then sells it to importers. In this case the name of the importer is not shown. It may be on the neck label.

The Trotanoy label indicates that the château is owned by the Château Trotanoy Company and shipped by a firm in Libourne, Jean-Pierre Moueix. It does not show that Moueix owns Trotanoy, but it does. Or rather, he does, since there really is a Jean-Pierre Moueix. Traditionally, the shippers have ended up owning many of the châteaux from which they buy.

The Trotanoy label also shows that Moueix sold the wine to Austin, Nichols & Co. Inc. in New York. Austin, Nichols, which is also a distributor, sells the wine to retailers who sell it to you, the consumer.

Baron Philippe: "I Am Rothschild."

THE VAST, bright room looks out through half-moon-shaped windows on the rolling fields of the Médoc. Ranged along one wall, amid a profusion of plants, are a priceless collection of pictures and sculpture—Kandinsky, Braque, Brancusi, Lippold. In a corner, Champagne cools in ice. There is scotch, gin, and a pitcher of tomato juice for those extraordinary Bloody Marys Americans seem to like.

One American, knowing when he is well off, heads for the Champagne. He is on his first sip when his host pads noiselessly into the room. "I am Rothschild," he said. "Let me freshen your glass."

Baron Philippe de Rothschild is about five-feet six-inches tall, stocky, but graceful as befits a former champion racing driver, a pilot, and renowned yachtsman. He looks well-fed, and similar to Picasso in middle age, say about 52 or 53. "I am 72," he said (1972), "and I also am said to resemble Louis Jouvet." Jouvet was a great French actor of a generation ago.

The brief encounter took place in a former stable that is now the main building, divided into offices, country home, and museum, of Château Mouton Rothschild, one of the most famous vineyards in France. This is a special year for Philippe de Rothschild—if not for the wine he makes—because he first settled in here as owner exactly 50 years ago.

"There was no running water, no electricity, no telephone," the Baron recalled. "It was primitive. It was not until the end of World War II that the peasants finally gave up their oxen for trucks."

The Médoc is primitive no longer. And behind the Rothschild estate's handsome 18th-century walls, are some of the most sophisticated winemaking plants in the world. While there are those here who make a pastime of gossiping about the Rothschilds, there are few who will deny the immensely important role this disarmingly simple man has played in their lives.

"His name is inextricably linked with the modern history of the Médoc," said Lionel Cruse. "When he goes, all of Bordeaux will feel the loss," said another grower, a fierce competitor of Mouton.

Right now, the Baron's daily routine would exhaust men half his age.

"From 7:30 A.M. until 1 P.M., I write," he said. "You may have read my translation of Marlowe's *Dr. Faustus*." Most of his effort at the

[33]

moment is devoted to translating Elizabethan poets and dramatists into French. Some of his work has received high critical acclaim.

After lunch there is the business of the château. There are four wines now: Château Mouton, of course; Château Baronne Philippe, which used to be called Château Mouton d'Armailhacq; Mouton-Cadet; and, more recently, Château Clerc-Milon, a Mouton property that lies to the north about half way between Mouton and its great rival, Baron Elie Rothschild's Château Lafite.

After the work of the wine business—most of which is now left to a large and highly professional staff—there is a swim in the new pool.

"Yes," the Baron said, "I installed the pool a year or two ago. Really, I needed something to lure my grandchildren down here from Paris."

There is one grandchild in particular, Philippe the nine-year-old son of the Baron's daughter, Philippine Sereys, who will someday inherit Mouton as Philippe did from his father, Baron Henri, and his father did before him. In fact, the Baron has adopted the boy so that, according to Jewish custom, the property may pass directly from father to son.

Baron Philippe is married to an American, Pauline Fairfax Potter, who, before their marriage in 1954, was a famous couturier on the staff of Hattie Carnegie. Baron Philippe's first wife was caught trying to escape Paris during the occupation and died in a German concentration camp. The Baron escaped to Morocco where he was jailed by Vichy authorities and returned to France. He escaped again and made his way to England, landing in France again during the Normandy invasion.

The Baroness Pauline does her writing between 1 A.M. and 3 A.M. The Rothschilds entertain vigorously at Mouton and she may spend an hour during the day selecting table settings for that night's dinner. To assist her, she has swatches of material from hundreds of table cloths and a picture file of her 180 sets of china.

Once the settings are chosen, the Baroness will call in the staff horticulturist. The Rothschilds reject the lush cultivated flowers which are standard at Bordeaux parties. They decorate their tables with natural plants. The arrangements are striking and it is not unusual to find huge fungi on the luncheon table or a handsome wild broccoli as a centerpiece at a formal dinner.

Unlike his more austere cousins who devote their lives to business and banking, Philippe has always concentrated on the arts and on wine. He was an early producer of talking films here in France and he has backed innumerable plays, ballets, and even theaters in Paris. His book for a ballet by Darius Milhaud, written in 1951, was revived in 1973 by the Nice Opera.

But his true concern has always been the wine of Château Mouton and, more specifically, having Mouton reclassified as a *Premier Crus* or First Growths. When the classification was made in 1855, four wines were listed at the very top: Lafite, Latour, Margaux, and Haut-Brion. Mouton was the first of the second growths.

Few wine experts here in the Gironde or elsewhere in the world deny that Mouton should be in the top rank. But other growers here are uneasy about any change. If there were to be a general reclassification, might they not drop in the list? None of them are willing to chance a genuine reshuffling.

Philippe had hoped that in 1972, his 50th anniversary at Mouton, there might be some attempt to change the long-standing ratings. But outside observers say there is little chance. In conservative Bordeaux, they worry about losing their own rating and they talk about the unwarranted popularity of Mouton-Cadet, by far the best-known of the Mouton wines. Even though it is merely a Bordeaux *rouge* and doesn't even rate the Médoc *appellation* it sells for around $4 in New York while other Bordeaux *rouges* command $2 or $2.50. Cadet, they say, hurts Mouton's reputation and narrows the chances for a change in rating.

Of course, no one would question the quality of the premier wine, Château Mouton Rothschild. Hugh Johnson describes it as "strong, dark and long-lasting." He says: "These wines reach into realms of perfection where they are rarely followed."

Perhaps someday,* Baron Philippe de Rothschild may win the first rank he and just about everyone else in the wine world believes he deserves. Until then, he may have to settle for his famous—and ironic —motto for Mouton: *Premier ne puis, second ne daigne. Mouton suis.* "First I cannot be, second I do not deign to be. I am Mouton."

Pauline de Rothschild died in 1976. In her memory, Baron Phillipe renamed Château Baron Phillippe, Château Baronne Phillipe.

---

* As the next piece relates, Château Mouton Rothschild was elevated to *Premiers Cru* in 1973.

A History in Labels

IT WAS the fall of 1945. The Germans had pulled out of Bordeaux long ago and it was time for the harvest. Almost as if in celebration of the end of the long dark night of war, nature provided one of the finest vintages of the century.

The war had meant tragedy for Philippe de Rothschild. His wife died in a German concentration camp; his property had been confiscated by the Vichy government and then occupied by the Germans.

But all that was past and he was back at Château Mouton vinifying one of the greatest of Mouton wines. To celebrate the war's end and the fine harvest, he designed a special label—thus beginning a tradition of special labels that has continued unbroken for 30 years.

The 1945 Mouton label featured a large gold V surrounded by a laurel wreath and grape vines. It bore the inscription: Année de la Victoire.

The 1946 label bore a small picture showing a dove of peace, with an olive branch in its beak, flying low over the vineyards, with the Gironde River in the background. Thus began the tradition of using a picture on each year's label.

The 1947 label was drawn by Baron Philippe's friend, Jean Cocteau, who started the tradition of using wine themes and Mouton themes, even in abstract or impressionist drawings and paintings. Cocteau's drawing showed a human figure with sheep's horns gazing fondly at a bunch of grapes.

Baron Philippe departed from tradition once, in 1953, to commemorate the 100th anniversary of the year when his great grandfather, Baron Nathaniel Rothschild, of the English branch of the clan Rothschild, bought Mouton. There is a picture of Baron Nathaniel and this inscription: "I dedicate this harvest to my great-grandfather, Baron Nathaniel, who bought the Domaine of Mouton on May 11, 1853; to my grandfather, Baron James, and to my father, Baron Henri."

Georges Braque drew a partially filled glass and a bunch of grapes for the 1955 label, and Salvador Dali produced a squiggly sheep for the 1958 bottle. Lippold came up with fireworks in 1959, and Henry Moore drew hands holding three gold cups for 1964. Dorothea Canning's satyr-like characters frolicked across the top of the forgettable 1965 vintage, and Marc Chagall did a light-hearted gouache with grape pickers, vines, and even a chicken for 1970.

[36]

Mouton Rothschild's label for 1973 vintage, château's first as a grand cru, features a Picasso drawing from Mouton's museum.

The 1973 label was a big one, literally and figuratively. It was the year when Baron Philippe won his 50-year-long campaign to have Mouton named a first growth and it was the year of Picasso's death. He chose a magnificent 1959 Picasso work entitled "Bacchanale" from the Mouton Museum and in a white band across the top of the label noted: In homage to Picasso (1881–1973).

Below the picture and the name of the château, it read: "Premier Cru Classe in 1973," then, under a gold coronet, he displayed the new Mouton motto: *Premier je suis, second je fus, Mouton ne change.* "I am first, I was second, Mouton never changes."

[37]

In 1974 Mr. Robert Motherwell became the first American artist to provide a label since Dorothea Canning, the wife of the late Max Ernst. He was not the last, however. Andy Warhol agreed to do the label for the 1975 vintage.

Change 1855?

EARLY in 1977 we reported on a tasting in Paris that attempted to open a new assault on the 1855 classification of the wines of Bordeaux. The article mentioned that Alexis Lichine had proposed an updating many years ago and that Baron Philippe de Rothschild had succeeded in having his Château Mouton Rothschild elevated from the first of the second growths to the status of a first growth, along with Châteaus Haut-Brion, Margaux, Latour, and Lafite.

Then I got into trouble. Innocently, the piece went on to say: "Still, 1855 remains sacrosanct. Purists even dismiss the elevation of Mouton, saying that it was a separate action and that 1855 remains intact." Within days, a letter arrived from Baron Philippe in London, who apparently reads all this stuff religiously.

"The 1855 classification sacrosanct?" he wrote. "Pray to whom? It was by no means legal, in fact merely a commercial list made up for the 1855 Paris exhibition, simply for shop-window purposes. On the other hand the 1973 classification is a government decree, genuine, legal and official.

"Purists? Who on earth are they? Names please! No one in the profession can be more 'purist' than we at Mouton, and can the French government be called 'impurist?' Those who cling to 1855 as sacrosanct and dismiss 1973 can only be disgruntled competitors whose 'purity' of judgment might be questioned.

"You are right to diagnose the fear of certain château owners that a new classification might precipitate their descent to a nether classification, as the cause of interminable delays of any reclassification.

"Champagne of the Garter." At the turn of the century each
bottle of this Champagne came with a pair of satin garters, for
men "wish to conquer hearts."

"The value which connoisseurs have put on Mouton through the
last half century, the price they willingly pay and have paid—top of
the five first—speaks for itself. The 1973 classification of the 'First
Growths' far from being in any sense a promotion is but a very
belated, well-deserved recognition of the unanimous verdict of those
connoisseurs the world over. Moreover, every expert knows the obvious reason for Mouton having been classified in 1855 as first of the
'Second Growths': the Château had been bought only two years
previously by a novice foreigner, my great-grandfather, an Englishman."

The problem here stems from the word "purists." It should have been clear from the outset that anyone who spends his time translating the Elizabethan poets into French would pick up a word like that. Okay, but the fact remains that many of the more traditional château owners and shippers cling tenaciously to the 1855 listings and regard what took place in 1973 as an aberration. Probably because they know in their hearts that one day the old order will change.

It isn't Mouton's reclassification that bothers them. No one denies that Mouton is a first growth. It is just that Mouton has opened the door to further change and, in spite of all the upheavals in the wine trade in recent years, Bordeaux remains resistant to change. We certainly do not regret writing the article. We regret using the word "purists." Perhaps "traditionalists" might have been better.

Hardly had the Baron's letter been read when another arrived, this one from Burgundy. Michel Couvreur, a shipper not previously known to us, who lives in the ironically named town of Bouze-les-Beaune, wrote to discuss another article that referred to the slippage in quality of Burgundy wines.

Mr. Couvreur agreed with that idea but wanted to add a few points. "The constant drop in quality in the Burgundies," was due also, he said, "to the doubling and even sometimes tripling of the yield from the same cultivated surfaces during the last two decades."

Moreover, he added, "It might also be contended that not only is Pouilly-Fuissé an 'American Wine,' but that the entire Burgundy vineyard region of the 'great names' is in its present condition as the direct and exclusive result of American buying methods."

He goes on to say that only Americans would believe that Burgundies blended from wines of several vineyards could be as good as the wine produced from the grapes of a single owner's vineyard. Any experienced Burgundy drinker knows that the reverse is generally true.

He also said that our distribution system, where the wine is bucked from importer's warehouse to distributor to retailer is a "death penalty" for delicate Burgundies.

"It perhaps still exists a tiny way to evade the death penalty—something like a Presidential pardon—that the American public becomes so reluctant to buy Burgundy wines (and possibly any expensive French wine) on the grounds of its quality or its price that the market would become extremely uncertain.

"This would make an end," Mr. Couvreur says, "to the teams of American buyers appearing for a few days in the vineyards, terrified by the mere idea that they could come back home with nothing bought."

What he is saying, of course, is that we Americans will buy anything, including wines that will ship poorly. Moreover, he says, we will pay anything for it. Thus, when there is a lot of money around, the growers double and even triple the yield they can get from their vineyards. This, of course, takes its toll on the quality of the wine.

Watery Burgundies from overproduced vineyards and corner-cutting vintners have become a fact of life. Whether it is the buyer's fault, the maker's fault, or the drinker's fault is hard to say. Probably everyone shares.

Rioja, the Best of Spain

THE FACT IS that the wines of the Rioja region of Spain are very fine wines. But beyond that, they are among the best wine bargains available (1977). If fine wine prices are beginning another upward climb, as many people in the trade believe, the wines of Rioja may play a more prominent role in everyone's wine drinking in the next few years.

There are excellent red Rioja wines in the shops these days for little more than $2 and very old bottles from the 1950's in a few places for under $10. Good wines from the 1960's are to be had for $4 and $5 and there are remarkable jug wines, not always easily obtainable, for less than their California counterparts.

The Rioja region is in the northern part of Castile, not far from the Pyrenees and the French border and a leisurely two-day drive from Bordeaux with time to stop at the Café de Paris in Biarritz.

This proximity to Bordeaux is important in the story of Rioja wines. The region produced good wine at least as far back as the Middle Ages, but it was the *phylloxera* epidemic in Bordeaux in the 1870's that changed winemaking in Rioja for the better. Many Bordelais wine producers fled over the mountains bringing their skills and modern techniques with them.

You will still find in Rioja *bodegas* where the grapes are
forced to release their juice by a manual winepress, worked
here in the traditional method.

Ironically, the Rioja techniques of today often resemble the Bordeaux techniques of a century ago. Long barrel aging, once a hallmark of the great Bordeaux wines, is still practiced in the Rioja. Two years in wood is rare now in Bordeaux; six years is not uncommon in the Rioja.

When wine rests for long periods in barrels, some of it evaporates. In France and California barrels are topped off with wine from the same vintage. In Spain, the producers believe the older wine is freshened and enhanced by the addition of new, or at least younger, wine.

This leads to some confusion about vintages. After a barrel has been topped off twice a year for six years or so, should it still bear the vintage year it had when the barrel was first filled? The Spanish think so. Besides, they say, there is only a bit of the younger wine in the barrel. So be it.

What this process does impart is a magnificent roundness and mellowness to the wine—we're talking about reds here, of course—and a lovely vanilla flavor that is the sign of aging in oak. Occasionally the oakiness is too pronounced, but not too often.

Sometimes drinkers expect the Bordeaux connection to imply a Bordeaux-style wine. The wine trade likes to foster this idea, too, so that the consumer thinks he is getting a Bordeaux at a bargain price. Not true—Riojas have their own style.

Rioja wines all are blends of "musts" from various grapes. The most common, the Tempranillo, often makes up 50 percent of the blend in a red Rioja. Second in importance is the Garnacha, the same grape that produces Châteauneuf-du-Pape in the Rhône Valley of France where it is known as the Grenache.

Rioja whites which, alas, often are allowed to stay much too long in wood, are made mostly of the Malvasia grape which shows up in so many Italian white wines. A Cune Monopole Dry sampled recently had the right touch of oak and was just acidic enough to put it in a class with a good white Burgundy without resembling a Burgundy at all. It was more like a fine dry California Chenin Blanc. Cune, incidentally is an acronym for Compania Vinicola del Norte de España. Its wines are well distributed in the New York City area and sell for under $3.50.

Some of the other Rioja shippers whose labels are to be found in the better shops in this country include: Bodegas Bilbainas, López de Heredia (Viña Tondonia), Marqués de Murrieta, Marqués de Riscal, Federico Paternina, and Marqués de Caceres. One note: look for the word *reserva* on a bottle of Rioja. Spain has been late in catching up with other nations with stiff wine-producing regulations. That change is now taking place. Meanwhile, the word *reserva* indicates that the wine was selected in the vintage year listed to be set aside for special aging both in the barrel and in the bottle.

Most of the best producers or *bodegas* are located in the Rioja Alta, the hillier and moister part of the region, in or near the town of Haro. In all, 38 *bodegas* are entitled to use the appellation, or as the Spanish call it, the *denominacion de origen*, of Rioja.

The lighter wines, those that more resemble Bordeaux, are shipped in Bordeaux-style bottles. The heavier wines go out in Burgundy-style bottles.

Rioja accounts for only a small portion of Spain's total wine production. Unfortunately, except for a few famous producers elsewhere in the country, few other Spanish wines can match the wines of the Rioja region in quality.

A great deal of wine is produced along the Mediterranean coast running southwest from Barcelona. The town of Panades, about halfway between Barcelona and Tarragona, is the home of the big wine firm of Torres, a label now quite familiar in the larger cities in this country. Torres Sangre de Toro is a powerful, rich red wine, more in the Rhône-style than Bordeaux or Burgundy.

While Spain's other wine regions may produce lesser wines they are far from being poor wines. Spanish Burgundy, which comes mostly from the Valdepeñas region south of Madrid, is probably the best jug wine in the world. Unfortunately, quality control is a problem and the wines can be excellent in one bottle and terrible in the next. Four or five years ago there was a greater abundance of cheap Spanish wine. If you can find it now—often in a straw-wrapped jug—it can be extremely good for the price.

Sommeliers—Endangered Species

WOULD I, the caller wondered, be interested in a quick junket to Atlanta? He wanted me to see something new and unusual—a Wine Wench.

Wine Wenches, he explained were the Hyatt Hotel chain's latest contribution to better living and fine dining. Wearing the ceremonial chain of the wine steward—and apparently not too much else—a Hyatt Wine Wench follows up the waiter and offers to help diners select a bottle to accompany their meal.

Sommeliers—Endangered Species

I didn't go to Atlanta and have yet to encounter a Wine Wench, but I have come across most of the handful of true sommeliers left these days. Wine Wenches notwithstanding, they have become a rare species, indeed.

Certainly the dean of New York wine stewards is Victor Puppin, at the Brussels. A venerable but still imposing figure in the regalia of his stewardship, Mr. Puppin presides over one of the better cellars in the city. I remember his first suggestion to me, some 20 years ago: a bottle of Quincy, to go with some chicken dish or other. I'd never heard of the wine before but that meal was the start of a long affair with the wines of the Loire.

Victor is a sommelier in the classic mold. Born in Venice, he worked in kitchens and dining rooms throughout Europe, picking up knowledge of wine along the way. In 1930, at the age of 24, he was made the wine steward at the Berkeley Hotel in London. Next came a stint at "21" in New York. Finally, in 1946, he came to the newly opened Brussels and has been there since.

One of the more serious problems of being a wine steward is getting the guest to reward you for your services. Most Americans and, in fact, most Europeans, have never dealt with a wine steward and are not sure how to react. Most just assume the sommelier shares in the tips of the waiters and captains. Not so. Many sommeliers are bitter about being ignored when the *pourboires* are handed out. Victor Puppin is not one of them. He has his own system and it is fascinating to watch. If his ministrations at tableside have produced nothing, he always manages to be at the door of the dining room when the party leaves. There is only one way to get out of the Brussels so he is well positioned. Even this ploy does not always work, but often it does. And, next time, the guest remembers that sommeliers, too, have to eat.

The great sommeliers of the past were more than wine sellers; they were wine buyers. Victor Puppin recalls how André Pagani, the founder of the Brussels, watched him closely for weeks, then told him: "It's all yours. Buy the wines and build a great cellar."

At the "21" Club, Mario Ricci, who followed Victor and who is now, himself in semiretirement, was also the wine buyer, in consultation with co-owner Jerry Berns, another serious student of the grape. Mr. Ricci has trained John Benevento to take his place. On most evenings, "21" will have two or three wine waiters in the various dining rooms, drawing on a cellar of the same calibre as the Brussels.

Most of New York's famous restaurants long ago dispensed with wine stewards, if in fact they ever had them. Lutèce, La Caravelle,

WINE TALK

Victor Puppin of the Brussels is one of the last of New York's true wine stewards.

The Four Seasons—they all leave the wine selection to the captains. "It gives the captain a chance to involve himself more intimately with the guests at his tables," said Paul Kovi, co-owner of the Four Seasons, "and it gives him a chance to make a better tip."

One reason for the disappearance of the sommelier is the simplification of restaurant dining over the years. The enormous meals of the Victorian and Edwardian eras were accompanied by a range of wines. Serious diners demanded the assistance of experts in orchestrating the succession of bottles. Today, meals are lighter and eaten more quickly. Only a handful of restaurant clients order two different wines with a dinner, and no special expertise is needed in selecting them.

Gone, too, are the vast cellars that were the mark of a great restaurant. Roger Chauveron, who now works in Florida, once recalled the first restaurant he worked at in Paris. Down in the *caves* under the street, there were separate cellars for the reds, the whites, and the Champagnes. And there was, of course, a man of great skill and learning to preside over them.

Robert Depardeau who was the captain/wine steward at Café Chauveron in New York before it closed has no sommelier at La Poullailer, where he is now maitre d'hôtel.

[46]

Sommeliers—Endangered Species

Even Taillevent, in Paris, which is reputed to have one of the greatest cellars of France, has no sommelier. The captains are knowledgeable and Claude Vrignat, the owner, is usually on hand to talk wines with the guests. A few of the old, classic restaurants in Paris still employ a wine waiter—Lucas-Carton and Maxim's, for example—but outside the city they are almost as rare as they are in this country. For one thing, the concept of a wine steward simply does not fit into the concept of the *nouvelle cuisine*, which is based on lightness and informality.

Another Paris restaurant that employs sommeliers is Fouquet's on the Champs-Elysées. One day a young chap walked into my office— an American—and said he was just back from Paris where he had worked as a sommelier at Fouquet's. In fact, he had; with almost no knowledge of wine. His job had been to urge the customers, most of them tourists, to drink wine. Moreover, he was told exactly which wines to urge them to drink each day. Technical problems were referred to an older, more experienced man. He was actually a shill, whose principal job was to move bottles. Not an altogether unworthy task because it did, after all, get people to drink wine.

There are a few younger sommeliers around—the knowledgeable type, not the wine hustlers. Perhaps the best example of the new breed is Kevin Zraly, the wine steward at Windows on the World, the highly popular place atop New York's World Trade Center.

Still in his mid-twenties, Mr. Zraly presides over a huge cellar and one of the most active wine businesses of any restaurant in the country. Windows on the World sells more than 10,000 bottles of wine a month.

Kevin Zraly got interested in wine in college and worked in a small but very wine-oriented restaurant in upstate New York. He grows some grapes on a place he owns in Ulster County, and has visited as many European vineyards and wineries as his schedule has allowed.

At Windows, Mr. Zraly works from a stock of about 10,000 cases of wine, held in the Trade Center's vast cellars. He works from three separate wine lists: a 25-item list at the bottom of the luncheon menu; a separate list for dinner; and a master list—actually a thick book— for the guest who is really into wines. All three lists are constantly being updated. Windows of the World is a businessmen's club at lunchtime and, for the members, Mr. Zraly fulfills some of the traditional roles of a sommelier. He buys wine for them through the club, stores it, and will recork a member's half-finished bottle and keep it for his next visit.

He holds regular seminars for the restaurant's mostly young staff and has initiated a series of wine lectures for members of the restaurant's luncheon club. Along with Alan Lewis, Windows' director, he has a hand in planning the menus at the Cellar in the Sky, a restaurant within a restaurant that features a fixed-price menu which includes three wines. The Cellar is a separate room adjacent to the main dining room of Windows.

But back to those Wine Wenches. A friend reports having dined and drunk well at the Hyatt Regency in Atlanta with a group of business associates. Everyone, he says, complimented the young woman on her wine suggestion. Afterwards, my friend asked her how she arrived at her choice. "Well," she replied, "the first one you mentioned, we have only three bottles of that. The one I suggested, I knew we had enough for your group."

The Wine Bars of Paris

IF YOU ARE A LAWYER and you have had a particularly wearing morning at the Palais de Justice, one of the most pleasant ways to recover is to slip out the back, walk through the picturesque little Place Dauphine and duck into the Tabac Henri IV on the Pont Neuf.

The Tabac Henri IV does a big legal trade because it is so close to the courts, but its fans are by no means limited to lawyers and detectives from the Quai des Orfevres. It is, simply, one of the best of the old-fashioned *tabacs* where really good wines are sold by the glass.

Owner Robert Cointepas has for years sought out the very best Beaujolais and lesser Burgundies to sell by the glass. Of course, you can have a bottle, too, but the beauty of little places such as the Henri IV is the fact that a visit and a taste of a good wine need not take up more than 10 or 15 minutes.

Mr. Cointepas deals directly with many of his suppliers. Indeed, he enjoys displaying on his bar flattering letters from them along with photographs of himself in the vineyards.

The Wine Bars of Paris

The wines of the day are listed on a blackboard, along with their prices. One afternoon recently we sampled a Beaujolais-Villages, a Morgon, and a Chinon, each of which sold for about $1.20 a glass. On some days, Mr. Cointepas may offer a Santenay or even an Aloxe-Corton by the glass. His whites may be mostly Mâcons, but he does have an occasional Auxey-Duresses or other good Burgundy.

To accompany his wines by the glass he offers a selection of good cheeses, pâtés, and sausages, all served on what is generally considered the best dark bread in Paris. A quick snack at the Tabac Henri IV can cost $3 but the quality is high and Mr. Cointepas presumably works on the assumption that the lawyers are all rich anyway.

There are still a dozen or so of these good little spots where a good glass of wine and a decent sandwich are to be had. La Tartine in the rue Rivoli specializes, as does Henri IV, in the wines of Beaujolais and the Touraine. They also serve good goat cheese and country hams.

Au Sauvignon in the rue des Saints Pères features Sancerre, Quincy, and, of course, Beaujolais, along with charcuterie of the Auvergne.

Le Sancerre in the avenue Rapp, over near the Eiffel Tower, specializes in the wine of the same name from vineyards owned by the same family as the *tabac*. One of the food specialties here is a fluffy omelette.

Ma Bourgogne at 133 boulevard Hausmann in the 8th Arrondissement offers a beautiful fresh Pouilly Fumé along with its other wines and specializes in the charcuterie of Saulieu, one of the great restaurant towns of Burgundy.

But of all these little spots, my favorite is a place called B.O.F. which stands for *beurre, oevfs, et fromage*—butter, eggs, and cheese. Without the periods you have a very naughty French word which means, well, never mind. B.O.F. is in the rue des Innocents, which used to be on the fringe of Les Halles, the great central market of Paris. It is an area where butter, eggs, and cheese were once the main commodity and the lifework of B.O.F.'s customers. It is rumored that this was also the busiest black market area in the city during World War II and the most wanted items were, of course, butter, eggs, and cheese.

Les Halles is gone, of course, and in its place is being built a vast agglomeration of convention halls, railroad stations, shopping arcades, parking garages, and restaurants, mostly underground. The old dingy streets on the perimeter are filling with American bars and boutiques. A tiny place like B.O.F.—there are four tables—cannot last much longer.

It's sad because B.O.F., according to people who know Paris well, is

[49]

really very little changed from what it must have been in the late 1800's. Indeed the ancient proprietor in his *bleu de travail* apron looks like a relic of a bygone age. He will give you a glass of Beaujolais or an old newspaper to read, but no water and no coffee. He will make you a sandwich on a miniature stove that pops out of a cabinet behind the miniature bar, but there hardly seems room to eat it.

It's too bad Malraux is gone. He might be induced to declare B.O.F., with its zinc bar, ancient bottles, and ineffable air of a bygone time, a national monument.

While they are more commercial, London is also a good city for wine bars and the idea is just beginning to catch on on this side of the Atlantic. The London Wine Bar in San Francisco, with its long and fascinating array of California wines plus some good European wines has been a success for several years now. It also serves as a retail wine shop.

Toronto now has a wine bar called Vines with about 100 different labels available by the glass, including wines from Germany, Canada, California, and France at about $1.20 a glass. The owner of Vines is said to be considering a similar venture in New York City where wine by the glass is still considered by most restaurants and tavern owners as something close to a license to steal.

Lafite—Tasting Ten Decades

THE HISTORY of Château Lafite-Rothschild can be traced back to the middle of the 13th century but it is unlikely that there was ever, in all that time, a tasting of Lafite wines as memorable as the three-day sampling held there in the fall of 1977.

There is always something slightly off-putting about accounts of tastings of very rare wines. The tone is usually patronizing. Look what I did that you will never be able to do. Okay, granted. But, every so often something happens that you feel you just have to tell everyone about. The Lafite tasting was one of these things.

Picture, if you will, a dinner in the ornate Empire-style dining room of the historic old château. The food? Nothing special: a steak, green beans, and some *ceps* (the local mushroom). But with it came these wines: Château Lafite-Rothschild 1959, 1949, 1934, 1900, 1888, and 1873.

Next morning, a warm, soft, early fall day, in a sunny room overlooking the vineyards, there was a formal tasting: rows of glasses, plates with bits of cheese, pencils and paper for notes. The wines: Lafite 1976, 1975, 1974, 1973, 1972, 1971, 1970, 1969, 1967, 1966, 1965, 1964, 1962, and 1961.

We had the afternoon off. Some slept, some went to the ocean to walk on the beach, a few of us went to explore an 11th century church. Then it was time for dinner, simple roast chicken. The wines: Château Lafite-Rothschild 1953, 1945, 1918, 1893, and 1869.

We finished up on Sunday morning with the second wines of two other Rothschild properties, Château La Cardonne, north of here, at Blaignan, an *appellation* Médoc acquired in 1973; and Château Duhart-Milon-Rothschild, which adjoins Lafite and which was acquired in 1962.

The wines: La Cardonne 1976, 1975, and 1974 and Duhart-Milon 1976, 1975, 1973, and 1971. The weekend ended at lunch Sunday with Duhart-Milon 1967 and Lafite 1955.

Oh yes, in case anyone felt deprived, each meal began with an informal reception and ended with coffee and cigars. The Champagne was Pol Roger and the Cognac was 1889 vintage, from the château's stock.

The purpose of all this was to celebrate what the Rothschilds see as a turning point in the history of Lafite, which they bought in 1868. There have been some staff retirements so there is a new *régisseur*, the man who is responsible for the vineyards and the winemaking. He is Jean Creté, who learned winemaking in Tunisia and has worked at several châteaus in the Bordeaux area. There is, too, a new general manager, Yves Lecanu, an amateur musician who, in his tasting notes, compares the wines to great musical compositions.

Even more important, perhaps, the tasting served as the public debut of Eric de Rothschild, an attractive, lively fellow of 37 who has taken over complete control of the operation of Lafite from his Uncle Baron Elie de Rothschild, just last February. (Elie had been in charge since the 1930's.) Lafite ownership is divided into six shares, all held by members of the Rothschild family. They are, for the most part, members of the French Rothschilds. Château Mouton Rothschild, whose vineyards adjoin Lafite, is owned entirely by Baron Philippe de Rothschild, who comes from the English branch of the clan.

Besides Eric de Rothschild, Mr. Creté, and Mr. Lecanu, the guests at the tasting incuded Guy Schyler, a member of an old Bordeaux family, who has represented Lafite when there are no Rothschilds in town; Dr. Emile Peynaud, a distinguished enologist and currently a consultant to Lafite; Daniel Lawton, a Bordeaux wine broker whose father once helped Clarence Dillon buy Château Haut-Brion; Abdallah Simon, an American importer who buys more Lafite than anyone in the world; and three writers: Odette Kahn, publisher of the *Revue des Vins de France* in Paris; Edmund Penning-Rowsell of *The Financial Times* of London; and myself.

As for the wines: It is hard to say there was a best in show because there were three leagues involved, maybe actually four: the very new wines, the contemporary wines, the older wines, and the very old wines. Of the new wines, I preferred the 1975, which had a lovely bouquet and the taste of oak. Professor Peynaud and several others preferred the 1976, saying it will eventually surpass the year-older wine. In the next group, 1961 was far and away the best of the lot. Some thought it the best wine in the tasting. It is still young. It might be another decade before it is ready to drink.

The 1959, a very famous vintage was thought by some to be the best of that decade. I preferred the 1953. It seemed to me to be a far richer, fuller wine, with a much longer finish, or aftertaste. The 1945, which incidentally sells for about $3,000 a case when one turns up, also got a few votes as one of the best of all. My feeling was that it had dried out and that while still a very fine wine, had no place to go but down.

The 1934 was a beautiful, soft, rounded wine; still very youthful, but lacking in the style and elegance of some of the others in the group. For me the 1929 was not only best of its group but the best of all the wines we drank. It was darker than some of the others, less obvious in either taste or bouquet, but it seemed to possess all the legendary elegance and finesse of the wines of Lafite.

The 1918 had a heavy, dark quality. I used the word "tarry" to describe it, a word used often in California. The French didn't know what I meant. So I dropped it.

Great old wines are often like older women about whom it is said: "She must have been fantastic when she was younger." Not the case with the old Lafites. Even the Bordelais, who remember châteaus and vintages the way some Americans remember long-forgotten baseball teams and players, were astonished at the youthfulness and vigor of the 1900 vintage and the wines from the last century.

In a blind tasting, most of us agreed, it would have been almost impossible to guess that these wines were as old as they were. It was

Worker sweeps floor area where tops of vats are visible. It is
in this area that the vats and presses are loaded with grapes.

difficult to distinguish between the 1953 in one glass and the 1873,
made 80 years earlier, in another. Of course, the fact that the wines
had rested in the Lafite cellar untouched since their bottling made a
difference. It is unlikely that old bottles elsewhere in the world will
match the quality of those here.

Appropriately, for me at least, the oldest of the old, the 1869 was
the best. Forget age, it was very simply a good bottle of wine to
drink. It had color, tannin, a beautiful youthful bouquet, and a rich
full-bodied taste. When you are only going to meet someone or something once in your life, it's nice that the encounter should be so
pleasant. Of this group, only the 1873 really showed its age. Eric de
Rothschild, with tongue only slightly in cheek, described it as "an old,
old, man, who has given up all his worldly goods."

Of the lesser wines, the La Cardonnes were simple wines of no
great repute, good for drinking very early in their careers. Of the
Duhart-Milons, the 1971 took plaudits from many of the group. I
found it to have a peculiar smell and an unpleasant taste. The 1967,
however, which was served later, with lunch, was an excellent wine, a
truly stylish Pauillac.

Needless to say, a tasting of this sort—and we're talking here just of
the Lafites—has some drawbacks. The basic level of quality is so high
that it is difficult to make any objective judgments. The 1965, a
brownish, indifferent wine, was my vote for the bottom of the list,

Antiquities in the caves of Château Lafite-Rothschild.

which, incidentally, we never drew up. "Ah," said Guy Schyler, "have it for lunch some day and you will change your mind." Maybe he was right, I doubt it. The 1969 was no prizewinner, either.

Is there any point in this sort of spectacle for anyone other than the participants? Not much, certainly. None of us are ever going to buy an 1869 or 1929 for that matter, and only a handful will ever taste the 1945. Why even a magnum of the 1961 costs around $350 nowadays. Most of us will never own or drink much new Lafite, either.

What, then, is it all about? This: There is a sweep of history in a tasting such as this one that ennobles any good bottle. It touches anyone who makes, sells, or drinks the best wines he can. In an age when cheapness and obsolescence are sought after and praised, Château Lafite tells us it doesn't have to be that way. And you don't have to be a wine drinker to understand that.

The Right Glass

REX MOTTRAM was a swine. Not that he did anything evil actually. He just happened to represent the modern, acquisitive, insensitive world in Evelyn Waugh's novel *Brideshead Revisited*. And he used the wrong glass.

In one passage, Rex and Charles Ryder, Waugh's alter ego, dine in Paris in 1925. Charles arrives early and orders. Montrachet 1906 with the sole and a Clos de Bèze 1904 with the duck. After a lemon soufflé, there is Cognac.

Writes Waugh: "The cognac was not to Rex's taste. It was clear and pale and it came to us in a bottle free from grime and Napoleonic cyphers. It was only a year or two older than Rex and lately bottled. They gave it to us in very thin tulip-shaped glasses of modest size."

" 'Brandy's one of the things I do know a bit about,' said Rex. 'This one is bad colour. What's more, I can't taste it in this thimble.' "

To Charles' disgust, Rex demands "a balloon the size of his head," and an inferior Cognac which he proceeds to have warmed over a spirit lamp. This is not about Cognac but about glasses. Waugh obviously took them seriously. Most wine lovers do.

There is a fellow here in New York who, two years ago, trekked a case of assorted Baccarat glasses into the National Park on St. John's in the Virgin Islands. He got them at a good price at St. Thomas and he really didn't relish drinking his wine any other way, even in a tropical forest.

Some years ago, at an informal lunch for four aboard a Swedish freighter tied up at Port Newark, each place was set with 12 Orrefors crystal glasses. "We probably won't use them," said the hospitable skipper, "but I like to look at them." In fact, by 5 P.M., most of them had been used, including the smallest, especially designed for aquavit.

Fine glassware is no affectation. A well-made glass is a handsome object by itself. Combined with the color of good wine and the play of light around a table, it becomes an integral part of the whole business of enjoying wine.

To be sure, Baccarat and Orrefors are expensive—up to $20 or $30 a glass. But good wine glasses do not have to cost a great deal. One of the best buys is made by the Colonial Glass Company of Weston, West Virginia and sells for $2.25 (1975) at the Pottery Barn here in New York City. It is a big tulip-shaped goblet that actually holds 20-ounces filled to the brim. It has many of the attributes of the more expensive glasses but can take most of the wear and tear of the average kitchen.

The basic rules for wine glasses are few: they should be stemmed, they should be big, and they should be clear. The stem keeps the hand's warmth from heating up the wine and it makes it easier to see what is in the glass. It is not necessary to hold the glass, as some fanatics do, by the base.

The glass should be big so that it can be filled halfway or less. This leaves room for the wine to be swirled around a bit to release the bouquet—assuming there is any. Also, it leaves room for the drinker to get his nose into the glass to enjoy that bouquet. Guests with larger noses should be served less wine. A good wine glass usually converges at the rim to concentrate the bouquet.

The only decoration on or in a wine glass should be the wine itself. No true wine glass is ever cluttered with Scotties, college seals, clever apothegms, or the monogram of the hostess.

Once, German wine glasses—or, more accurately, glasses for German wine—had green stems. This was to give the drinker the impression that the wine had more color than it really did as he looked down into the glass. The Germans have learned how to give their wine the color they want and green stems have largely disappeared.

The worst wine glasses are the tiny four-ounce ones often found in inexpensive Italian restaurants. Why anyone would use them is a mystery. Even the most modest restaurants in Italy provide a decent-sized glass, even if it is a chipped tumbler. Perhaps the idea is to have the customer work up an appetite by constantly pouring the Chianti.

Needless to say, wine glasses are a problem for restaurants. Commercial dishwashers are not kind to them; either are waiters or customers. The usual compromise is a fairly thick eight-ounce all-purpose glass that can take a beating. Where elegant glasses are used, breakage is going to be part of everyone's bill.

For home use, a 10- or 12-ounce glass is adequate for every occasion. The so-called Bordeaux-style can be used for any kind of wine from Champagne to brandy. The Burgundy-style is best for table wines.

Champagne is not supposed to be served in the flat, saucer-like glasses endemic to most weddings. They are for ice cream or shrimp. The true Champagne glass is tall and thin and is called a flute. It makes the Champagne look better and last longer.

The big 20-ounce goblet mentioned above is actually a combination of the flute and the Bordeaux glass. It can be used for everything. It is strong enough for everyday use and still looks striking at a dinner party. They can be cleaned in a dishwasher but it is safer and they look better when done by hand.

There are some very cheap wine glasses around. They look pretty good at first but they have a thick lip—called a bead—around the rim. Using them is like drinking from a cheese jar. They might be just the thing, though, if you are looking for something to fling into the fireplace.

Snifters, by the way, are perfectly acceptable for brandy, Evelyn Waugh notwithstanding.

A Few Wine Courses

IN THE FALL, there are two important crops in the wine world. One is grapes, of course. The other is students who flock to wine appreciation classes. Harriet Lembeck, who runs one of the best in New York City often sells out her 15-week course weeks before the first session.

Behind me as I write are five shelves, floor-to-ceiling, filled with "how-to" wine books. Sometimes it seems that more people thirst for wine knowledge than for wine. Still, every time another wine book or another notice for a wine course arrives, I hearken back to something Alexis Lichine said years ago: "There is no substitute for pulling corks." It's true. If you don't sniff, taste, and look at the stuff, all the books and courses in the world are not going to be of much value.

Which is not to say the courses and books are not valuable. Anyone with a basic knowledge of wines, self-acquired, would do well to take a good course and get things straightened out in his head. But wine is no different than a lot of other things we become interested in and enjoy. If you choose to become an opera singer you must study singing. But if you want simply to enjoy opera you just go to the opera. It is not necessary to read three volumes of Ernest Newman on Wagner to enjoy *Die Meistersinger*. You don't have to write a paper on Strindberg to enjoy the theater.

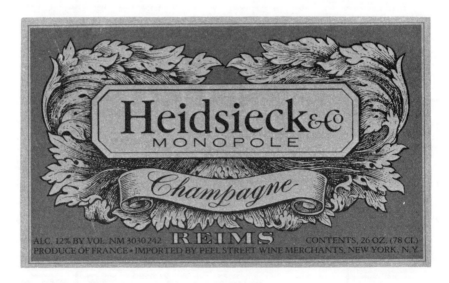

There are lots of people who buy wine by the book. They know the names of the châteaus and vineyards and they know the best vintages. Wine merchants all have stories about customers who order Romanée-Conti and Château Lafite-Rothschild, and Château d'Yquem only because they have heard that they are the best and they can afford them.

A few years back, a big supply of the 1968 vintage of Château Lafite-Rothschild came on the market. It was heavily advertised at $4 a bottle. Lafite at $4 a bottle? Could this be?

It could and was. But 1968 was a mediocre year in Bordeaux and the wine was nothing to write home about when it was bottled. It was not bad. In really bad years, Lafite and other first growth châteaus bite the bullet and sell the wine off anonymously. No, the 1968 was not bad, but neither was it particularly long-lived. In 1971, the best of the 1968's were rather pleasant Bordeaux. But that was it. They had nowhere to go but down.

By 1975, all those unsold cases stood a good chance of turning to vinegar overnight. So, there was a big advertising push and, just like that, all the 1968 Lafite was sold.

At $48 a case, there were literally dozens of better buys around, in lesser-known Bordeaux, in good Burgundies, even in California Cabernets. What some people had always known and the rest of us suspected was true: people do buy labels.

(An interesting sidelight: comedian Dan Rowan, a very serious wine man, told me that once when he and Dick Martin were playing Las Vegas, he was shown a warehouse full of Lafite 1968. "They put it on the menus for the junketeers," he said. "The high-rollers who get free trips in exchange for what they leave at the tables. The wine is listed at $60 a bottle and the suckers think they're making a killing when the house gives it to them for free.")

Label-buying has spawned a whole new breed of wines. Blue Nun, Grande Marque and Mouton-Cadet are all inexpensive blends that change little from year to year, can be produced in huge quantities, and are backed with expensive promotional campaigns. They are for confirmed label-buyers and new wine drinkers who are still unsure of themselves. Good wines all, but rarely exciting, and never bargains. Somebody has to pay Stiller and Meara.

My own feeling is that wine courses, even the simplest, can be confusing to the totally uninitiated and, in some ways, only serve to turn them off. Which brings us back to Alexis Lichine and his dictum about pulling corks.

There is no doubt that the more wine you drink the more you will learn. The problem is that people tend to stick to a wine they like. Thus, even though they are pulling lots of corks, the wine is all pretty much the same.

Accordingly, we have devised an all-purpose course that requires no books and no classroom time and yet is bound to teach the faithful adherent a good deal about wine. It does cost a few dollars, though. Here is what you do: Pick out a well-stocked wine shop that you can use comfortably and frequently. Walk in unannounced. Head for the red-wine section and select a bottle of French red wine for $4 or less. Do not tell anyone in the store what you are doing. Pay for the wine, take it home and drink it with dinner. If possible have dinner with someone else, so you can ask questions such as "What do you think about the wine?," and "I don't know, what do you think?"

The next day, return to the store and buy an Italian red wine in the same price range. Repeat the same process. This time, the discussion will be more penetrating. One of you can say: "It seems different than the one we had last night."

Go through the same routine the next day. In fact, do it ten times. Not necessarily on consecutive days, but certainly on days close enough so that you remember the previous bottle. Try a Spanish wine, then a California wine, then a New York wine. Then go back to France and try a different bottle than the first one. Do the same with Italy. And Spain.

Very soon, you will have acquired a modest wine vocabulary; you will recognize the vast differences in styles of wine; you will have endured a couple of clinkers that you can avoid in the future; and you will have gained confidence in a liquor store. Suddenly, there will be a logic, a rightness to all those forbidding shelves. You won't be an expert, but you won't be a nervous fool, either.

Then it will be time to move on to the whites. This might be more difficult, unless you don't mind eating fish and chicken fairly regularly. Again, start with France. Try a Muscadet, a Chablis, a Mâcon, a wine from Alsace, a Graves. Try the whites of Germany, Italy, Spain, and California. Again, stay in the $4 area.

Some may prove to be too sweet, some too dry, some too bland. Decide for yourself. Then, if you wish, repeat the same process all over again with sparkling wines or rosés. Just bear in mind that playing around with Champagne is a very expensive game.

The beauty of this process is that you develop your own opinions, your own judgments. Later, you can compare notes with friends or with teachers. It is important not to stop along the way. Many people search until they find a wine that suits them, then stay with it for years. Nothing wrong with that, unless you are really interested in extending your knowledge of wine. Then you must forge ahead. Make a note of the ones you like. Then, when you've finished trying new bottles go back and get a case or two of your favorites.

Now, when you buy a bottle for $8 or for $2.50, you have an excellent frame of reference for judging it. Moreover you will be surprised to discover how accurate your judgment is, compared with the opinions of experts. There is nothing hidden in wine; it's all in the bottle waiting for you to find it, just the same as any veteran taster.

If along the way, you become curious about the sources of the wines you are quaffing, pick up a copy of Hugh Johnson's *World Atlas of Wine*, which is in paperback for under $10. The time for books and wine courses is after you have learned a little on your own.

Lafayette, We Are Here

IN A BLIND TASTING held in Paris during 1976, several California wines triumphed over some of the best France has to offer. More startling: the judges were French.

The tasting was arranged by Steven Spurrier, an Englishman who runs a wineshop and the Académie du Vin (where the tasting took place), a school for tourists and Frenchmen alike, in Paris. The wines were limited to two types. The white-wine comparison put California Chardonnays against Burgundy whites, all of which must, by law, be made from the Pinot Chardonnay grape. The red-wine category pitted California Cabernet Sauvignons against only Bordeaux reds, in most of which the Cabernet Sauvignon grape is the principal constituent.

The French judges voted the 1973 Chardonnay from Château Montelena and the 1973 Cabernet Sauvignon from Stag's Leap Wine Cellars the two best bottles in the tasting. Both wineries are relatively new; both are located in California's Napa Valley.

WINE TALK

The judges at the tasting were Pierre Brejoux, Inspector General of the Institut National des Appellations d'Origine; Michel Dovaz, Institut Oenologique de France; Aubert de Villaine, co-director of the Domaine de la Romanée-Conti; Claude Dubois-Millot, commercial director of *Le Nouveau Guide*, a popular gastronomic magazine; Odette Kahn, director of the prestigious *Revue des Vin de France*; Pierre Tari, proprietor of Château Giscours; Raymond Oliver, owner of the restaurant Le Grand Vefour; Jean-Claude Vrinat, owner of the restaurant Taillevent; and Christian Vanneque, wine steward at the Paris restaurant La Tour d'Argent.

The California Chardonnays in the tasting were: Château Montelena, 1973; Spring Mountain, 1973; Chalone Vineyards, 1974; Freemark Abbey, 1972; Veedercrest Vineyards, 1972; and David Bruce, 1973.

The French entries were: Meursault-Charmes (Roulot) 1973, Beaune Clos des Mouches (Drouhin) 1973, Bâtard-Montrachet (Ramonet-Prudhon) 1973, and Puligny-Montrachet Les Pucelles (Domaine Leflaive) 1972.

Except for Drouhin, the names in parentheses are the proprietors of the Burgundy estates where the wine was produced. Drouhin is the name of a wine shipping firm in Beaune that, in this case, probably purchased the wine from several owners in the Clos des Mouches Vineyard, then blended and bottled it in the Drouhin cellars.

Each judge was asked to evaluate the wines as to color, bouquet, palatability, and balance and to give each a numerical rating on a scale of 20 possible points. The results: Château Montelena, 132; Meursault-Charmes, 126.5; Chalone Vineyards, 121; Spring Mountain, 104; Beaune Clos des Mouches, 101; Freemark Abbey, 100; Bâtard-Montrachet, 94; Puligny-Montrachet, 89; Veedercrest Vineyards, 88, and David Bruce, 63.

Regular readers of mine will recall several other similar comparisons in which the American Chardonnays bested their French rivals. In both instances champions of the French wines argued that the tasters were Americans with possible bias toward American wines. What is more, they said, there was always the chance that the Burgundies had been mistreated during the long trip from the wineries.

What can they say now? The judges included some of the leaders of the French wine establishment and there is always the chance that the American wines suffered during their long trip to France. Could Mr. Spurrier have rigged the tasting—providing lesser bottles of the Burgundies? The names—among France's elite—do not indicate that. Moreover, Mr. Spurrier's business consists of selling French wine, mostly to Frenchmen. Aside from the considerable publicity he stands to pick up, there seems to be no reason why he would want to incur the wrath of French wine chauvinists.

The fact is that the best American vineyards and wineries can produce extraordinary wines. Admittedly, the wines in this tasting are from the premium wineries, are in extremely short supply, and cost a great deal of money—anywhere from $6 to $20 a bottle. But the same is true of the Burgundies.

Mike Grgich, the winemaker at Château Montelena, said yesterday he made about 1800 cases of the 1973 Chardonnay, all of which has been sold. The wine was fermented extremely slowly and spent six months in French oak barrels before bottling. His 1974 Chardonnay—another 1800 cases—will be released in August. But, Mr. Grgich said, "The one to watch will be the 1975. I think it will be the Chardonnay of the century." There will be about 5,000 cases of the 1975 Château Montelena, because as Mr. Grgich said, ". . . I just couldn't stop people from bringing in more and more fantastically good grapes."

In the red-wine category an American wine came out on top again. The results were: Stag's Leap Wine Cellars, 1973, 155.5; Château Mouton Rothschild, 1970, 155; Château Montrose, 1970, 150; Château Haut-Brion, 1970, 145.5; Ridge, 1971 Mountain Range, 133.5; Château Léoville-Las-Cases, 1971, 123; Heitz Cellar, 1970 Martha's Vineyard, 114.5; Clos du Val, 1972, 111.5; Mayacamas, 1971, 107; and Freemark Abbey, 1969, 106. (All the American wines were Cabernet Sauvignons, and Mountain Range and Martha's Vineyard were made from grapes from selected vineyards.)

The results, even though they were an enormous compliment to little Stag's Leap Wine Cellars, deserve closer examination. For one thing, only one judge, Mrs. Kahn, picked Stag's Leap Wine Cellars as the top wine and she gave it 15 points. One other judge, Mr. Oliver, joined Mayacamas, Montrose, and Stag's Leap in first place, giving each of them 14 points.

Two judges, Mr. Vanneque and Mr. Brejoux, put Haut-Brion first, each with 17 points, and Mr. Vrinat paired Haut-Brion and Montrose for first. Beyond that, there was little unanimity. Mrs. Kahn gave Ridge 7 points out of 20, Freemark 5, and Clos du Val and Heitz each an ignominious 2. But Mr. Tari gave Ridge his top vote, 17, Heitz 15, and Freemark, grouped with Haut-Brion and Montrose, 14.

Mr. Vanneque gave Clos du Val and Stag's Leap 16.5 each, and Ridge 15.5, but the Mayacamas, to which Mr. de Villaine gave 12, he gave only 3. Mrs. Kahn gave Mayacamas 13.

In short, there was very little consistency. Stag's Leap generally rated high, Mayacamas and Freemark generally rated low. The French tasters were generally kind to Mouton and Haut-Brion.

Is such a tasting a valid judgment on the quality of the wines involved? Probably not. Make no mistake, they are all extremely good wines. But the comparisons may not be fair. Not too long ago, there was a tasting involving a group of first growth Bordeaux of the 1970 vintage. Included were several California Cabernets one of which got high marks from the tasters, all of them men with years of experience in the wine business. It turned out to be a Sebastiani nonvintage Cabernet from California's Sonoma Valley. Was it better than, say, the 1970 Haut-Brion? The French wine had only begun to develop. It may require at least a dozen years to reach its peak. The California wine was ready to drink then.

Where will the Stag's Leap 1973 Cabernet be when the 1970 Mouton reaches its peak, possibly 20 years from now? Is it fair to put the Ridge 1971 against the Clos du Val 1972? Should a 1970 Montrose be on the same table as a 1971 Léoville-Las-Cases? And should these second growths be judged with first growths?

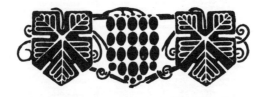

Monarch, the Manischewitz Maker

PASSOVER seemed like the appropriate time to do a story on Manischewitz, probably the most famous name in kosher wine. Then came a letter from one of their agents outlining some of the more unusual facts about the company, which made the story that much easier to do.

The most unusual fact, for openers, was the fact that Manischewitz is a food company. It does not make a drop of wine. The Certificate of Kashruth, which guarantees that the wine is kosher, says Manischewitz Wine Company, but there really is no such company. It is the Monarch Wine Company and it is certainly one of the more fascinating wine operations around.

Monarch, the Manischewitz Maker

When Monarch started up just after Prohibition ended, its founders decided that they would try to get the Manischewitz name, already well-established, for their line of kosher wines. Even then, they had no intention of limiting themselves just to kosher wine. An arrangement was made which is still in effect. Monarch simply pays a royalty to Manischewitz for the use of its name.

Monarch is a full-scale winery but it is not located in a vineyard or anywhere near a vineyard. It is in the Bush Terminal in Brooklyn, in the shadows of the Verazzano-Narrows Bridge. The vineyards are upstate. They stretch from the Finger Lakes to the shores of Lake Erie.

The contract growers bring their grapes at harvest time to two Monarch processing plants at Dunkirk and Fredonia, south of Buffalo. There the grapes are pressed into juice that is frozen in bulk and retained until it is needed at the winery in Brooklyn.

Most wineries use their equipment once a year, after the harvest. Then the presses, sorters, stemmers, and fermentation vats are cleaned and left to wait until the next harvest. At Monarch, wine is made the year around. "Generally, we make wine every month except July," said Monroe Coven, Monarch's bearded, professorial, chief oenologist. "This gives us the efficiency of 11 wineries, or perhaps, a winery 11 times our size."

A winery even twice as big as Monarch's would be difficult to imagine. It encompasses four very large city blocks between Second Avenue and the harbor at 45th Street. Much of the area is warehouse space, but the winery alone is vast.

Actually, there are two wineries: one for still wines and one for Champagne. For an addition to the Manischewitz line, Monarch is the fourth largest producer of Champagne in the United States. Almost all of it is private label, that is to say, the Champagne is the same, but Monarch puts many different labels on it to satisfy customers around the country.

Many fans of Monarch's Champagnes and other sparkling wines do not know they are drinking something made by the makers of Manischewitz. And they certainly do not know their Champagne is kosher—kosher for Passover.

In fact, everything made in the Monarch plant is kosher for Passover. The entire winemaking process is supervised by Rabbis Jacob Cohen of Congregation Ohev Shalom in Spring Valley, New York and Jehoseph H. Ralbag of Congregation B'nai Israel on East 77th Street in Manhattan. Every one of the 400 employees who physically handles any Monarch wine is required to be an observant Jew.

Keeping such a vast winery—it produces some five million gallons of wine a year—kosher presents some problems. For example, Mr. Coven and his staff are cautious about referring to the cultures used to create fermentation as yeast although that is what they are. "Yeast connotes leavening," Mr. Coven said, "which is not kosher. Of course, that has nothing to do with wine, but still, we talk about cultures instead of yeast."

Monarch is also very careful about bringing nonkosher food into the plant. As a result, employees get two meals a day, breakfast and lunch, both strictly kosher, and both supplied by the company. "Besides," said Chester Moss, production director, "there is no place to eat around here, anyway."

According to Meyer Robinson, Monarch's Secretary and Treasurer, only about 10 percent of Manischewitz wine is sold to Jews. What's more, more of it is sold at Christmas than at Passover. In Puerto Rico, according to company figures, Manischewitz outsells the most imported wine from Spain by two to one, and it is shipped regularly to most major cities in the world, including Bangkok, Tokyo, and Hong Kong. "We even sell in Germany," Mr. Robinson said. "Isn't that something—Manischewitz wines in Munich, Germany?"

Monarch officials believe they are second in size only to Gallo among privately owned wineries and first when it comes to diversity. "We have our grape wines, an entire line of fruit wines, and we even make our own vermouth," Mr. Robinson said. "We sell table wines we buy already bottled in California, and we import from France, Italy, Germany, Spain, Austria, and even Japan, under the Tytell label." Robert Lourie, Monarch's Director of Imports, said the firm is the sixth largest wine importer in the country.

Monarch's advertising budget is large, particularly at Passover. But the company's favorite commercials were ones it got free. When Astronaut Eugene A. Cernan paused during his first moonwalk and looked at the incredible surroundings, he exclaimed, for all the world to hear: "Man, oh Manischewitz!" And he isn't even Jewish.

Israel's Wines

FOR MOST Jewish families, the Passover Seder is a time for traditional wine as well as traditional food. In this country, traditional wine has come to mean the sweet, heavy wines made almost entirely from Concord grapes, most of which are grown in New York State.

Most of the so-called kosher wines are doctored with sugar, partly to make them sweeter and partly to offset the unusually high acidity of the Concord grape. In recent years, some efforts have been made to cut the sweetness of these wines, in response to the growing sophistication of American wine drinkers. Even so, they still bear little resemblance to the drier table wines that have become so popular.

Increasingly, many Jewish families combined religious tradition and contemporary taste by serving Israeli wines during the Passover season. Israeli's winemakers produce some 27 varieties of wines, all of which are available in this country and all of which are, necessarily, kosher.

The Israeli wine industry, from vines to bottles, is government-owned, so there is no problem about brand choice: they all bear the Carmel Wine Company label. Carmel dates back only to 1952 when the firm was founded in the United States to market the wines. A similar firm has been doing the same thing in Great Britain since 1897. The United States and England are the two biggest customers for Israeli wines, but they are also sold in about 30 countries.

Wine was produced in Palestine at least 2,000 years before Christ, and Biblical references to wine and vineyards are almost too numerous to mention. In fact, wine apparently was more plentiful than water and was used to wash houses, and as medicine and dyes.

Roman legions tore up most of the Palestinian vineyards in 70 A.D. and those that were replanted were destroyed during the long years of Arab conquest before the Crusades.

According to Alexis Lichine's *Encyclopedia of Wines*, the modern story of Palestinian wines began in 1870 when an agricultural school was founded at Mikveh with a program that included experimentation with wine grapes. Some Christian monastic orders were growing grapes in the country and, in 1880, German Templars planted large tracts of land in the Carmel district with vines from the Rhine Valley.

Around the same time, the first Zionists were beginning to arrive in Palestine and some of them, underwritten by Baron Edmond de

Rothschild, began planting vineyards and by 1890, some 7,000 acres of grapes were in cultivation.

In 1906, the Rothschilds turned the wineries over to the growers. The cooperative they founded still exists. In fact, it produces some 75 percent of all Israel's wines.

The cooperative has two major facilities, one at Rishon-le-Zion, near Tel Aviv; the other at Zikhron Ya'agov, a few miles south of Haifa. Not until the establishment of Israel, however, did the nation's wine business begin to prosper.

The influx of thousands of immigrants, some of them trained viticulturists, led to vastly increased domestic consumption of wine and, by 1950, to a doubling of the wine grape acreage. Today, there are some 10,000 acres of vines in Israel.

Here in the United States, the Israel wine industry hopes to build a market for Carmel wines both as holiday wines and as table wines for any meal. Promotional efforts recently have dwelt heavily on the original Rothschild influence and, in fact, there are Bordeaux qualities to the Israeli wines. But they are wines of the Mediterranean basin, much more akin to the wines of Greece or Cyprus. To burden the wines by forcing a comparison with Bordeaux is unfair to them. They should be drunk and appreciated in their own class.

Carmel wines are widely available in this country, particularly in metropolitan areas. The best-known include Adom Atic, a Burgundy type, Avdat Red and Avdat White, blended along Bordeaux lines; Partom, a Port style, and Sharir, a Sherry. There is a Champagne, there are brandies, liqueurs, even a gin and a vodka. One of the brandies, of which there are reputed to be only 2000 bottles extant, was released just for Israel's 25th anniversary. It comes in a blue satin bag and is called, appropriately, Carmel 25th Anniversary Brandy.

There is another way to enjoy Israeli wine: own your own vineyard. An outfit called Israel International Corporation will sell you a half-dunam share of a vineyard near Zikhron Ya'agov. Your deed, the company claims, entitles you to 10 cases of your own wine, with your private label, every year. Israel International is in Greenwich, Connecticut. Rubin Dobin, one of the promoters, said the company is also buying land near Nazareth and Bethlehem.

Corkscrews—The Long, Hard Pull

THERE ARE supposed to be people who, lacking the appropriate tools, can grasp a wine bottle with one hand, swat it vigorously on the bottom with the other and send the cork flying across the room—with no loss of the contents.

For most of us, this kind of bravado is interesting to contemplate but completely impracticable. Unless the wine we plan to have at dinner is a 39-cent Muscatel with a screw-on cap, we need a corkscrew.

There is probably no more aggravating, frustrating, annoying little household tool than the corkscrew. Who among us has not, with the entire family watching, given that last expert pull and gotten nothing but shredded cork? Who has not ended up pushing the cork into the bottle or, in a demonstration of total ineffectuality, been unable to budge the damn thing at all?

Wine has been around some 6,000 years or so but bottled wine as we know it dates from the turn of the 17th century. Corks were not new then but they were just stoppers, jammed into a bottle temporarily and pulled out by hand—or possibly by teeth, the way John Wayne does it with a bottle of redeye.

When the concept of aging wine came into vogue it was followed quickly by corks that would stay in the bottles indefinitely. These corks had to be pushed all the way in. Of course, they couldn't be pushed all the way in unless there was some way to get them out. Enter, the corkscrew, or bottlescrew as it was known for many years.

The French call it a *tire-bouchon*—cork-puller—which is a bit more accurate. As we shall see, not all the devices that extricate corks from bottles use a screw.

Old prints show bewigged gentlemen wrestling with bottles using corkscrews not much different than those we use today. We must assume then, that they became just as angry as we do now when their corkscrews didn't work. Would that the science of cork-pulling had developed over the years as well as the art of winemaking.

Not that modern science has ignored the problem. No novelty shop worth mentioning is without its supply of clever corkscrews. Generally they can be found under a sign saying "party equipment," and they are grouped with equally useless bottle and can openers, glass swizzle sticks, and cocktail napkins with bawdy inscriptions.

[69]

Often these corkscrews are not screws at all but dangerous devices designed to feed gas into the bottle through a vicious-looking needle of the type used for spinal taps and giving horses illegal injections. The gas, from a carbon-dioxide pellet, is supposed to push the cork effortlessly from the bottle.

The only time I tried one of these devices, the bottle exploded. It was an old-fashioned Chianti bottle, almost covered with straw, so the glass did not fly as far as it might have. But the wine went right through the straw and all over the dinner table. Later I learned that these CO_2 cork extractors are not to be used on Italian Chianti-type bottles or on German wine bottles. The German bottles, it seems, tend to have weak spots that will give under the extra pressure.

I was surprised, recently, to see my friend Andrew C. McNally, the fine wine expert for Heublein Inc., take one of those lethal CO_2 extractors from his tool kit as he prepared to open a cache of very old wine bottles. Mr. McNally approaches the opening of a bottle the way a surgeon approaches opening someone's head, so I decided that if anyone should have one of those things it should be him. As a matter of fact, he never used it that day. "Only on special occasions," he said, declining to amplify.

Just a few weeks ago, one of the better-known department stores in New York was pushing another pressure gadget for opening bottles. This one had to be pumped once the needle was inserted in the cork. The young woman demonstrating the device matter-of-factly pulled cork after cork without ever interrupting her sales pitch. A lot of people were buying them, too. Not me. I wouldn't touch one of them with a ten-foot pole. There would always be that thought in my mind as the pressure built up: Which is going to go first, the cork or the bottle.

For me, the most efficient of all corkscrews is the common one with a wooden capsule, a wire helix (the screw part), and two wooden turners, like small propellers, on the top. The smaller turner pushes the helix into the cork; the second one, using tremendous leverage, pulls the cork from the bottle. I've never know this type of corkscrew to fail on a normal—that is, not dried out—cork.

The standard waiter's corkscrew, the kind that looks like a penknife and, in fact, often has a small penknife blade, is not one of my favorites. Its advantage is portability. It folds up into a very small package. But unless the helix is good, and most of them are not, this style corkscrew can fail at critical moments. It will rip through a dry cork or a soggy one, leaving most of the cork in the bottle and, subsequently, even tougher to remove.

Corkscrews—The Long, Hard Pull

Not dangerous, but frequently inefficient, is the contraption with two sidearms that go up as the point goes into the cork and are then pulled down to extract the cork. The business end of these gadgets is usually an awl, that is, a straight metal shaft with a worm-like edge. They frequently pull right out of the cork without budging it from the bottle.

About eight years ago, in a liquor store in Carmel, California, I discovered a tray of what looked like small chrome tongue depressors in a bowl on the counter. "It's the best cork-puller in the world," the clerk said, and showed how it worked. It had two steel prongs that must be wiggled down between the bottle and the cork. Then they are twisted sideways and up, bringing the cork with them. At $1.25, I couldn't resist. I still use it almost exclusively.

The Ah-So, as this particular cork-puller is called (although it comes from Germany, not the Orient), is not as good as the double action corkscrew, but it is the lightest, most portable of all—and the simplest. It works on old corks, wet corks, and corks that have been chewed up by other corkscrews. It takes a little practice to get used to the Ah-So, but it's worth the effort. Oh yes, it is not $1.25 any more. Some places get $6 for it, but it can still be found for around $3.

The utter simplicity of the Ah-So is entirely out of keeping with the great corkscrew tradition. The Victorians, besides being great claret drinkers, were also gadget-happy and some of the combinations they contrived that included corkscrews almost defy the imagination. In 1855, for instance, a design was patented for a device that, besides a corkscrew, included a nail scissors, a rasp, an ear picker, and a cigar piercer. In 1882, one appeared that was combined with a pocket cigarette-making machine, a knife, a buttonhook, and a spring-bit screwdriver.

Inevitably, people would begin to collect old corkscrews and just as inevitably, they would form themselves into a society. The group is called The International Correspondents of Corkscrew Addicts and it is headed by Brother Timothy, the Cellar Master of the Christian Brothers Wineries in California. Brother Timothy bears the title of "Right" in the I.C.C.A. It comes from the old adage: "I'd rather be right than president."

Do not think for a moment, though, that that sort of levity characterizes the affairs of the Correspondents. Corkscrew collecting is a serious affair involving considerable sums of money. Corkscrews, for one thing, have become a regular part of Christie's and Sotheby's auctions in London.

Brother Timothy's collection, known as the Christian Brothers Collection, presently more than 1,300 corkscrews, some of them more than 200 years old. His rarest, made by William Pitts of London in 1805 or 1806, includes a nutmeg grater. According to Brother Timothy, the nutmeg probably was used to disguise poor wines.

Brother Timothy's collection—parts of which are usually on display at the Wine Museum in San Francisco—is based mostly on esthetic appeal. Other collectors prize corkscrews for their mechanical prowess, or lack thereof. One Connecticut man prides himself on owning three of the most useless corkscrews ever made.

Corkscrews, good ones, have sold at auction for up to $400. (Brother Timothy once bartered 10 cases of wine for one.) Prices inevitably must go up. Traditionalists deny it, but the chances are that one day, corks will disappear. Even now, the supply barely meets the demand. The great, two-and-a-half-inch corks of the past are no more, even in the most famous Bordeaux bottles. Champagne producers make no secret of the fact that they would welcome a substitute for the cork that now costs them up to 40 cents for each bottle they fill.

When corks do disappear, corkscrews will, of course, become totally useless. And because of the perversity that lies at the basis of all things, they will immediately become more valuable.

Meet Petite Sirah

IN 1976, I wrote about a great buy in a California wine: a nonvintage Cresta Blanca Petite Sirah which was available at the time for under $2.50 a bottle. Cresta Blanca was having distribution problems at the time and readers experienced a great deal of frustration in trying to find the wine.

The story made some people angry but also made a few adventurous readers interested in learning more about Petite Sirah. It is safe to say that their efforts were not unrewarded. Petite Sirah is another of those grapes, like Zinfandel, that California has taken to itself and produced something special.

As far as anyone can tell, the Petite Sirah is a relative of a lot of grapes that make their home in the Rhône Valley of France, particularly one called the Duriff. There is also a French Sirah, from which the famous Hermitage is made. The California version may or may not be a close variation of that one, too.

Unless you happen to be working for a doctorate at the University of California or the University of Bordeaux, really, what difference does it make? The fact is that the Petite Sirah, once a lowly blending grape thought to produce best in hot climates, has turned out, in recent years, to be the source of a whole new class of wines.

Not surprisingly, the California Petite Sirahs bear the same relationship to the more elegant wines, such as Cabernet Sauvignon, as the Rhône Valley wines in France do to the more elegant wines of Burgundy. There is nothing particularly subtle about Petite Sirah. It is a strong, dark, powerful wine—a Percheron compared to a racing thoroughbred.

Even some of the best Zinfandels outclass most Petite Sirahs but that might not be for long. Some of the more recent versions of this wine are surprising in their sophistication. Most of this style, it should be noted, comes from aging in small oak casks. There are those who say that almost any wine will taste good after a few months in a new barrel, but wood undeniably does something worthwhile to Petite Sirah.

There are light Zinfandels and heavy Zinfandels, even *rosé* and white Zinfandels, but no one—at least not so far—has attempted to make anything out of Petite Sirah other than a solid red wine. True, some of the Petite Sirahs from California's hotter climes are softer and lighter than the big wines from the north coast but even the lighter ones make for a considerable mouthful of wine.

According to Norman Roby, a veteran observer of the California wine scene, the Concannon Vineyard at Livermore was the first to produce a varietal Petite Sirah—a wine made from at least 51 percent Petite Sirah grapes—back in 1961. It was a huge, rich wine, according to Mr. Roby, because it came partially from vines planted by the Concannons in 1911 and whose fruit, over the years, had been blended into the winery's "Burgundy."

At about the same time, Lee Stewart, the founder of Souverain, was experimenting with a varietal Petite Sirah. The wines found a limited but appreciative audience and were continued. Later in the decade, other wineries experimented with their own Petite Sirahs and more and more growers, the men who supply the wineries, began to plant more Petite Sirah vineyards.

Today, there are a dozen or more Petite Sirahs on the market, a number of them in fairly wide distribution. One of the more outstanding has to be the 1974 Mendocino from Fetzer Vineyards. It is a big tannic wine but there is plenty of fruit to balance things off. At around $4.50 (1977), it is a fine way to get to know this kind of wine. There is a Mendocino 1974 Special Reserve, too, but I have not tasted it. The crafty Californians probably hoard it all.

A much softer, rounded Petite Sirah is the Sonoma Vineyards 1973. You'd probably say that this is a more refined type of Petite Sirah but it does have fullness and flavor and at around $3.50 it is an interesting buy. Mirassou has produced a fine, deep, Petite Sirah from Monterey and Santa Clara grapes and Souverain recently released its 1974 Sonoma Petite Sirah which, it claims, is better than the 1973, a rather appealing wine in its own right. Souverain has gone through a number of mutations since Lee Stewart came out with one of the first of the modern Petite Sirahs in 1964, but the heritage is there and the wine is a good one.

Simi's 1972, made from Alexander Valley grapes exclusively, is a lighter version of the traditional north coast Petite Sirahs, and Ridge's 1974 York Creek—made from grapes grown in a vineyard in the Napa Valley—is a classic Ridge Vineyards wine: dark, intense and rich, and still young.

Eli Callaway, the controversial proprietor of Callaway Vineyards down near San Diego, recently sent along a magnum of his 1974 Petite Sirah with the admonition that it be left for 30 years. In the bottle it appears to be an extremely dark purple wine. I will report further on it in June, 2007.

Zinfandel, the Mystery Grape

WE HAD a Merlot fad, we almost had a Petite Sirah fad, and Cabernet Sauvignon is always a bit faddish, but there is always one red wine grape that is popular with the true California wine enthusiasts: the Zinfandel.

The only place in the world you will find the grape is in California and how it got there nobody really knows. For almost a century, everyone was convinced that it had been brought here by Agoston Haraszthy, the improbable Hungarian who founded Sauk City, Iowa, Buena Vista Vineyards in Sonoma County, and later allegedly was eaten by crocodiles in Costa Rica.

There are some indications that the grape was here before Haraszthy arrived in the mid-1800's, but whatever its origins it has become one of the best-known grapes grown in this country. That has to be at least partly because it produces such good wine.

The Zinfandel grows well in any region suitable for the true European wine grape varieties—and a lot of hotter regions where other varieties, such as Cabernet Sauvignon, do not. Thus, Zinfandel can be found in almost every wine-growing section of California, from the blazing-hot Central Valley around Bakersfield to the coolest vineyards of Mendocino County, hundreds of miles to the north.

The range of Zinfandels produced reflect this wide diversity of soils and climates. In 1976, at the Los Angeles County Fair, 43 Zinfandels were entered and they represented almost as many styles of vinification.

For many years, the Zinfandel was considered a lesser grape and was used for jug wine, for blending into other wines, and for shipping east, as fruit, for the home winemakers of New York and Boston. Today, Zinfandels are vinified with all the skill and care of the finest Cabernet and the results show it.

August Sebastiani says Zinfandel should possess a distinctive "bramble" flavor, but only he and a few other people know what the flavor of brambles is.

Most wine lovers, including the oenologists at the University of California, say the Zinfandel flavor at its best is reminiscent of blackberries. In any case, it should be about halfway between the Cabernet Sauvignon and the Pinot Noir grape in terms of tannin—that astringent taste that is part of any great wine—and the wine should be fruitier than the best Cabernets.

PRODUCED AND BOTTLED BY
SHERRILL CELLARS, WOODSIDE, CALIFORNIA

ALCOHOL 12½ % BY VOLUME

1974

ZINFANDEL

CALIFORNIA

Zinfandels can resemble Cabernets if they are made the same way. Indeed, a fine Ridge Vineyards Zinfandel has five times the finesse and elegance of some second-rate Cabernet. But a great Cabernet is always better than a great Zinfandel. What's more, it probably will last far longer. Few Zinfandels improve after four or five years of age.

Bob Thompson, one of the more astute observers of the California wine scene, believes that the best Zinfandels come from Sonoma County, where old Agoston Haraszthy made so much of the grape back in the 1860's. But he also believes that the best in Sonoma County come from the Russian River region, a good stretch north and west of the old Buena Vista Vineyards.

If anything, it is too early—by about 20 years—to say where the best Zinfandels come from. Ridge makes one entirely from grapes from the Shenandoah Valley in the foothills of the Sierra Madre. Sutter Home, which makes only Zinfandels, brings many of its grapes from the Deaver Ranch in Plymouth, 120 miles east of the Napa Valley winery.

David Bruce makes magnificent Zinfandels from Monterey County grapes and Bernard Fetzer has a little gem of a light Zinfandel made entirely from grapes from Lake County, east of his winery in Mendocino.

The Bruce 1972 was, to my mind, the finest of 11 Zinfandels at a tasting put on by some colleagues in the Wine Writers Circle. The label did not signify, but the wine gave every indication of being a late-harvest wine, that is, one made from grapes left on the vine to their peak of ripeness. It was inky-dark, intensely flavored, and highly tannic, with a rich, powerful bouquet. It was a wine to be savored by itself, like a Port and, as such, probably didn't belong in a tasting of table wines. Which may be why so many others at the tasting preferred the Clos du Val 1973 and the Ridge Lytton Springs 1973. Clos du Val is produced by a young man, Bernard Portet, who grew up at Château Lafite-Rothschild in Bordeaux. He attempts to make wine in the austere, subtle way of Bordeaux but he still manages to achieve an intensity in his wine that is strictly California. Ridge, which in some years produces five or six Zinfandels, all from separate vineyards or grape-growing regions, is consistently the finest of all Zinfandel winemakers. The depth and range of the wines from this one producer are truly amazing.

This particular tasting was a wealth of riches, which is a bad thing to say. It sounds more like shilling to the trade than an exercise of critical judgment. Even so, most of the wines were very good. I found a 1972 Parducci slightly oxidized but still worth drinking and a 1972 Sutter Home, with a very soft, ripe raspberry flavor, to be delightful.

A Christian Brothers nonvintage Brother Timothy Special Reserve was a big-bodied wine with a rounded finish—which means to me that the tannin is less noticeable and the harshness is gone. This comes from blending several vintages.

A 1973 Simi and a 1973 from Burgess Cellars both seemed closed in, that is, they had not yet developed enough to be fully enjoyed.

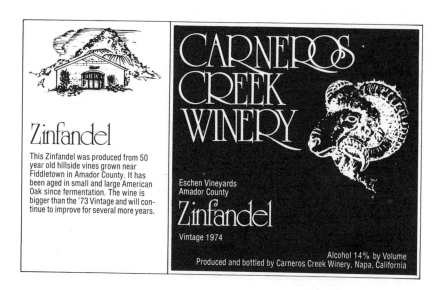

Zinfandel

This Zinfandel was produced from 50 year old hillside vines grown near Fiddletown in Amador County. It has been aged in small and large American Oak since fermentation. The wine is bigger than the '73 Vintage and will continue to improve for several more years.

CARNEROS CREEK WINERY

Eschen Vineyards
Amador County

Zinfandel

Vintage 1974

Alcohol 14% by Volume
Produced and bottled by Carneros Creek Winery, Napa, California

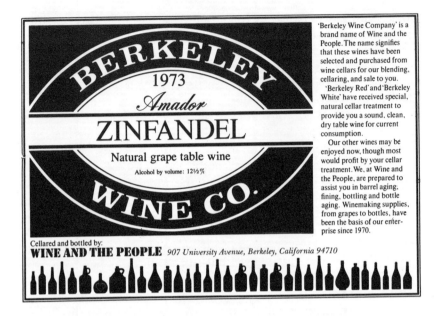

Both were well-made wines, however. Another year of bottle age would have made a difference.

A 1973 from Dry Creek Vineyards was another big wine with a dark, garnet color and intense bouquet and flavor. It had a particularly pleasant, spicy aroma. Finally, there was the 1974 Zinfandel from Château Montelena, the current darling of the new wineries. It was a wine of great finesse and style—not as overpowering as, say, the Ridge, but a wine in the sophisticated Bordeaux style. Before the covers were removed, I thought it was the Clos du Val.

For a change, this was not just an academic tasting of unobtainable California wines. Most of the wines are available in the New York area at the better wine shops although probably no store will carry them all.

The Cellar at "21"

PETE KRIENDLER once told me this story: Three men came into the "21" Club one night with women who did not appear to be their wives. Obviously bent on making a big impression, the men brushed aside the wine list and asked for "the oldest bottles in the house."

"We have a lot of old stuff down in the cellar," Mr. Kriendler, one of the owners of "21" said. "We don't know what condition it's in and we don't really know what it's worth. So I made a deal with them: some very old wine—1876, 1899—one hundred bucks a bottle, no returns. They drank it, that's all I know."

The story is pure "21": casual, unorthodox, but with lots of style. The tale also discloses something that even some of "21's" scotch-drinking regulars do not know: The restaurant has one of the great wine cellars in the city.

There may be doubts about some of the old bottle (they are listed on the wine card as "Château l'Inconnu"), but there is no question that it is possible, at 21 West 52nd Street, to call up from the depths an 1876 Lafite, an 1874 Latour, or an 1869 Mouton. There are no ancient Burgundies, of course, but the card does list plenty of 1966's, some beautiful 1961's, and many wines from the Domaine de la Romanée-Conti in the 1955 vintage. It is safe to say that no French restaurant in the city can match the selection of great French wines available at "21."

Among the people who are aware of what treasures lie in wait belowstairs at "21" are a number of canny Frenchmen. When Baron Philippe de Rothschild comes to New York, he heads for René Dreyfus's restaurant, Le Chanteclair, because both men were daredevil auto racing drivers 50 years ago. But when Philippe Cottin, the Baron's manager at Château Mouton, is in town, he heads for "21."

One reason for the depth and variety of the "21" *cave* is the restaurant's longevity. Wine cellars are not created overnight. To be able to offer 1955 Burgundies, you have to have purchased them in 1957. Which is exactly what the club's head wine steward, T. Mario Ricci, did. Late in 1977, Mr. Ricci, who is in semiretirement, and co-owner Jerry Berns were selecting and buying their 1975 Bordeaux—wine which will not appear on the list for three or four years.

The "21" legend was created by two-fisted—and well-heeled—drinkers such as John O'Hara and Robert Benchley. Less well-known

Many of the regulars at "21" have their own bins full of vintage wine.

is the fact that the tradition of fine wines goes back to the club's earliest days. It's origins were in Greenwich Village where Jack Kriendler and his cousin, Charlie Berns, opened a speakeasy called The Red Head, around 1922.

The Red Head was the precursor of a succession of places that culminated in the opening of the present "21" on New Year's Day, 1930. One of the features of the speaks run by Jack and Charlie was good food, decent liquor, and, even in the depths of Prohibition, good wines, often spirited off ships in the harbor in the dead of night.

With the coming of Repeal, beer and whiskey flowed freely once again, or at least a bit more freely than it had under the Volstead Act. At "21" the wine cellar also benefited from the new dispensation. "The emphasis was French in those days," Pete Kriendler recalled, "and my brother tried to match the wines to the menu. He began the tradition of laying down good bottles."

John Karl Kriendler did more than that. He began acquiring rare old wines at estate sales. Some of the oldest bottles in the "21" cellar today are there because of canny purchases more than 40 years ago.

Jack Kriendler began the tradition of good wines at the "21" club, but it was his younger brother Mac—Maxwell—Kriendler who became the connoisseur. "I first met Mac Kriendler with Orson Welles on the Riviera in the 1930s," Alexis Lichine said recently. "We talked about wines, of course, and the next thing I knew, we were in Burgundy, tasting, tasting, tasting."

In those days, Mr. Lichine was associated with the late Frank Schoonmaker. Later, they went separate ways and both became suppliers and wine consultants to the club. Both, in fact, appear in photographs in Marilyn Kaytor's lively history of the restaurant, titled "21."

"Mac became the enthusiast's enthusiast," Mr. Lichine said. "He began buying wine in *tonneaus* (barrels holding about 1200 bottles) and having it bottled especially for "21.""

After the War, when Alexis Lichine was putting together his syndicate to buy Château Lascombes in Bordeaux, the group included Mac Kriendler and various "21" regulars such as banker Gilbert Kahn. The château later was sold to an English firm but the "21" wine card still lists Lascombes '57, '61, '66, '70, and '71. It also lists Château Prieuré-Lichine, Mr. Lichine's personal property, in the 1964 vintage. What's more, the bar wines at "21" are both Lichine wines. The white is a French Pinot Chardonnay under the Alexis Lichine label and the red is a new wine simply called Alexis Lichine Red Table Wine, which is a soft, attractive Bordeaux, just appearing in the United States.

[81]

BONNES-MARES

APPELLATION CONTROLÉE

RÉCOLTE

1973

MIS EN BOUTEILLES
DANS MES CELLIERS

BERNARD GRIVELET

NÉGOCIANT-ÉLEVEUR AU CHATEAU A CHAMBOLLE-MUSIGNY (COTE-D'OR)

BOTTLED IN FRANCE

"LONGE PROSPICIO"

Chateau Bottled table wine	Outstanding Growth
1 Pt. 8 Fl. Oz. - Alc. by vol. 13%	Produce of France
IMPORTED BY **LEONARD KREUSCH INC.**	MOONACHIE, N.J.
Sole Agent for U.S.A.	

Among the owners, Jerry Berns is the resident wine expert. Nothing is poured in the house that he has not tasted and approved. A serious student of wine, he slips away from the club in the afternoon for tastings whenever he can.

In the dining rooms, the most likely candidate to assume Mario Ricci's mantel is John Benevento, a waiter for ten years at the old Forum of the Twelve Caesars before coming, in 1971, to "21." "I spotted him right away," said Mr. Ricci. "He was a good wine man then, he's a better one now."

Many "21" customers know exactly what they want. Some even keep stores of their own wine in the club's cellar. Burgess Meredith has a superb collection of Burgundies, for example, and there are quite a few bottles with notations such as: "Miss Nancy Tucker from Daddy. To be opened after wedding."

There are, of course, many customers who do not know what they want and it is the sommelier's job to help them out. "You size them up," said Mr. Benevento. "You find out what they are eating and suggest something in the appropriate price range. Sometimes you guess wrong and get a guy who says, 'I wanted a bottle of wine—I didn't want to buy the place.' "

Are bottles ever returned? Rarely, according to the sommeliers. "Our job is to intercept the bad ones, before they get to the guest," Mr. Benevento said.

"Edward G. Robinson once made me take back a magnum of Château Gruaud-Larose," Mr. Ricci said. "I asked him if it was bad or if he just didn't like it. He said he just didn't like it."

Wine is not cheap at "21" but it is less expensive than at some other restaurants in the city because many bottles are priced based on a markup of the original cost rather than on current replacement value. Of course, for many wines in the "21" cellar, such as those 1955 Burgundies, there is no replacement value.

Probably the stiffest wine tab in the place is for a glass of bar wine. With tax, the price is $3.14 or not much less than the cost of a full bottle at retail. I mumbled something to that effect on being presented with my bill one afternoon. My companion straightened me out. "You're not buying a drink," he said. "You're renting space at the most famous bar in the world."

Thomas Jefferson, Wine Lover

THE BICENTENNIAL was not a total loss—we've discovered Thomas Jefferson. Earlier this year we learned that he enjoyed eating, collected recipes, and tried to improve the quality of what he and his friends consumed in Virginia and at the White House.

There has always been an indication that Jefferson loved wine. Part of the traditional wine lore is a selection of his letters in which he praises the wines of Château Haut-Brion and Château d'Yquem. Now, thanks to the diligent efforts of some latter-day *vignerons* in Jefferson's state, Virginia, and some skilled historians, the third President's close association with wine is better known.

We always knew, for example, that Jefferson was impressed with

Bordeaux. It turns out that he loved his Burgundies, too. On January 22, 1789, when Jefferson was in Paris as Ambassador to France, he wrote to M. Parent, his shipper in Beaune:

"For a few weeks, sir, I have been meaning to ask you for a shipment of Meursault wine. But the season was rough so that I thought it best to wait until it relents. It was long in coming so now I have urgent need for it. Therefore, I would appreciate, dear sir, you shipping me 250 bottles of wine of goutte d'or Meursault.

"I got so used to Mr. Bachey's 1784 that if he still has some, I would prefer it. If he is out of it, be kind enough to supply the best available in this class of wine. . . ."

On February 16, M. Parent replied from Beaune. "A shipment of four baskets in bottles, packed in straw, and stringed up and marked PS No. 1 and 3 and 4, one of which contains twenty-five Boncretien pears that I sent you because I believe they must be rather scarce in Paris after the hard frost of last winter. There are 248 or 249 bottles in the four baskets, which left the 14th and should be received later in the month or by the first of March at the latest."

Parent went on to tell Jefferson that he had got the last of the 1784 but that the price had gone up and that it was not from Mr. Bachey—"He has only '87 vintage available and they are not very good, red nor white. . . ."

Parent went on to say that Bachey still had some of the 1788 goutte d'or but that he wanted 500 pounds for it and half already had been sold. If Jefferson wanted any, Parent advised, he had better order soon. The more things change, the more they remain the same.

Jefferson wrote back on March 11 to say that he had received the four baskets of Meursault but, he added:

"The Bachey wine you sent has made me a bit demanding. The shipment I just received from you was not as perfect. I would have thought it was a year other than 1784, if you hadn't told me it was that year." Nothing like keeping the *négociant* on his toes.

Perhaps Jefferson was a bit harsh with his Burgundy shipper because of some of his experiences in Bordeaux. There he worked through John Bondfield, the American consul in that port city. To a friend in Virginia looking for an agent in Bordeaux, Jefferson, writing from Paris, recommended Mr. Bondfield.

"If wine is your object," Jefferson wrote, "he is a good judge of that. He supplies me, as he had before done Doctor Franklin, with very good.

"They cost now 30 sous a bottle and 2 livres (pounds) when 3 years old, which is the age before which they should not be drank. . . ."

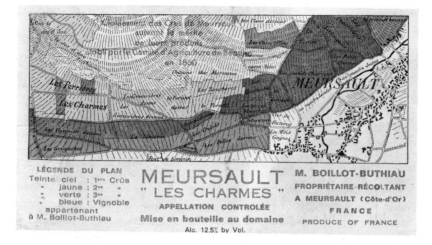

LÉGENDE DU PLAN
Teinte ciel : 1ᵉʳˢ Crûs
" jaune : 2ᵉˢ "
" verte : 3ᵉˢ "
" bleue : Vignoble
appartenant
à M. Boillot-Buthiau

MEURSAULT
" LES CHARMES "
APPELLATION CONTROLÉE
Mise en bouteille au domaine
Alc. 12.5% by Vol.

M. BOILLOT-BUTHIAU
PROPRIÉTAIRE-RÉCOLTANT
A MEURSAULT (Côte-d'Or)
FRANCE
PRODUCE OF FRANCE

In May 1788, Jefferson wrote to Bondfield to say that some Sauternes he had ordered had arrived safely and to request 125 bottles of the 1784 "vin d'Hautbrion" from the Comte de Fumelle, who then owned the Haut-Brion property.

On June 28, Mr. Bondfield replied that the "125 bottles of Haut-Brion shall be shipt by the first ship that sails from hence for Rouen or Havre." The sea route was then safer and quicker than the overland roads.

But in October, Bondfield was writing to Jefferson apologizing for the fact that the wine had been sent to someone else by mistake. "The vintage and a wedding we have had in our family," he wrote, "captivated me most of this fall in the country that in truth I had lost sight of the Comte. . . ."

Bondfield tried to make amends but, apparently, Fumelle sensed the fix he was in. "The Comte has only four hogsheads of 1784 on hand," Bondfield informed Jefferson in Paris. "I offered him 600 livres (pounds) for one of them which he refused.

"I am to have two cases of the first hogshead he draws off," Mr. Bondfield went on. "It is too much to pay three livres in Bordeaux for a bottle of Bordeaux wine, but so great has been the demand for that vintage that the holders obtain that exorbitant price."

Poor Bondfield had to worry for a couple of months. But in December, Jefferson put him at ease. "The accident of the Haut-Brion wine," he wrote on December 14, 1788, "is of no consequence; and if you should not already have received or engaged for more to replace it, I can do without it, because I have asked leave to take a trip to

America which will occasion my absence from hence during the next summer.

"My hope is to sail in April and return in November. You will therefore be so good as to send me the bill for the Sauternes. This proves a most excellent wine, and seems to have hit the palate of the Americans more than any wine I have ever seen in France."

Jefferson never returned to France. But he never lost his interest in wine. He bought vines from the greatest vineyards in Burgundy and Bordeaux and imported skilled vineyardists to cultivate them. They died, of course, from the *phylloxera*.

These excerpts are from a fascinating book called, *Jefferson and Wine* published by the Vinifera Wine Growers Association at The Plains, Virginia. They are a small group of growers and winemakers who have succeeded in doing what Jefferson attempted almost two centuries ago: to grow the great *vinifera* vines of Europe in the soil of the Eastern United States.

Great Rieslings—Theirs and Ours

ARE CALIFORNIA WINES as good as European wines? Better? The argument goes on endlessly. What's more, it is going to become more heated as more and more European winemakers come to this country to study our winemaking methods while our young oenologists spend more time abroad trying to learn old-world secrets.

One of the best ways to find out what is going on is to hold blind tastings. I say one of the best because blind tastings are not always accurate. As, for example, when wines of the same year are compared despite the fact that California may have had a great harvest and France a poor one.

One of the best of these tastings was held in this country in 1978. It compared the very finest of late-harvest Rieslings from California and Germany. Late-harvest Rieslings have been a specialty in Germany for many years but are a relatively recent development in this country.

These are wines made from grapes that have been left on the vines well past the normal harvest time. This permits the fruit to grow even riper, increasing the sugar content, and producing a rare, concentrated sweet wine. The very best of these wines are made from late-harvest grapes that have been attacked by a mold, the *botrytis cinerea*, that eats through the skin of the grape and allows water in the juice to evaporate. This concentrates the sweetness and the flavor even more.

In Germany, there are different levels of quality among the late-harvest wines. The first is "Spätlese," which merely means late harvest. Next is "Auslese," which means a late harvest of specially selected bunches of grapes, particularly those affected by the *botrytis*, called, in German, *edelfäule*.

Then comes "Beerenauslese," which means specially picked, late-harvest single grapes, and finally, there is "Trockenbeerenauslese," which refers to an infinitesimally small number of these specially selected individual grapes that are left on the vine until they are almost dried out (*Trocken* means dry). A bottle of Trockenbeerenauslese can sell for $175 and not lack for buyers.

Peter Sichel, whose family has been in the wine business in Germany for 200 years and who knows his rare Rieslings as well as any man, had been impressed recently by the extraordinary quality achieved in late-harvest wines by some California producers.

So not long ago, he gathered 16 bottles of rare wines, four from California and four from Germany and invited some friends and colleagues for a blind tasting.

There were four "flights" of wines, as they say in the trade: four Spätleses, four Ausleses, four Beerenausleses, and four "Trocks." American wineries are not permitted to use terms such as Auslese and Spätlese, so they were paired with German wines according to their sugar content, which is almost always listed on the label.

Each group of four included one wine from the Mosel, one from the Rheingau, one from Napa Valley, and one from either Sonoma or Mendocino Counties. The tasting was characterized as "informational," but, of course, no one could resist rating the wines they were tasting.

In the lower categories, no one had any trouble identifying the Mosel, the Rheingau, and the California wines, and there was general agreement, certainly on the Spätlese level, that the German wines outclassed the Californians.

The most skilled tasters had no difficulty with the Ausleses either. (In fact, several of the tasters, including David Peppercorn and his wife, Serena Sutcliffe, both English wine consultants and both holders of the title Master of Wine, identified every one of the German wines unerringly. Most of the rest of the group were not so lucky.) However, for most of the tasters the differences among the sweetest wines, at least where origin was concerned, were extremely hard to detect. In many instances, wines were assumed to be German because they were the best, and then turned out to be Californian.

The tasting was clearly a triumph for the American producers of late-harvest Rieslings, particularly for Richard Arrowood, the young winemaker at Château St. Jean in Sonoma, who had a wine in each of the four groups. His wines were regularly assumed to be the very finest of the German entries.

The unanswered question in this particular tasting was: How will the wines develop? All were from the 1976 vintage and these concentrated, sweet wines should develop considerably over the next five years. The German ones almost certainly will. How the Californian wines will fare, no one knows yet. Mr. Sichel has put away samples of all 16 and has vowed to recreate the same tasting in 1983.

Here are the wines in the Sichel late harvest tasting:

Spätleses: Château St. Jean Mendocino County selected late harvest from the Cole Ranch; Raymond Vineyard Napa Valley estate bottled; Waldracher Krone (Mosel); and Schloss Groensteyn Spätlese Rüdesheimer Klosterlay (Rheingau).

Ausleses: Château St. Jean Mendocino County selected late harvest from the Victor Matheu Vineyard; Burgess Cellars Napa Valley; Bernkastler Badstube (Mosel); and Eltviller Sonnenberg (Rheingau).

Beerenausleses: Château St. Jean Sonoma County individual bunch selected from the Jade Mountain Vineyard; Freemark Abbey Napa Valley Edelwein Gold; Piesporter Goldtröpfchen (Mosel); and Höchheimer Domdechaney (Rheingau).

Trockenbeerenausleses: Château St. Jean Alexander Valley (Sonoma) individual bunch selected from the Robert Young Vineyard; Joseph Phelps Vineyards Napa Valley selected late-harvest from the Stanton Estate; Zeltinger Sonnenuhr (Mosel); and Schloss Eltz (Rheingau).

Côtes-du-Rhône

FREDERICK WILDMAN tells the story of Albert Lebrun, at the time President of France, and his foreign minister, Aristide Briand, arriving for lunch at La Pyramide, that extraordinary temple of gastronomy in Vienne, half an hour's drive south of Lyon.

The presidential party had telephoned ahead and, when the group arrived, the proprietor, Fernand Point, was waiting at the head of the steps into the restaurant. Question of protocol: Would Mr. Point walk down to receive his guests? The President of France solved the problem by striding up the walk and presenting himself to the master of French cuisine. Presidents of the Republic come and go. There was only one Fernand Point.

That's the way it is in the valley of the Rhône. "We have been here since time began," the vines and the river and the old sunbaked towns seem to say. "Come to us if you choose. We will not go to you."

It's true. How else explain the fact that the great wines of the Rhône are so little known? Someone is always praising Burgundy. Libraries are written about claret. Even Alsatian Riesling is better-known than Hermitage. Even the best-known wine of the Rhône, Châteauneuf-du-Pape, is discussed more than it is drunk, not only in this country but in England, where French wines are revered, and, alas, in France itself. Who among us actually has ordered a Rhône wine in a Paris restaurant?

Oh, there are a few clever souls around. There is a small group of Americans who own—or did the last time I checked—a vineyard in the Côte Rôtie, in the town of Ampuis, across the river and just downstream from Vienne. They produce a fine wine. Not only are these chaps into superb wine, they also manage to hold their annual meetings at La Pyramide.

Not all of us can own one of the Rhône's vineyards, nor can we all do business over *gratin queues d'écrevisse* along its banks. But we can certainly drink its wines. The Rhône begins high in the Swiss Alps. It races through Geneva and tumbles to the valley floor near Lyon. There it joins the Saône River, makes a left turn and cuts through one of the oldest parts of France on its way to Marseilles and the sea.

The Côtes-du-Rhône extends from Lyon to Avignon. The vines grow on both banks in hard, granitic soil, in vineyards probably first planted by the Greeks. The wines, to quote Alexis Lichine, "are not subtle; they are big, rough, and heady, with a strong, almost pungent perfume and they are tamed only by long imprisonment in the bottle."

Which may explain why we know so little of the Rhône wines. The trend in recent years has been to lighter wines. Burgundies come to us thin and mean and clarets often can pass for *rosés*. I remember one of George Meredith's heroes, probably Richard Feverel, laying down Burgundies for a new-born son. Were he to do that today, the boy would need to drink the wine when he was three.

Not so with Rhône wines. Rhône wines last and last and improve with age. The Côte Rôtie—roasted slope—where those lucky Americans have their vineyard—produces the northernmost and, to some, the most elegant of all the wines of the Côtes-du-Rhône. Côte Rôtie is a strong wine, but nowhere as big as Hermitage or even some Châteauneuf-du-Pape. Hugh Johnson says Côte Rôtie is the region's most complex and most rewarding wine. A good Côte Rôtie really isn't even drinkable until its had four years in the bottle.

A fine Hermitage from one of the best vineyards will last as long as any great Médoc, improving with the years. A rich, vigorous wine when young, it acquires real subtlety with age. Hermitage, the king of Rhône wines, once was more acclaimed than it is today. Grown on a single hill overlooking the river at Tain-l'Hermitage, it is made mostly from the Syrah grape. It needs five years in the bottle and can easily last for 25. Many last 50 years and more. There is some white wine made, and there are those who say a big, robust Hermitage Blanc is the only wine equal to Szechuan food.

Châteauneuf-du-Pape has all the body of Hermitage and lots of good, dark color, but it ages much more rapidly. Alas, some of the vintners in this part of the world are going the way of the Beaujolais to the north, making their wine light for early consumption. The best Châteauneuf-du-Pape are made in the old, inky-dark, heavy style and reach their peak at seven or eight years. Clos St.-Pierre, Château Fortia, and the Domaine de la Solitude are just a few of the better properties.

The cognoscenti love to exclaim over the most obscure of the Rhône wines. "What," they exclaim in mock dismay, "you've never had a Château Grillet?" A Condrieu? A St.-Péray or a Cornas? Château Grillet is a single, privately owned estate. The smallest *appellation contrôlée* in France, it produces a white wine made entirely from the Viognier grape. It is a full-bodied white that ages like a red. Only about 800 gallons are made each year. Even so, if you feel some day you must have one, most of the better shops have a bottle around.

Almost as exclusive, but with, it is said, a bit less finesse, is Condrieu, made from the same rare Viognier grape. Average production from vineyards just upriver from Grillet is about three times as large as Grillet. Most of the Condrieu is drunk at Le Pyramide and a few other great restaurants in Lyon. St.-Péray is a white from the country just south of Hermitage. Cornas, its red neighbor, is another long-lived wine.

But stay these rarities for the moment. The Rhône is a river of wine in a land of abundance. Think of Bresse chickens, Charolais beef, Reblochon cheese, and the provenance of nearby Périgord. This is no place to be concerned with rarities. This is the home of good, sturdy Côtes-du-Rhône, year in and year out, the best buy in inexpensive French wine.

Côtes-du-Rhône when applied to wine is a generic name covering the lesser wines of the entire region. Some 120 separate *communes* are entitled to the *appellation* and they can use it for white, red, or pink wine. The whites are undistinguished compared to, say, the Chardonnays produced in the Mâcon region to the north. The *rosés* are best drunk where they are made.

In the southern part of the region, 14 *communes* are entitled to the *appellation* Côtes-du-Rhône Villages. Chusclan and Sablet are two seen in this country.

Back in 1972 and 1973, when French wine prices were going out through the roof, good solid Côtes-du-Rhône were to be had for half the price of some lesser Beaujolais. The price spread is not so great now, but Côtes-du-Rhône is still a fine bargain. What's more, the weather in the Rhône Valley is invariably better than it is north of Lyon. Whatever vintage you find is liable to be at least fair.

Of course, Côtes-du-Rhône is a simple wine and while it is sturdy and full-bodied, it is not meant to last as long as its most illustrious neighbors. Two or three years is about all the age it needs.

My own favorite among the lesser Côtes-du-Rhône wines is Gigondas. Until a few years ago, the wines of Gigondas, which are soft and full, were entitled only to the Côtes-du-Rhône Villages *appellation*. Now it has its own. The wines are similar to the lighter style Châteauneuf-du-Pape which are produced only a few kilometers away, but they are usually half the price.

The Best of Sonoma

IT LOOKED LIKE the kind of room they set up in a high school for blood donations: folding tables covered in white, a curtained-off area for the technicians, and lots of people walking around in ill-fitting white coats.

In fact, it was a room in the Veterans Memorial Auditorium in Santa Rosa, California, set aside for the biggest wine-judging this part of the California wine country had ever seen. Santa Rosa, about 60 miles north of San Francisco, is the county seat of Sonoma County, and along with Napa to the east and Mendocino to the north, one of the three most famous wine counties in California.

The judging, which involved 17 different varieties of wine and more than 140 different entries, was held during October, 1975 as a preliminary event in the Sonoma County Fair Harvest Festival. The results were announced Saturday, the second day of the three-day festival.

Sonoma County winegrowers have, with only a few exceptions, long taken a back seat when compared with their more glamorous neighbors across the line in Napa. This event was one step, it was hoped, in a campaign both to upgrade the wines of Sonoma and the reputation of the Sonoma winemakers.

The judges selected were the legendary André Tchelistcheff, Moscow-born and French-trained oenologist who was chief winemaker at Beaulieu Vineyards in Napa for more than 30 years; Dr. Harold Berg, retired chairman of the Department of Enology and Viticulture at the University of California; his successor, Dr. A. Dinsmoor Webb; actor Burgess Meredith, wine connoisseur for many years; and television comedian Dan Rowan, who owns one of the largest wine collections in the Los Angeles area with an emphasis on California wines. There were also four wine writers, Robert Balzer of *The Los Angeles Times*, Ruth Ellen Church of *The Chicago Tribune*, Alexis Bespaloff, author of numerous wine books and articles, and, finally, myself.

The director of the judging, Professor George M. Cooke, a University of California viticulturist, opened the first session with a discussion of the ground rules. The first day's tastings would, he said, be for the retention or elimination of the wines offered. Awards would be made by retasting on the second day of those wines held over.

At 9:30 A.M. the judges, resembling aging internes in their white jackets (for protection from wine spills) went into the hall for a brief break. When they were called back 13 glasses were arranged at each place; 12 with samples of the first wine, the blend of inexpensive white wines known in California as Chablis. The last glass was filled with water. Each glass was marked with a number and each judge had a form with the corresponding numbers, space for notes, and his final decision. In addition each judge had a stack of soda crackers, a big chunk of sourdough bread, and a plastic bucket for spitting out each taste.

Spitting is a decidedly unromantic, but very necessary part of the wine experience. Assuming a judge needs two or three mouthfuls of each sample to make a decision, a tasting of 140 wines would have to degenerate into a really monumental drunk.

By 10:10 A.M. the Chablis had been done. The judges, voting on each sample, had eliminated seven of the 12 entries. (On the next day, they were to eliminate one of the remaining five, awarding three bronze medals and one silver.)

A group of 11 *rosés* was followed by lunch. Then came, in order, French Colombard, Chardonnay, Burgundy, Pinot Noir, Zinfandel (the biggest group with 16 entries), Cabernet Sauvignon, and, winding up just before 6:30 P.M., Petite Sirah.

The judges retained 55 wines for award judging on the second day. The second session began promptly at 9 A.M. with the five remaining Chablis and followed the same order, except that three new classes that had not been tried on the first day were brought in. They were Sauvignon Blanc, Gamay Beaujolais, and Napa Gamay.

During the second day, the samples were fewer but the discussions were longer and often heated. Mr. Tchelistcheff and Mr. Rowan were the mavericks, often disputing the decision of the majority with enough sophistication and knowledge to change a vote. To everyone's surprise but their own, Drs. Berg and Webb often differed diametrically in their assessments of individual wines.

By the end of the day, 55 medals had been awarded: three gold, 11 silver and 41 bronze. The winners broken down by types of wines were:

CHABLIS

> *Silver:* Dry Creek Winery (Idlewood Vineyards). *Bronze:* Simi Winery, 1973; Geyser Peak Winery (Voltaire label); Souverain, 1973.

WINE TALK

CHENIN BLANC
> *Silver:* Pedroncelli Winery, 1974; Simi Winery, 1973; Korbel and Bros., 1974. *Bronze:* Souverain Cellars, 1974; Souverain Cellars, N.V. (nonvintage).

GREY RIESLING
> *Silver:* Souverain Cellars, 1973. *Bronze:* Sonoma Vineyards, N.V.; Korbel and Bros., 1974.

JOHANNESBERG RIESLING
> *Gold:* Château St. Jean, 1974. *Silver:* Sonoma Vineyards, 1974. *Bronze:* Souverain Cellars, 1974; Pedroncelli Winery, 1974; Simi Winery, 1973.

SEMILLON
> *Bronze:* Trentadue Winery, 1972.

ROSÉ
> *Silver:* Simi Winery, 1974 Grenache Rosé. *Bronze:* Korbel and Bros., N.V.; Souverain Cellars, 1974.

FRENCH COLOMBARD
> *Silver:* Souverain Cellars, 1974. *Bronze:* Sonoma Vineyards, 1974; Hacienda Winery (Estancia Vineyard), 1974; Souverain Cellars, 1973 (Colombard Blanc).

PINOT CHARDONNAY
> *Gold:* Hacienda Winery, 1974. *Silver:* Souverain Cellars, 1974; Geyser Peak Winery (Voltaire N.V.). *Bronze:* Dry Creek Winery, 1974; Sonoma Vineyards, 1971.

BURGUNDY
> *Silver:* Kenwood Winery, 1972; Trentadue Winery, 1973. *Bronze:* Pedroncelli Winery N.V.; Foppiano Winery N.V.; Korbel and Bros. N.V.

PINOT NOIR
> *Silver:* Geyser Peak Winery (Voltaire). *Bronze:* Buena Vista Winery, 1971; ZD Wines, 1972; Souverain Cellars, 1973.

ZINFANDEL
> *Gold:* Hacienda Winery, 1973. *Bronze:* Grand Cru Vineyards, 1973; Dry Creek Winery, 1973; Buena Vista Winery, 1972; Kenwood Winery, 1972; Sebastiani Winery, 1972.

CABERNET SAUVIGNON
> *Silver:* Pedroncelli Winery, 1972; Buena Vista Winery, 1969. *Bronze:* Foppiano Winery, 1971; Souverain Cellars, 1972; Kenwood Winery, 1972.

PETITE SIRAH
> *Silver:* Kenwood Winery, 1973. *Bronze:* Souverain Cellars, 1973; Dry Creek Winery, 1973.

SAUVIGNON BLANC
> *Silver:* Dry Creek Winery, 1974. *Bronze:* Château St. Jean, 1974; Korbel and Bros., 1974.

GAMAY BEAUJOLAIS
> *Silver:* Sebastiani Winery, 1973. *Bronze:* Dry Creek Winery, 1974; Sonoma Vineyards, 1974.

NAPA GAMAY
> *Bronze:* Geyser Peak Winery (Summit label); Sonoma Vineyards.

A Zinfandel produced by Hacienda Winery won a special merit award. It was a light, almost *rosé* wine that bore little resemblance to the other 15 Zinfandels submitted by Sonoma wineries, but had great merit on its own.

The number of awards was relatively small compared to some industry-oriented judgings where very few entrants come away empty-handed. "The system has its faults," said one winery owner after the judging, "but I'd rather this than one where 30 Zinfandels are rated one through 30. How can anyone honestly say this wine is number 17, that one is number 23, and that one is number 30?"

The judges knew the wines they tasted only by number and learned the results at the same time as the contestants. They never did learn the names of the wines they eliminated. "They will never be made public," Professor Cooke said. "Only the winemakers themselves know who they are."

Style became a matter of some importance during the judging. For example, the two top winners among the 11 Johannisberg Reislings were both wines made from late pickings. Wines with considerable residual sugar and evidence of *botrytis*—the special mold that occasionally attacks the grapes in the fall and concentrates their sugar content. The question was: Should these two sweet wines be judged in the same way as those Johannisbergs which had been vinified dry? Similarly, some Chenin Blancs are vinified dry, others with some sweetness. Should they be judged in the same category? And what about the wide range of Zinfandels—from the big tannic wines made to be drunk ten years from now to the light, fresh ones, ready now?

These are questions for the Sonoma officials to ponder before the next judging. More immediate is the problem of buying these wines. Most of the award winners are fairly large commercial wineries whose products can be found in the East. But distribution is chancy and quantities usually are small.

Some, like Hacienda, which walked off with two of the three gold medals, are so small that they sell most of their production right at the winery. (Hacienda, a new winery, is owned by Frank Bartholomew, former head of United Press International, who rebuilt the Buena Vista Winery, Sonoma's most famous, before reselling it.) This raises another question. Should national publicity be given to wines that, for all practical purposes, no one can buy? Probably. After all, how many people can go out tomorrow and buy a 1961 Mouton Rothschild? Nevertheless plenty has been written about 1961 Bordeaux and will be written in the future. Fortunately, the wines of Souverain Cellars —which walked off with 12 medals—can be found in many shops in major cities outside California. Actually, the burden is on the California wineries. If they want national recognition, they are going to have to give the rest of us a chance to drink their wines.

Friedrich Engels' Favorite

IN 1865 pollsters in England and Germany set out to probe people's basic likes and dislikes. According to David Resnick, an assistant professor of government at Cornell University, two of the people who replied were Karl Marx and Friedrich Engels.

Marx, according to Professor Resnick, played it straight. His idea of happiness was "to fight," his idea of misery was "submission," his heroes were Spartacus and Johannes Kepler, the astronomer, and his favorite color was—red.

Engels hoked it up and put together a series of humorous answers for Marx's daughter Jennie, rather than submit his own. In reply to the happiness question he wrote: Château Margaux 1848.

Says Professor Resnick: "The Soviet editor of the edition I found this in provides the following footnote about Château Margaux 1848: 'A sort of wine. The date is an allusion to the revolutionary events of 1848.'

"The least the decadent capitalist press can do," Professor Resnick goes on, "is to help our Soviet colleagues. To call Château Margaux a sort of wine at the very least betrays a certain lack of sensitivity; but assuredly 1848, while no doubt a great year for revolution, refers to vintage.

"From biographers we know that Engels had a penchant for enjoying himself and there is every reason to believe that he knew what he was talking about. My question is, simply: Was Château Margaux a great wine? It would give me no small amount of satisfaction to fire off a letter to the editors in Moscow correcting this serious misunderstanding of Engels' work. . . .'"

Well, in fact, 1848 was a good year for both revolutions and wine. The famous classification of 1855 was still seven years in the future but there was no doubt that the preeminence of Margaux, along with Lafite, Latour, and Haut-Brion, the four châteaus that were named first growths in 1855, had been established long before.

In 1788, when the French Ambassador to the Court of St. James's retired, he asked Christie's, the auctioneers, to sell off his cellar. Among the items were 15 dozen bottles of "Ch. Margau" which were knocked down for 49 shillings a dozen (Lafite went for 66 shillings a dozen). In 1815, in a sale held a month after Waterloo, Margaux was sold in London for 112 shillings, sixpence a case, and the Lafite, 100 shillings.

In 1848, Margaux was owned by a French-Spanish banker named Aguado, the Marquis de las Marismas. By acquiring the château in 1836, he became the first of the rich bankers to buy a Bordeaux château. He was followed by the Rothschilds, the Pereires, and the Foulds.

I could find no specific mention of the 1848 Margaux, but records of the Bordeaux wine trade indicate that it was an excellent vintage for the region, which almost always means that it was even better for the first growths. It was a big harvest and the picking began on September 20, which is about average in the Médoc. The wine, according to the old records was "exquisite, rich, and full-bodied."

All of which would seem to indicate that old Engels was right on the dime when, 17 years later, he declared that happiness was a '48 Margaux. If the description was accurate in the old records, the wine should have been at its peak in 1865.

The Soviet editor was probably wrong on several counts. After all, the revolution of 1848 was something of a bust. In fact, its failure prompted Engels to return to England where he spent 45 years as a successful businessman, bankrolling much of his friend Marx's writing and research. Since he found no conflict in those two roles, there is every reason to assume that, like any bourgeois London businessman, he kept a decent cellar.

If there was some sentimental attachment to the 1848 vintage it may have stemmed from the fact that that was the year Engels and Marx published the *Communist Manifesto*.

Harvest at Monbousquet

IF the 1973 grape crop in France is the largest in 50 years, as most of the experts are predicting, some of the thanks must go to Kintilla Heussoff.

Kintilla is a 19-year-old student of architecture at the University College of Dublin, in Ireland. She is also one of the more attractive grape pickers this season at Château Monbousquet, a 100-acre estate and vineyard about five kilometers from the center of the world-renowned wine community, St.-Emilion.

Alain Querre, the young proprietor of Monbousquet has been hiring students to pick his grapes for many years. "I would never do it any other way," he said. "They are enthusiastic, dependable, and fun. They bring the outside world here to Monbousquet and we hope they bring a little of our world back with them to their homes."

This year, most of Monbousquet's pickers are Irish. In other years the group—usually about 40—has been more evenly divided among Irish, Americans, Dutch, Italians, and, of course, the French. This year there were no Americans although several American girls, students in Paris, were expected for a few days at the very end of the harvest this coming week.

At Château Monbousquet, the student grape pickers are paid
little, but the food and wine are just fine.

WINE TALK

In the vast Bordeaux wine district, of which St.-Emilion is a part, there are some 7,000 separate estates, farms, and châteaus which must be picked approximately at the same time every year. Since the work lasts no more than three weeks or so, local people can't be counted on to do all the work. Nor can other parts of France be called on; they have their own grape crops.

So, pickers are imported from Spain, which is only a few hours' drive, and from Italy. Gypsies are recruited and then local people fill out the ranks, particularly on weekends when whole families make a holiday of working in the vineyards.

"The local people who are available for the full *vendange* are often the dregs," Mr. Querre said, "and workers from other countries often have little interest in the work." There are other problems, as well. At Château d'Angludet, near Margaux, in the Médoc, owner Peter Sichel thought himself fortunate to find a large group of gypsies looking for work just before the harvest. Then, one night, in the gypsy camp, two rival leaders went for each other with knives. The issue was settled with one group leaving in the middle of the harvest.

The going rate this year (1973) has been about 40 francs (about $9) a day (60 on Sunday) with three meals. Even the local people are given the makings of three meals to bring home and cook if they wish. A picker is paid if it rains but he must stay in the fields, in the rain. This is to prevent him from driving 20 kilometers (12 miles) to where the sun is shining to make a few more francs for himself.

Alain Querre pays his young students 35 francs because he also houses them. The pickers sleep in two separate dorms in a partially remodeled 16th-century farm building. They eat in a common dining room in the same building and no one could be found to complain about the French country cooking. Elizabeth Milburn, a Londoner who is not a student but a young civil servant, said she had picked grapes in the Loire Valley one year but that the experience at Monbousquet was much superior.

Part of the young people's enthusiasm may stem from Mr. Querre's extreme generosity with his wine. Helen Keane, a music student at Trinity College in Dublin, said she had never even drunk wine before coming to St.-Emilion but that she was up to about a quart a day.

"You don't make any money at this," said Michael Moloney, 22, a student at Jesuit Belvedere College in Dublin. "After you pay your fare you have just about enough for one hell of a night's drinking in Paris on the way home." Most of the Manbousquet pickers will earn about 500 francs for their efforts since few stay for the entire harvest.

Most of Monbousquet's students came at the suggestion of friends who had been there in previous years. Few do the harvest here more than two or three times. "It's an experience, a good one," said an Irish youth, "but then, I guess, you want to try other things."

Some proprietors are not interested in student pickers. "You have to train new ones every year," said Martin Bamford, one of the managers of Château Loudenne in St.-Estèphe north of Bordeaux. But many grape growers besides Alain Querre do use them.

Most of the young people come to the area by train from Paris. The nearest mainline stop to St.-Emilion is Libourne and on days when the harvest is about to begin, the station is a chaotic scene. Hundreds of boys and girls, many with backpacks and almost all with long hair and blue jeans, pour off the trains chattering in six or seven languages. The proprietors wave placards with the name of their estate or château, much as do camp counselors in Grand Central Station in New York.

Of course, many students simply drive out from the University of Bordeaux 30 miles away, but Mr. Querre prefers not to use Bordeaux students. "They are never as enthusiastic as the people from other countries," he said.

Work begins in the fields around the old château at 8:30 A.M. Lunch, an hour and a half, is at 1 P.M. and the day ends at 6:30. There are also breaks in midmorning and midafternoon when the women of the château bring bread, cheese, salami, and wine out to the fields. After dinner there are songfests with students from each country contributing songs. Usually a few of the boys slip away to St.-Emilion in search of what one girl called "greener fields." What they usually get, according to Mike Moloney, is hangovers to take into the vines the next morning.

Let the Wine Breathe

"LETTING THE WINE BREATHE" is one of those stilted phrases that cries out for a George Price cartoon. Of course, wine does not breathe. It oxidizes, and the oxidation can be good for the wine or it can be bad depending on the circumstances.

Robert Daley wrote a story some years back about drinking a very old bottle of wine at a French country inn. The trip, the meal, everything, had been planned around this rare bottle from the 19th century. As the moment to open the bottle approached, the tension mounted. A hush fell over the guests, beads of sweat stood out on the proprietor's brow. Then the cork was drawn. The bouquet was beautiful—but ten minutes later the wine was dead, finished.

The wine was a relic. It had been preserved long past its time. When the air hit it, it crumbled like some artifact from an Egyptian tomb. This wine happened to be extremely old. Much the same thing can take place with far younger wines. An English wine enthusiast made some tests a few years ago, using various first growth—the very best—Bordeaux wines from the early 1950's. They were decanted and left to rest. In general, they improved for about 15 minutes—bouquet, taste, color, everything. Then they went downhill. In most cases they were dead an hour after they had first been opened. Air, someone said, is the enemy of wine. With older wines it is usually the conqueror, too.

French winemakers who come to this country usually spend most of their time in French restaurants plugging their product. So, in 1974 twelve California Cabernet Sauvignons were served at a luncheon here for a St.-Emilion château owner, just to introduce him to some of the best American wines.

By general agreement, the best of the lot was the 1969 from Freemark Abbey. One of the poorest, it seemed at first, was the 1966 Robert Mondavi Cabernet Sauvignon. This was a disappointment because the 1966 Mondavi was already something of a legendary wine. But a strange thing happened; an hour after the guests had left, the host and the Frenchman retasted some of the wines. The Mondavi was excellent. It had needed only more exposure to the air to bring it up to its peak. A week later, Mr. Mondavi was encountered in a restaurant here and told of the tasting. "If you used my 1966," he said, "I hope you opened it early." Actually, all the wines had been opened about an hour before the lunch.

Let the Wine Breathe

All wines will oxidize and go dead but, for the most part, only red wines need to "breathe." As the tendency to drink wines young grows stronger, "breathing" becomes more important. It speeds up the aging process.

Most reds will benefit from some exposure to air before drinking. For some it is an absolute necessity, particularly the expensive Chiantis which are becoming more popular in this country. The best Chiantis are called "Classico" and "Classico Riserva." These wines usually can be opened four hours before being used and sometimes even that is not enough to make them easy to drink. They are very hard wines and should probably have 20 years in the bottle.

Some people say the best way to aerate a wine is to pour it into a decanter. This way all the wine comes in contact with the air as it goes from one bottle to the other. There are other experts who say decanting is mostly for getting rid of sediment in old wines and that all the air any wine needs it will get sitting in a large wine glass waiting to be drunk.

It is difficult to come up with any rule of thumb regarding wine breathing. Usually, opening a bottle 30 minutes before it is to be used will suffice, assuming that is, that the wine has been in the bottle long enough.

Thus a famous—and expensive—Bordeaux that has been in the bottle ten years may only need 30 minutes of exposure to air. The same bottle opened five years earlier might have needed far more time to breathe, although to open a great Bordeaux five years before its time is never a good idea. Infanticide, one expert calls it.

Bottles that are opened and then unfinished can be a problem. If at all possible, it is best to store the unfinished wine in a smaller bottle. A half-finished magnum has a lot of air in it to work on the remaining wine. If the wine is poured into a standard wine bottle and recorked, there is almost no air in it to cause harm. Some people recommend that gallon jugs of wine be decanted into regular wine bottles for the same reason. In most cases, however, sticking the jug in the refrigerator is sufficient. Just remember to pull it out in time so that you are not drinking cold red wine with your meal.

To Decant or Not Decant

A READER inquired recently: "Why don't you write anything about decanting wines?" Simple. Because it is possible to drink wine for years and never encounter any that has been or needs to be decanted. Still, there are some misconceptions about decanting and this is as good a time as any to discuss them.

To begin with, decanting is not a pretentious rigmarole invented by pretentious aficionados. That is, it is not supposed to be. Decanting a bottle of Beaujolais is pretentious; decanting a 20-year-old Bordeaux is not.

The main reason for decanting is to separate the wine from the sediment. Most good old red wines throw some sediment. Young wines such as the Beaujolias do not. It is, of course, entirely possible to drink these wines without decanting them, but it requires careful pouring. The pronounced shoulder in a Bordeaux wine bottle acts as a built-in receptacle for sediment, but the business of tipping a bottle up and down to fill a group of glasses inevitably results in some sediment escaping and being mixed into the wine.

If the wine is decanted, only one pour, done hopefully with a steady hand, is required. What's more, experts decant over a candle or electric light so they can spot the sediment as it begins to come through the neck of the bottle into the decanter.

This can be expensive. Sometimes the sediment begins to come through when there is still a quarter of a bottle of wine left. A good sommelier will leave the bottle. When the sediment settles again, a less than fastidious drinker may find a glass of wine he had not counted on.

White wines are almost never decanted because they almost never have any sediment. Sometimes there are a few cream of tartar crystals in white wine but they are harmless and not worth going through the fuss of decanting to eliminate.

Red wine sediment is made up of tannin, pigments, and, sometimes, tiny quantities of mineral salts. Large amounts of sediment are removed while the wine is aging in vats or wooden casks and for inexpensive wines this is enough.

But fine wines destined for long life will begin to throw more sediment starting anywhere from three to ten years after they are bottled. Sometimes, as in the case of some great Rhône wines, there is so much sediment that, if they are kept for many years, they must be rebottled. This is true, too, of some rare Italian wines from the Piedmont.

People who collect fine old Bordeaux take great pains to insure that these irreplaceable wines reach their table in good shape. Thus, a bottle is carried from the cellar on its side, just the way it had been lying in the rack. Then it is stood upright, maybe for 24 hours, to let the sediment sink to the bottom. Finally it is decanted.

Incidentally, this is where those straw baskets one sees in some restaurants come in. They are meant to carry the old bottles from the cellar. Some purists insist that the bottle should be returned to the basket if the wine is not to be decanted. Another group, let's call them the upright school—say this is not necessary. If the wine is decanted, the question becomes moot—at least until someone comes up with a basket for decanters.

Sediment is the principal reason for decanting, but not the only one. Decanting can actually make a harsh younger wine more palatable.

The act of pouring the wine from the bottle to the decanter aerates it. Another word for aeration is oxidation and another word for oxidation is aging. This is particularly helpful with younger Bordeaux wines that should be ready to drink but are not. This is the case also with wines such as Chianti Classico, where the bottlers often recommend that they be opened four hours or so before using. Decanting can speed up this mellowing process.

With very old wines—or poorly made wines—decanting can be a risk as well as an aid. Some old wines are literally killed by fresh air. It is not uncommon to open an old claret or Burgundy, exclaim over its excellence, then have it turn flat and dead in 15 minutes or less. This can happen in the original bottle. Decanting will only hasten the wine's demise.

There is another kind of wine that gets decanted from time to time: inexpensive California jug wine. The jugs, particularly the gallon size, are ungainly and take up a lot of space on the table. Decanters or carafes are more attractive and easier to handle. And they may fool the guests if that is your pleasure. There is every possibility, however, that the gallon jug may one day go the route of the nickel beer. More and more, the winemakers seem to be concentrating on the half-gallon size. There is an obvious marketing advantage to the half-gallon bottle, of course. Most of the better-known jug wines now sell for about the same in the half-gallon as you used to get the full gallon for.

Bollinger, the Great Tradition

THERE IS said to be a family in Ay, France whose men have worked in the wine fields and cellars, in a direct line of descent, since the 13th century. People who know Ay and its inhabitants say this kind of devotion to the vineyards and the Champagnes they produce is not unusual. There is certainly nothing to distinguish the tiny village from the other communities in the Valley of the Marne. Like them, its streets are narrow and quiet, its buildings heavy and gray, and its people friendly but reclusive. And, like them, its true worth is hidden in the vast chalk *caves* under its streets where millions upon millions of bottles of Champagne age slowly in the cool darkness.

Ay is not really the center of the Champagne area. That would have to be Epernay, or perhaps Reims, both a few kilometers away. But Ay is the home of Bollinger, which some experts, including the British writer Cyril Ray, who devoted a book to it, consider the finest of all Champagnes.

The house of Bollinger is not the largest in Champagne. It boasts some three miles of *caves* while Möet et Chandon has 17, and sells some 15 times the quantity that Bollinger sells. In fact, of the dozens of shippers in the area, Bollinger is about 12th in volume and fourth in shipments to the United States.

If there is anything that distinguishes Bollinger, that sets it apart, it is the fact that until the summer of 1972 it was run by one woman, Madame Jacques Bollinger, for more than 30 years. Even after her retirement, Madame Bollinger, was still an enormous presence in the offices, cellars, and fields of her firm.

"I am not quite ready to give it all up," she said in 1972, sipping Bollinger before the fire she keeps burning year-round in her vast living room here. And her presence at the biweekly tasting sessions was a must. "She has fifty years of tasting experience," said her nephew, Christian Bizot, an officer of the firm. "That is about twenty years more than any of the rest of us on the tasting committee."

Madame Bollinger could hardly disassociate herself from the firm, even if she chose to. Her home is literally part of the Bollinger complex of buildings. The new wine in casks sits in cellars across a little street; the old cooperage is in the same courtyard, the endless *caves* wind directly beneath her kitchen, and the Bollinger vineyards, which she inspected daily on her bicycle, begin a few meters away.

[106]

"Bollinger runs itself, really," Madame Bollinger once told guests. "The only task is to maintain the highest level of quality." She has done this in the past—and her successors, Christian Bizot, and Claude d'Hautefeuille, another nephew who is president of the firm, continue in the same tradition of devotion to the most painstaking and expensive methods. For instance, French law says that nonvintage Champagne must remain in the bottle one year. The average in the trade is about two and a half. Bollinger keeps its wine in the bottle four and a half years. The law says vintage Champagne must spend three years in the bottle; Bollinger's spends five and, in fact, the last bottles of any vintage to be shipped from the Bollinger cellars will have spent seven years in the chalk tunnels under Ay.

The Bollinger firm was founded in 1829, although its antecedents went back at least another 100 years. The first Bollinger, Joseph Jacob Placide Bollinger, actually started as a front for someone else. The business belonged to Athanase Louis Emmanuel Comte de Villermont, an admiral in the French navy, whose family had owned vineyards in the Valley of the Marne for more than a hundred years. As a nobleman, he could not openly engage in trade, so the firm of Bollinger was organized with the understanding that the name de Villermont would never appear on papers or on the bottles.

Joseph Bollinger, who had been a salesman for another Champagne firm in the area, later married a daughter of the Comte de Villermont and gradually took over the business that bore his name. Some of the present Bollinger vineyards and *caves* date back to the Comte de Villermont and the first Bollinger, who was the grandfather of Madame Bollinger's husband, who died in 1941.

Madame Bollinger was born Elizabeth (Lily) de Lauriston in Touraine, the daughter of a wealthy cavalry officer and country squire, and a descendant of John Law, the legendary Scotsman who fled a murder charge in England to become France's Minister of Finance and creator of its first system of paper currency.

Madame Bollinger's husband took over the firm in 1918 on the death of his father. He married Elizabeth de Lauriston in 1923 and as Cyril Ray has said: "She married not only a dashing young wartime airman (he had won the Légion d'Honneur and the Croix de Guerre as a French aviator)—she married also a great wine."

The young woman learned eagerly and at her husband's death 18 years later, was more than qualified to take his place. She slept in the Bollinger cellars during Allied bombings and, as soon as the war ended, began the job of rebuilding the firm.

Like most Champagne shippers, Bollinger buys much of its grapes from independent growers in the region. But since the war, the firm also has increased its own vineyards by 60 percent. And, from the days of the German occupation, when the Germans carried off much of the Champagne and banned shipments to most markets, trade has increased to the point where Bollinger's annual production of about 100,000 bottles is sold in 80 markets around the world.

"For the first time in a century and a half, there is no Bollinger among the officers of the firm," Madame Bollinger said, "but the Bollinger spirit is still here. That will never change."

Madame Bollinger died in 1975.

How Much Is Enough?

A BOTTLE OF WINE for two people, either at home or a restaurant, is one thing; wine for a large dinner party is something else again. As Thanksgiving approaches each year even those people who never give dinner parties give dinner parties. Only they are called family dinners.

More and more people are serving wine with big family gatherings and, understandably, hosts and hostesses who have not served much wine before spend a considerable amount of time trying to decide what wine to buy. Don't. It doesn't matter much what wine you serve as long as it isn't too sweet to go with food.

Do you, like most people, serve turkey at Thanksgiving? Fine. Turkey is the great all-purpose wine food. Are you into slightly sweet German wines such as Blue Nun? Perfect for Turkey. Do you go for those also slightly sweet Portuguese *rosés*? They're not bad with turkey, either.

I'd prefer a light Burgundy, but Beaujolais, slightly chilled, is a fine turkey wine and there is nothing wrong with serving a good Bordeaux, either.

No, the type of wine is really not your problem—but quantity is. Most people who are new to wine, still associate it with spirits, and spirits are something you were taught to pour sparingly. The classic situation is this: a man or woman enters a liquor store, tells the clerk there will be 12 for dinner on Thanksgiving and asks for a good wine. The clerk whips something off the shelf and proclaims it to be absolute perfection for the family feast. How much is it? Five dollars. Okay, I'll take two.

Which means everyone gets a thimbleful at dinner. This is primarily the clerk's fault. Knowing he was dealing with a neophyte, he should have recommended a jug of Gallo Hearty Burgundy, a gallon of inexpensive Chianti, or some other sturdy but inexpensive wine. One of the most pleasant moments at any dinner party for me comes at the end when I tell the guests how much wine they consumed. With a long, convivial meal, it is not at all unusual to count up two empty bottles for each guest. It's particularly fascinating when most of the guests are people who had announced earlier that they really are not wine drinkers.

In part, the hesitancy to buy a lot of wine for a dinner is based on economics. The gallon-size bottles solve that. Even with today's prices, excellent California wines in gallons (or now three-liter) bottles can be had for a price that works out at under $2.00 per fifth.

But often there is an ethical consideration, too. Is it right to pour so much wine down the throats of your guests, even if they are relatives? A man who drinks a bottle of wine over the course of a three-hour meal invariably is in far better shape than the man who downs three martinis before a business lunch.

If you choose to serve German wines, the problem of too much drinking diminishes still further. They usually contain about nine percent alcohol by volume. In Germany last year, I met a restaurateur who had just served lunch to a group of New Zealand and Australian winegrowers who were touring the Rheingau. There were 29 of them in the group. After they boarded the bus to continue their trip, he counted 91 empty bottles. "They were in good spirits," he said, "but they certainly were not drunk."

Wine is meant to be drunk. There are drunkards who drink wine, but they would be drunkards whether they had wine or not. The reason wine has been man's favorite beverage since the dawn of time is the fact that it does not make one drunk. Its alcoholic content is perfectly balanced by the pace at which we eat and the amount we eat.

Reservations about alcoholic content are understandable in newcomers to wine. The problem of spending too much is easier to resolve. The simple fact is this: there is no need to spend a lot of money on wine, regardless of who is coming to dinner.

WINE TALK

There are still a few boorish types around who might turn their noses up at lesser wines, but they are rare and they only do it if they can see the label first. I have never met a true wine lover, and that includes the owners of great châteaus and famous California wineries, who does not get immense pleasure from drinking the simplest of wines in good company.

There is an old story about Voltaire writing to the original Louis Latour to compliment him on his wines. "I serve your Beaune to all my friends," he wrote, "but your Volnay I keep for myself." Great wines are meant to be shared with one, two, or three friends, who really appreciate them. In such instances, the wine is central to the gathering. At big parties or dinners, unless they are for wine societies, the wine is meant to enhance the gathering, not dominate it. There is no need to bring out great bottles.

My favorite dinner is one where the wine, whatever it is, flows freely. Then, at the end, if the host is a wine man, or if I am the host, there might be a moment to produce one or two special bottles. It is amazing sometimes, how people who profess to know nothing about wine at the outset of the meal, immediately notice the difference in the new bottles.

Try never to serve a wine you have not tasted yourself beforehand. If you are going to serve jug wine, pick up a couple of inexpensive decanters and fill them as needed for pouring at the table. Don't make excuses for what you serve. Most guests will be looking to you for a cue before talking about the wine. If you think it's good, so will they.

Wine prices have been going up, but there are good buys around, even if you don't want to serve jug wine. Most good wine shops are selling little known Bordeaux châteaus in the 1973 vintage at reasonable prices. Beaujolais prices are going up but there are some good 1976's—a superb year in Beaujolais—in the $4 category. Don't forget California. There are some excellent Zinfandels and California Burgundies at moderate prices. Remember to ask for the case price if you can afford a case; it brings the price down even further.

Drinking wine by the bottle is obviously more expensive than by the jug. But there is nothing that imparts a feeling of well-being to a meal as readily as casually opening another bottle when the guests get thirsty.

A Cognac Episode

NINETEEN SEVENTY-FOUR was the 250th anniversary of Remy Martin, one of the great names in Cognac. This makes the company older than George Washington and a great deal older than the United States.

All of which called for something special in the way of a birthday celebration. That something special was readily available: a special bottling of what has come to be known as the Anniversary Cuvée: a blend of Grande Champagne Cognacs, none of them less than 50 years old and some more than 100 years old.

The blend went on sale in this country during 1974 for a cool $275 a bottle. There were only 2,000 bottles available here, out of the 38,000 produced, and they were snapped up very quickly. If you were "lucky" enough to get one of the 2,000 bottles you also got a certificate giving the number of your bottle and some background on what you were drinking.

Cognac, like so many other things we have come to accept as staples of the good life, was born out of hard times. When Arabs controlled the Mediterranean, wine drinkers in the Low Countries turned to the Charente, for their rather harsh wines. When the Mohammedan hordes had been driven back and the rich wines of the Mediterranean once again were obtainable, the wines of the Charente went begging.

That is when the winemakers hit on the idea of distilling the wine into a spirit. In fact, the word *brandy*, is derived from the Dutch phrase for burnt wine. As a distilled product, the wine gained a market around the world, borne by the sailors who came to the area, more for the salt from its marshes than for its wines.

According to André Heriard-Dubreuil, chairman of Remy Martin, it was the English sailors who first acquired a taste for brandy and made it almost a national drink in Great Britain. The British carried French brandy to the Orient and today, according to Mr. Heriard-Dubreuil, Hong Kong is one of the prime markets for great brandies.

Cognac is simply the finest brandy. Except that there is nothing simple about it. There are six Cognac regions, beginning with Grande Champagne. Then come Petite Champagne, Borderies, Fin Bois, Bon Bois, and finally, Bois Ordinaires. Blends from all these regions can be considered Cognac. The best, obviously, are from the Grande Champagne area exclusively.

Much of the secret of Cognac is the aging in oak barrels made from the forests of Limousin about 75 miles east of the Charente region. Any Cognac must have two years in oak. Most have three and the best have five or more.

Cognac is distilled only in pot stills, which means one batch at a time, the way water is boiled in a kettle. Most lesser brandies are made in a continuous still that somewhat resembles the radiator in your car.

Two distillations are required. The end product is clear and colorless and each gallon represents 10 gallons of wine originally poured into the still.

All Cognac is brandy, but only the brandy made in the six regions defined by French law can use the name Cognac. There are Italian, Spanish, Greek, German, and Russian brandies, but only one Cognac. And only one Cognac costs $275 a bottle—Remy Martin's Anniversary Cuvée.

A Wine Hustle Is Not a Dance

THEY NEVER LET UP. First it was someone pushing a rare old Cognac for $275 a bottle. Now it is a chap in England. He wants to sell you some Château Mouton Rothschild, 1971. Buy 50 cases and he will throw in a week in London, Paris, and Bordeaux with hotels, sight-seeing, and a meal in a three star restaurant, as yet unnamed.

The cost? A mere $350 a case, F.O.B. Bordeaux (that, of course, brings the basic price to $17,500), and if you have checked the freight rates for 50 cases of wine from Bordeaux to wherever you are, plus customs, and other aggravations, you know you will have your hands full.

But that is not all. You have to accompany your wine. If you send it off by itself, you have just become an importer, a class of men recognizable for their nervous tics and singular lack of longevity. Since no one in his right mind wants to become an importer, you must find someone to "clear" your wine. That is, someone who will go through the motions of importing—for a fee—before turning the wine over to you.

This most ambitious of promotions is the creation of Southard & Co., a London firm of importers. More particularly, it seems to be the special project of a Mr. Lionel Frumkin, Southard's Managing Director.

The project first appeared in an advertisement in *The Wall Street Journal*, presumably on the grounds that *Journal* readers have already been softened up by so many other extraordinary proposals. "Buy the Baron's Red Gold," the ad said, "and get a free trip to Château Mouton Rothschild.

"In the mellow serenity of the cellars at Château Mouton Rothschild belonging to Baron Philippe de Rothschild, lie case upon case of the magnificent 1971 vintage." And so on.

Well, there is no question about the case after case thing. Mouton is in the same boat as everyone else in Bordeaux. They simply cannot move the 1971's (or the 1972's). Except, of course, for those wines sold at incredible prices in the speculative madness of the early 1970's to importers and even retailers who can't unload them either.

There is also the question of quality. There are those wine experts who say that some of the 1971's will be even better than the very fine 1970's. But there are others who remain more skeptical—who find, in fact, that lesser 1971's have already begun to fade.

But away with black suspicion. Let's assume that the 1971 Mouton is excellent. Right now, Sherry-Lehmann in New York is selling the 1970, the known quantity, for $247.85 a case.

Mr. Frumkin notes that his offer is for one person. "If you purchase 100 cases," he explains, "this will entitle you to bring your wife, girl friend, or any other nominated person."

Let's see. At his price, the trip for you and your other nominated person would cost $35,000. Buy the 1970 in New York for $24,785 and you will save $10,215 off the top. The New York price, remember, includes duty, shipping, and, if they like your looks, some help in loading the 100 cases in the back of your car.

By even the most conservative estimate, you still will have about $12,000 to make that trip for two to London, Paris, and Bordeaux. A meal in a three star restaurant? You can eat all week in three star restaurants with that kind of money. As for Château Mouton, well, you are always welcome there to visit the cellars and the museum. Baron Philippe probably will be in California getting a tan, but his staff will be on hand, eager to meet the fellow (and his wife or girl friend) who bought 100 cases of Mouton, and who is throwing all that money around in downtown Bordeaux.

This is obviously the silly season in the wine world. While someone in England is offering a $12,000 trip "free," up in Canada they are pumping wine into cardboard containers for sale to Californians.

According to *Advertising Age*, a trade publication, Valley Rouge Wines, Ltd. of Winnipeg, is offering a cardboard gallon container with a plastic liner filled with wine. As the wine is poured out— through an attached spigot—the bag collapses. No air gets in, they say.

The wine in this thing is Californian—at least in the California market. Elsewhere, Valley Rouge sells Canadian wines, including one called Baby Duckling. North Dakota, Michigan, Minnesota, and Ohio are Valley Rouge markets, according to *Advertising Age*.

Valley Rouge's general manager, Hugh Sutherland, is quoted as saying that the cardboard and plastic combination has been a smash in Australia. Maybe so. A few years back, Nicolas, the big French wine company, tried a cardboard container for wine in France. Within a few months, crates of leaky cardboard containers began piling up in the Nicolas warehouses on the edge of Paris.

The box and bag combination is probably a quantum leap ahead of the Nicolas efforts. What's more, it's undoubtedly cheaper, easier to handle, more sanitary, and all that kind of thing. But I, for one, can't call it progress.

Mary Ann Graf

MARY ANN GRAF is in her early 30's and just getting over her first big crush. Of grapes, that is. Miss Graf is the head winemaker at the Simi Winery in Healdsburg, California, probably the only woman in the world to hold that title.

The function of the winemaker is unique—particularly in a winery

SIMI

SINCE 1876

SONOMA

ZINFANDEL
1973

Alcohol 13 % by Vol.
Produced and Bottled by SIMI Winery, Healdsburg, California, U.S.A.

such as Simi which is dedicated to high quality wines. The winemaker decides when and what to pick, how to crush, how to ferment, how long to age, and when to bottle. If the winery bottles ten wines, each of these functions will differ for each wine. And a mistake at any stage of the process can rarely be rectified.

In the fall of 1973, under Miss Graf's supervision, the Simi crew crushed 1,500 tons of grapes and produced about 275,000 gallons of wine. One third is white wine and the rest red. Most of the red is Cabernet Sauvignon, the king of California wines.

In early January, 1974, Mary Ann Graf and her fellow workers were clarifying the 1973 reds to prepare them for aging. They were also preparing for a February bottling of the 1973 whites and continuing to bottle some 1972 reds that have been in oak casks for a year.

"We tasted the 73's on Monday," Miss Graf said, "and the Cabernet was, well, overwhelming. It will last 10 or 15 years." The whites, too, looked promising, she said, particularly the Gewürztraminer and Chardonnay. This is good news at any winery, but particularly for the winemaker. If something has gone wrong, the winemaker bears the responsibility. Like a football coach, the winemaker is paid to come through each season with a winner.

WINE TALK

There are still plenty of things that could go wrong with the 1973 vintage, but for Mary Ann Graf, the worst is over and, as a new winemaker, she has won her spurs. "She has as far as I'm concerned," said Simi's owner Russell Green. "I'm very proud of her."

"Let's say I'm a little more confident now," Miss Graf said, cautiously. "I don't have to go by other people's stories—and exaggerations—now that I've been through it myself."

"I remember those days and nights during the first fermentation," said Russ Green, laughing. "Mary Ann was up and down ladders, running from tank to tank. She could tell how the fermentation was going just by listening to the wine bubbling inside."

Miss Graf was born in the wine country in Sherlock, near Sacramento, but she never lived on a farm as a child. "My father taught agriculture," she said, "and I wasn't entirely a city kid, either. But I had no idea I'd ever end up doing this."

Mary Ann entered the University of California at Davis in 1961 with vague plans for a career in food science. "I got into a wine appreciation course because I thought it was a basket-weaving sort of thing," she said. "Then I got hooked." She graduated in 1965 with a Bachelor of Science degree in enology. The Davis branch of the University of California, incidentally, has one of the most famous schools of enology in the world.

Miss Graf spent four and a half years with the Gibson Wine Company near Sacramento, a producer only of fruit wines. "I just got bored with fruit wine," she said. "I wanted to try my hand at the good stuff." Her next job was with United Vintners at Asti, but she was no closer to "the good stuff." She was assigned to product development and worked on the creation of Annie Greensprings, an apple-based wine.

Then came a brief stint at Tiburon Vintners, now known as Sonoma Vineyards, working for the owner, former Broadway dancer, Rodney Strong. "I worked through the 1972 crush," Mary Ann said, "then, last March, Russ Green called me."

The Simi Winery is on the old Redwood Highway just north of the center of Healdsburg, about 60 miles north of the Golden Gate Bridge. The winery was founded by the Simi brothers in 1876. They gave it the name Montepulciano after the town in Italy where they were born. The old name, which was hardly ever used, can still be seen weathering away on one side of the main winery building.

Russell Green, who was once the president of the Signal Oil Company in Los Angeles, bought the winery in 1970. He had spent his summers in the nearby Alexander Valley since childhood and had

Mary Ann Graf working at the Simi Winery in Healdsburg,
California.

grown grapes there since 1958. His first wines came from the 1970
crop, but not until now has he considered the wine good enough to
bear a vintage date. The 1973's will be the first, under Russell Green's
ownership, to have the year on the label.

There are some other Simi vintages in the handsome stone cellars.
They were made by the Simis themselves and date from the middle
1930's. Russ Green found them when he took over. There are Cabernets and an unusual wine made from the Carignane grape which is
usually employed in making cheap wine.

The old ones were so good that Mr. Green and Miss Graf have
decided to keep up the old Simi tradition of producing a Carignane
wine. Other wines in the Simi line—all of which can be found at one
time or another in better wine shops on the East Coast—include:
Zinfandel, Gamay, Burgundy, Beaujolais, the Cabernet Sauvignon,
Pinot Chardonnay, Johannisberg Riesling, Gewürztraminer, Chenin
Blanc, Chablis, Cabernet Rosé, and Grenache Rosé.

In one respect, Mary Ann Graf has been enormously lucky, working at Simi. André Tchelistcheff, a legendary figure in the California wine industry, is serving as a consultant at Simi. During his more than 30 years at Beaulieu Vineyard in the Napa Valley he, perhaps more than any other man, became identified with the finest in California wines. Now retired from Beaulieu, he has worked side by side with Mary Ann at Simi. "It's been a really unbelievable education," she said.

Miss Graf has little interest in feminist activities, nor does she consider herself a pioneer in her job. "There are other women in the business," she said, "and more will be coming along.

"Women have a lot to offer in this field," she went on, "but they are intimidated by the product. They are certainly as capable as men of being discriminating about wine."

Are there any special qualities women might bring to the wine business? Miss Graf thought for a minute. "I doubt it," she said. "For instance, women are supposed to be so meticulous. But I'm not a particularly clean person. You should see my lab; there's junk all over."

What about the future? "I don't think I'd like a management job," Mary Ann said. "Give me my wines and let me baby them along. I'm not too crazy about children, but the wines are like children. Some develop into fine adults in spite of you, some have better breeding than others. It's like having a whole population to work with."

French and Kosher

SOME YEARS AGO, I wrote a piece about a Lutheran winemaker in the Alsace region of France who annually turns his cellars over to a rabbi from nearby Strasbourg. The rabbi, with the aid of some theological students, then proceeds to make some 5,000 cases of kosher Alsatian wine.

To this parochial school product who had come to think of kosher wine as something sweet and heavy and made from Concord grapes, or perhaps a wine made in Israel, the Alsatian story seemed unique.

Apparently, however, quite a bit of first quality kosher wine is produced in Europe, particularly in France. A reader, Albert Baumgarten of Manhattan, wrote that he once lived in Strasbourg and has fond memories of the kosher wines made under the Koenig label. But, he added: "Virtually every large Jewish community in France has a similar arrangement with a local vintner. Thus there are good Bordeaux wines made under the supervision of the Bordeaux rabbinate, Mâcon wines from Lyon and a Champagne. . . . A Swiss vintner produces a Fendant de Sion and a kosher Johannisberg, and there are several Italian kosher wines."

According to another reader, the Consistoire or Beth Din of Paris, France's principal rabbinical authority, authorizes and supervises the production of a number of kosher wines from North Africa and one from the Bandol area of southern France.

This reader, who asked not to be identified, said that a few years ago, the chief rabbi of Paris, Meir Jais, had "several rivals who entitle themselves variously" and who authorized the production of kosher wines on their own.

"About ten years ago," he wrote, "two of Rabbi Jais' competitors declared a temporary truce long enough to rent a Champagne factory in Epernay. Under the direction of the regular foreman, they bought the best grapes available and together with their students manufactured a dry Champagne which they distributed under competing labels, Sion and R.N. Laxner."

The reader, who claims his own knowledge of wines is limited solely to kosher varieties, said he and some friends who know wine tasted a bottle of the kosher Champagne. "They were polite about its quality," he wrote, "probably more so than the wine deserved, since it cured my curiosity about Champagne, definitively."

The laws governing the production of kosher wine in France are strict. No non-Jew may enter the *chais*—where the wine is made— during the vinification. And if the vineyard from which the grapes come is owned by a Jew, nothing but grapes may be grown in it. In many smaller communities, farmers will plant fruit trees or even grain between the rows of vines. If the vineyard owner is not a Jew, this rule does not apply.

In France, under Napoleonic law, the various Consistoires or Beth Din are empowered to impose a tax on the production of kosher products. Thus, each bottle of kosher wine becomes a source of income for the groups that control them.

One complaint voiced by those who wrote in about the Alsatian wines was the apparent impossibility of buying them in this country. Some said they had tried to convince importers to bring them in but with no success.

This may change within the next four or five months. Duc de Provence, a New York importer, recently arranged to be the U.S. representative for a kosher Côtes de Provence which may arrive here in the fall (1973). Some 500 cases of the nonkosher version are presently en route here and Alvin Lukashok, president of Duc de Provence, said he is having a new label prepared for the kosher version, which is already sold in France. Both a red and a *rosé* will be available.

The production of the Duc de Provence wines is under the supervision of the rabbinate of Paris, according to Mr. Lukashok. If the wine is any good, it will be the first time Orthodox Jews and any others who demand a strictly kosher wine will be able to drink anything other than the sweet American Concord types or the Israeli wines.

Mr. Lukashok, whose father-in-law is a member of the Marseilles Beth Din and who helps supervise the making of the wine, said the kosher version may actually be better than the nonkosher.

It is axiomatic in the wine business that the cleaner the equipment is, the better the wine and, as Mr. Lukashok said, "Nothing was ever cleaned as well as the *cuvée*—the fermentation vats—used for the kosher wine."

A Forgotten Wine—Cahors

IN THE DAYS when the English ruled Bordeaux and most of Acquitaine, the Médoc was covered with marshes and bogs and its wine was often thin and weak. To give it body and strength, it was often blended with a deep, powerful wine from the up-country. That wine was Cahors, one of the legendary wines of France.

Cahors was known as *vin noir du haut pays*, the black wine from the high country, because of its intense red color. By contrast, the Bordeaux wines were distinguished by their light color and became known as clairets—or clarets as they are still called in England.

Cahors is a small city (with two one-star restaurants in the Michelin guide) on the Lot River in south central France, about 80 miles north of Toulouse. The Lot is a tributary of the Garonne River which flows past Bordeaux and which made it easy to ship the Cahors wine to the blenders.

Cahors has fallen out of style in recent years, partially because of the trend to lightness and partially because it is a wine that requires a great deal of aging to bring to perfection and no one seems to have the patience to wait. The best of the wines of Cahors are vinified the way they were hundreds of years ago, some of them spending 30 or 40 years in wooden casks before being bottled.

The result is a wine that, in Frank Schoonmaker's words, is "slow-maturing, remarkably long-lived, firm but not harsh," with an "unmistakable distinction and a cachet all its own." The Cahors wines are made almost exclusively of the Malbec grape, which is used in Bordeaux now to soften some of the classified growths which are made mostly from Cabernet grapes.

Cahors is a very ancient wine-growing area. It was known to the Romans long before the birth of Christ—Horace wrote of it—and it was one of the first wine regions where the farmers thought to plant the vines in even rows. Originally, even in Bordeaux and Burgundy, the vines were permitted to grow randomly on the ground.

François I sent to Cahors for a *vigneron* to plant and cultivate the royal vineyards at Fontainebleau, and Rabelais was a great fan of the black wine. In the 19th century, *phylloxera* hit the Cahors vineyards particularly hard and many of the ancient vines, some of them 100 years old, were destroyed. Today only a few *vignerons* make the wine in the old way, aging it for years in wood, but there are a few and, now and then, some of these wines actually find their way to this country.

Interestingly enough, while Cahors was eclipsed by more popular wines both in France and elsewhere, French viticulturists did not forget it. Long known as the king of the V.D.Q.S. wines, Cahors, in 1971, was awarded its own *appellation contrôlée* designation. V.D.Q.S. stands for *vins délimités de qualité supérieure*, wines of high quality, made under strict government control, but not up to *appellation contrôlée* standards.

A few years ago, the French writer Philippe Couderc spoke of having a 1964 Cahors with a cassoulet at Chez Proust in Paris. The wine, the dish, and in that case, the restaurateur, Robert Lamazere, who has since moved on to better things, all came from the same part of France. Before that, Mr. Couderc said, Cahors had always been too dark, too heavy, and too rich in tannin for his taste. But the '64 Clos de Gamot was, he said, a revelation, and he looked into the making of the wine. He found that it had been made by the same family in the same cellar for more than 500 years and he made plans in 1970 to visit the Clos de Gamot to taste their 1893, then still available.

The best way to sample this unusual wine is to go to Cahors, which is one of the lesser known, but truly beautiful, parts of France. And, too, this is the ancient land of Périgord, where the food is second to none.

Besides the Clos de Gamot, two of the better known Cahors are made by Jouffreau and Tesseydre. There is a large cooperative at Parnac, called Les Caves d'Olt, about 15 miles from Cahors but within the Cahors wine area which makes about half of all the Cahors wine.

Finding Cahors wines in this country is not easy. Two of the biggest wine shops in New York City do not even mention Cahors in their most recent and quite extensive catalogues. But it is possible to stumble across some in a small store where the owner has forgotten about it and no customer thought to buy it. If you're lucky enough to find one, by all means buy it. As Philippe Couderc wrote: "It starts slowly and finishes well."

What Goes with Bordeaux?

EVERY liquor store clerk has heard it: "I'm having twelve people for dinner. We're starting with prosciutto and melon, and the main course will be rack of lamb. What wines do you suggest?"

But how many butchers have heard a customer say: "We're having twelve people for dinner. I want to serve a 1973 Puligny-Montrachet with the first course and a 1966 Château Pichon-Lalande with the main course. What meats do you suggest?"

More people build their meals around their wines than one might suspect. And not just connoisseurs, either. It might be that someone came through with two special bottles at Christmas time. Or it might be a bottle that had been saved for years, waiting for a very special occasion. Or, for people who are serious collectors, it might be the time to drink some older bottles, before the wine begins to decline.

Wine societies such as the Chevaliers du Tastevin, the Commanderie de Bordeaux, and the Confrérie de St.-Etienne, literally spend months deciding what foods to serve with their most cherished wines. Subcommittees gather regularly to sample dishes that might be served at some major dinner.

Some years ago, I was invited to attend one of these testing meals. A prominent group had decided to hold a dinner built entirely around the sweet wines of Bordeaux: Sauternes, Barsac, St.-Croix-du-Mont, and Loupiac among them, if memory serves.

In Bordeaux it is customary—if not exactly the rage—to serve Sauternes with pâté before a meal and with Roquefort cheese afterwards. And, in fact, the combination of the intense sweetness of the wine with the texture and flavor of these foods can be fascinating. Of course, the Sauternes makers believe that sweet wines will accompany anything—or almost anything—and the group planned a meal to see if they were right. I didn't think they were and the subsequent lack of enthusiasm for sweet-wine dinners leads me to believe that few others did, either. It was a good example, however, of just how the wines can be the most important part of a meal.

Actually, there are no rigid rules about what kind of food should be served with, say, a 1966 Bordeaux, or a bottle of Champagne, or a very old Burgundy. There are a few foods, though, that are really anathema to wine and, of course, there are combinations of foods that make it a waste of time to open a wine bottle. Serve barbecued spareribs with a delicate old claret, for example, and you will never even taste the wine.

My friend Howard Hillman has drawn up what he calls a "least wanted" list of foods that do not go with wine. Taken from his book *Diner's Guide to Serving Wines*, here they are:

Artichokes, asparagus, bananas, candied vegetables, chocolate, citrus juices, coffee, tea, cranberries, egg yolks, hot spices (chili, curry, horseradish, mustard, etc.), molasses, oily fish products (canned tuna, anchovies), pickles, pineapples, the onion family (especially garlic), sugar (vis-à-vis dry white wines), tomatoes, and vinegar.

WINE TALK

Of course, some items are less hostile to wine than others. Garlic, for instance. Cooking a leg of lamb with garlic does not mean there can be no wine with the meal. At least, I hope not. And I'm certainly not going to forego that nice cheap Chianti I like just because there is an anchovy in the pizza.

Having dispensed with foods that are suspect regardless of what the wine may be, let's look at some various wines and what foods might enhance them.

Red Burgundies: almost any red meat will complement a robust Burgundy. If you have a particularly fine bottle, say a great Chambertin or a Richebourg, it would be well to balance it with a simple cut—not something with a heavy sauce, because the sauce will tend to obscure the complexity of the wine.

The same is true for rare old Bordeaux, incidentally. When old wines are tasted at meals at Château Lafite-Rothschild, for instance, the meals are kept purposely simple so as not to intrude on the wines.

Many wine enthusiasts, particularly in France, serve game birds with their best bottles. Generally, with exceptional Bordeaux and Burgundies, young game birds are simply roasted and served with their own juices. Lesser wines can be used with heavier game— venison, hare, and so forth, because with these rich meats, the power of the wine is more important than the finesse. Game is often used to accompany great Rhône wines such as Hermitage and good Châteauneuf-du-Pape.

Italian connoisseurs like to serve game with their big wines: Barolo, Chianti Classico Riserva, and Brunello di Montalcino. Some Spanish wines such as the better Riojas—Marqués de Murrieta and Marqués de Riscal—and the top-of-the-line wines from Torres, near Barcelona, also are set off to their best advantage by dark, game meats with pronounced tastes.

The best of the California reds, the great Cabernet Sauvignons from the north coast counties possess all the subtlety and distinction of the great reds of Europe and should be paired with foods with the same care. Some of the newer wines, those from Monterey County and some bottlings of wineries such as Ridge and Callaway, which is near San Diego, are of such intensity that they can stand up to the richest meat dishes and most powerful cheeses.

Beaujolais is a fresh, fruity wine—or should be—and is best paired with lighter foods: turkey, roast chicken, hamburgers, tartar steak. The better Beaujolais—Fleurie, Brouilly, Morgon, etc.—can be considered in the same class as the lighter Burgundies such as Santenay, that is, they can be matched with almost any red meat dish. This is

Since even before 1855, Château Lafite-Rothschild has led the honor roll of the first growths of Bordeaux.

particularly true of the 1976 Beaujolais, the one currently on the market and the best in many years. It is a richer, darker, more intense Beaujolais than most wine lovers have experienced in a decade.

Traditionally, white wines are paired with white meats and fish. The lighter reds have been moving in on white wines where most of the lighter meats are concerned: veal, poultry, pork, even ham. But dry white wine is still best for fish. It has the extra acid needed to complement the oilyness of most fish.

The great white Burgundy wines: Bâtard-Montrachet, Chevalier-Montrachet, the best Meursaults, white Hermitage, and the *premier cru* Chablis should be set off by the best fish dishes: lobster and crab in rich sauces, and Coquille St. Jacques. The finest Chardonnays of California should also be considered in this group. Some of them are even more intense than the Burgundies. I know one connoisseur who delights in serving Gallo Chablis Blanc with elegant seafood dishes. He insists that this heavy-bodied and slightly sweet wine, if thoroughly chilled, stands up to any rich fish sauce.

Alsatian whites, Riesling, and Gewürztraminer in particular, are as yet little-known in this country but their intense flavor needs to be offset by good solid food. Traditional Alsatian dishes point the way: choucroute, sausages, smoked pork, and ham hocks, for instance. I would love to have once again the ice cold Reisling I enjoyed at the Maison des Têtes (or Kopfhaus, if you prefer) restaurant in Colmar. The dish chosen to go with it: sliced breast of roast pheasant on a bed of choucroute (sauerkraut) that had been steeped in Champagne.

Chinese food, in my opinion, does nothing for Alsatian wine and vice versa. With the fiery Szechuan and Hunan cooking much in vogue, beer is almost a necessity. I prefer it even with Cantonese cooking. If you must have wine with Chinese food, consider Hermitage white, a big powerful wine that may be a match for the meal.

German wines, despite Blue Nun's claim, do not go with everything, except for the most uninitiated wine drinkers. The drier ones go well with poultry and white meats; the best of them should be savored alone or with nuts or fresh fruit. They are magnificent apéritif wines.

The same is true of the great French sweet wines mentioned above. They are excellent with foie gras and some cheeses; they are even better with fresh peaches or pears.

Finally, Sherry. In Jerez, where the only true Sherry is made, it is invariably paired with seafood—but only the pale Fino Sherries and only when they are ice-cold. It is particularly suited to shellfish and fish with rich sauces.

Beautiful Bouscaut

IN 1967, a group of American businessmen came to Cadaujac, France —a little town on the southern outskirts of Bordeaux—and bought themselves a wine business.

Most of the new owners of Châteaux Bouscaut had done well in the bull market of the sixties and when they insisted that they were not interested in tax dodges or instant cachet, people smiled knowingly. Over ten years later, the Société Civile du Château Bouscaut is still no threat to the Rothschilds up north in the Médoc but its owners have every right to tell their friends "We told you so."

Foreign ownership is nothing new in Bordeaux. The city itself was owned by the English for 300 years. To the north of the city, in St.-Estèphe, Château Loudenne has been owned by Gilbey's, the gin people, since 1875. Château Latour, one of the five first growths is owned by Englishmen and, right here in the Graves district, Château Haut-Brion, another of the first growths is owned by the American Douglas Dillon.

The American group, headed by Charles Wohlstetter, Chairman of Continental Telephone Corporation, and Howard Sloan, a New York insurance man, came in with no wine business background and very little wine expertise. But they knew what was happening in the wine world and they had the assistance of the ubiquitous Sam Aaron, wine salesman par excellence, who had set up the deal.

They also were very lucky. First, they were able to hire Jean Delmas to run the place. Delmas, a native of the Bordeaux area, is also the manager of Château Haut-Brion which is about 15 minutes away over the back roads.

A big, solid Frenchman who speaks fluent English and enjoys skiing in the Alps and travelling in the United States in the off-season, Mr. Delmas has modernized the entire winemaking process at Bouscaut. Old vines have been replaced and the blend has been changed.

The older Bouscauts were made up of 10 percent Malbec grapes, 45 percent Merlot, and 45 percent Cabernet Sauvignon. Now the combination is 5 percent Malbec, 15 percent Merlot, and 80 percent Cabernet. The Cabernet was increased, Mr. Delmas explained, "For elegance, finesse, and a longer life."

The weather also has been kind to the new owners. Bordeaux can be harsh on its growers and the Graves district which is wooded and

Worker cultivates vineyard in front of Château Bouscaut, a
Bordeaux vineyard purchased by Americans in 1967.

more subject to frosts can be the harshest of all. In fact, the Americans' first vintage, 1968, was bad. It was sold off in bulk and not a
bottle was filled. But 1969 was a good year, 1970 was a superb year,
1971 was good, and 1972, well, Jean Delmas predicted it would be
okay. "An average year," he said, a bit guardedly. Every bottle of the
1969 was sold. The 1970's and 1971's also are completely sold and in
January, 1973 they had not yet left the property. The 1970's were only
being bottled then, and the 1971's were still in casks in the Bouscaut
chais.

In 1970, Château Bouscaut produced 18,000 cases of red wine and
3,000 of white. The next year there were 11,000 of red and 2,000 of
white and, in 1972, 15,000 of red and only 1,000 of white. This is from
40 *hectares*—about 99 acres. Château Mouton has about 60 *hectares.*
"We will have 45 eventually," Mr. Delmas said, "but first we will go
for quality, then quantity."

To date, Mr. Wohlstetter, Mr. Sloan, and their associates have spent about $2 million to purchase and modernize Château Bouscaut, including the original purchase price of $1.35 million and about $400,000 for the cellar of old wines, both from Bouscaut and other châteaus, dating back to 1918. The updating has not been limited to the fields and the winery. The handsome château, parts of which date back to the 18th century, has been completely redone and, by Bordeaux standards, which are extremely high, it is a handsome place.

Set in a huge park, at the end of a long pebbled drive under massive trees, the house is at its best on the night of a big dinner party, when every vast room is ablaze with light and the windows are mirrors in the reflecting pond before the front door.

Much of the wiring and plumbing were replaced after a fire by the previous owner, Robert Place. But the interiors were done completely by a decorator the owners had not expected: Mrs. Jean Delmas.

Bordeaux châteaus owners are, in the main, wealthy and they set a vigorous social pace. The round of formal dinners hits its peak during the early fall and the owners, many of whom live in Paris the rest of the year, vie with each other to put on elegant parties.

To the surprise and delight of the new Bouscaut proprietors, they found themselves swept easily into the châteaus round and they try when possible to do their share of party throwing. One problem: Few of them can spare more than a few weeks a year to spend in Cadaujac.

In addition to evening parties and dinners there is a regular round of luncheons and receptions for troops of visiting American wine lovers, tasting societies, and, of course, friends of the owners. Sometimes this kind of hospitality backfires. Allan Meltzer, a New York public relations man recently removed to Florida, was at Bouscaut when an American doctor called from Paris. "I'll be arriving tomorrow with my wife and two daughters," the medical man said. "We'll need two rooms."

"I'd never heard of the guy," Mr. Meltzer said. "I told him he was welcome to drop in and that I'd be happy to show him around. But I made it clear that Château Bouscaut is no hotel."

Restaurant Prices

PEOPLE can get very worked up over restaurant wine prices. Write a dozen stories about retail prices—nothing but yawns. But drop in a few lines about what the restaurants are doing and the mail pours in.

Usually there are a few wine lists, from places where the prices are reasonable. Once in a while there is an angry rejoinder from some restaurant man who points out, reasonably enough, that he has to make a living. And then there are the stories from people who simply feel that they have been had.

After a recent article that complimented several restaurants on their wine lists, in came a reply from one of them, La Vielle Maison in Florida. Thanks for the plug, it said in effect, but why did you say that some of our prices were high? After all, we use Baccarat crystal and we have to add 75 cents a bottle to cover breakage. Another restaurant man wrote that he spent $3,000 a year on glasses and that he, too, factored that into the price he charges for wine. A random thought: should the customer pay the extra freight if the dishwasher breaks the glasses?

A most interesting letter came from Kenneth Parker of Greenwich, Connecticut, a man who is obviously very serious about his wine.

"My wife and I enjoy eating out in New York but almost every evening is ruined for me when the wine list arrives. The ridiculous markups upset me."

Mr. Parker wrote to a dozen of the best-known and most expensive restaurants in the area asking if he could bring his own wine and be charged a corkage fee. Only two of them answered, The Four Seasons and Le Cygne, and both turned him down.

"Although I've done it on occasion," he goes on, "I can't really enjoy a bottle of wine that I have paid someone $20 to $40 to open. Add to that the sullen looks you get when you exclude the inflated price of the wine when calculating the tip and it makes the experience unpleasant."

Mr. Parker has compiled some statistics to show how wine prices are increased in restaurants. He uses the current retail price (1978) which, in most instances, is far more than the restaurant paid for the wine, and probably more than the current replacement price. The figures apply only to Bordeaux and only cover half a dozen restaurants but they do represent the often haphazard pricing policies of most deluxe restaurants in New York and in other major cities.

Restaurant Prices

CHÂTEAU	PRICE	RESTAURANT	MARKUP	PERCENT MARKUP
Latour 1966	$30 (retail)			
	70	La Cote Basque	$40	133
	68	Four Seasons	38	125
	45	La Cremailliere	15	50
Brane-Cantenac	13 (retail)			
	32	La Caravelle	19	146
	26	La Cremailliere	13	100
Gruaud-Larose 1967	8.50 (retail)			
	18.50	Four Seasons	10	120
Lafite-Rothschild 1970	24 (retail)			
	90	La Caravelle	66	275
	65	La Cremailliere	41	175
	54	Four Seasons	30	125
Cheval Blanc 1970	22 (retail)			
	56	Four Seasons	34	155
	50	La Caravelle	28	127
	50	La Cremailliere	28	127
Beychevelle 1970	13 (retail)			
	22	La Cremailliere	9	75
	30	La Caravelle	17	130
Gruaud-Larose 1970	9 (retail)			
	16	La Cremailliere	7	78
	21	La Caravelle	12	133
	25	La Cote Basque	16	178
Figeac 1970	9.50 (retail)			
	21	La Caravelle	11.50	120
	18	La Cremailliere	8.50	90
Haut-Brion 1970	20 (retail)			
	60	La Caravelle	40	200
	45	La Cremailliere	25	125
Latour 1970	25 (retail)			
	65	La Caravelle	40	160
	55	La Cremailliere	30	120
	45	Cafe Argenteuil	20	80

CHÂTEAU	PRICE	RESTAURANT	MARKUP	PERCENT MARKUP
Talbot 1970	$8 (retail)			
	22	La Cote Basque	$14	175
	25	La Caravelle	17	212
Cos d'Estournel 1970	8 (retail)			
	25	Cafe Argenteuil	17	212
Margaux 1970	23 (retail)			
	65	La Cremailliere	42	183
	54	Four Seasons	31	135
Palmer	11 (retail)			
	38	La Caravelle	27	245
Talbot 1971	8 (retail)			
	25	Cafe Argenteuil	17	212
	21	La Caravelle	13	163
l'Angelus 1971	7 (retail)			
	18	La Cremailliere	11	157
	15	La Caravelle	8	114
Beychevelle 1971	8 (retail)			
	22	La Caravelle	14	175
	22	La Cremailliere	14	175

Having published Mr. Parker's interesting compilations, it is only fair to add that his premises are not always exactly on the mark. You do not pay the markup just to have someone open the bottle. You pay for having it purchased and stored. You pay for having it properly served and you pay for the restaurants total investment in keeping a good cellar. Also, you do not pay if the wine is bad or, in some cases, simply not to your liking.

Not including the wine in the tip is also questionable. After all, the restaurant probably didn't bake the bread but that is part of the meal, isn't it?

Standard markups usually are around 100 percent of the replacement cost. Many smart restaurateurs are finding that lower margins on wine are paying off handsomely in terms of increased wine sales. However this may not be possible in the deluxe restaurants Mr. Parker favors, or at least uses in his figures.

The overhead in these restaurants is simply enormous and the owners are continuously seeking ways to cover it. Increasing wine prices is one of the easiest. It's either that or the food, they say, claiming that their clientele gets more upset about increases in food prices than they do over high wine prices.

Still—$25 for a bottle that can be replaced for $6; that is a bit much.

A Winery on the West Side

ONE OF the rarest Italian wine labels in the world, Castello dei Tredenari doesn't even come from Italy. And, as a matter of fact, it really isn't even Italian. It is the house label for the wines of Lee J. Tredenari, one-time circus roustabout, taxi driver, ad agency executive, and independent fellow.

Mr. Tredenari has been making wine in the basement of his townhouse on West 103rd Street—hardly one of the world's great viticultural regions—since 1967. You can't buy Tredenari wines and that's a pity because, given the obstacles he must overcome, the stuff he makes is not bad—not bad at all.

The old immigrant winemaking tradition is almost dead in the city. The old men who used to go down to the freight yards and buy California grapes by the case are all gone now and the younger people are not interested.

"Why should they?" Mr. Tredenari asked one day recently while swirling a glass of his 1974 in his dining room. "The jug wines from California are very good and the price of grapes just goes up and up." When Lee Tredenari's father made wine in South Philadelphia years ago, the grapes cost $1 a box. To make his 1976 vintage Mr. Tredenari paid $12.50 a box.

"And the grapes aren't much good," he said. "There was a lot of rot." He buys Grenache and Zinfandel and vinifies them into a blend

Vino Rosso
Dalla Cava dei Castelli

Tredanari
1975
Vino Prodotto ed
Imbottigliato nel Castello

The label is on bottles of wine produced by Lee J. Tredenari
in the basement of his town house on West 103rd Street in
New York City. His house is pictured on the label.

of his own. He also buys mixed white grapes—"I have no idea what
they are"—to make his white wine.

By law, he is allowed to produce 200 gallons a year, and so he does.
The end product goes into the old coal cellar under 103rd Street for
aging and, after a few months, is poured into bottles Mr. Tredenari
gets from his son-in-law, the manager of The Sign of the Dove, the
New York City restaurant. Each normal vintage produces several
hundred bottles, many of which leave the Tredenari ménage under
the arms of friends.

Lee Tredenari was born in the part of South Philly that also
spawned Fabian, Frank Guerrera of the Metropolitan Opera, and
Eddie Fisher. "My sister went out with Buddy Greco," Mr. Tredenari
said. As for Mr. Tredenari, he was successively, a Golden Gloves
contender, a pipefitter's helper, and an infantryman.

After service in Europe during World War II, he helped found a
G.I. taxicab company in Philadelphia. It was crushed by the organized taxi companies. Next came three years at the University of
Pennsylvania and a year at Temple University. He spent some time
studying television and radio and then got a job as a disc jockey in

Lancaster, Pennsylvania. By 1948, he was doing a late night stint on a Philadelphia station.

He broke into television about that time by cleaning up after the elephants on "The Big Top," moved up to director, and then went off to direct the first telecasts of the Chicago Symphony Orchestra. Later he did commercials for John F. Kennedy, Lyndon B. Johnson, and Hubert Humphrey, this last as head of radio and television production at Doyle Dane Bernbach, the advertising agency.

About ten years ago, restless and getting ready to chuck the everyday routine, he decided to make some wine. He still had the ancient equipment his father used in Philadelphia. That led to planting his own vineyard.

"I had some property up in Carmel," he said. "It seemed like a great place to grow grapes." After studying a bit, Mr. Tredenari decided to plant French-American hybrids, crosses between the elegant wine grapes of France and the tough winter-resistant vines of the American northeast.

"It went all right at first," Mr. Tredenari said. "But when the vines began to bear, it was a disaster. The birds got it all." In one weekend, hordes of birds flew in and decimated his three acres of grapes. "We salvaged about five pounds of grapes from three acres," he said. "So we went back to the Hunts Point Market to buy what we needed."

In 1971 Lee Tredenari dropped out of the working world. He'd made some money and he wanted to reassess his life. "I wanted to see where this wine thing would take me, for instance," he said.

New York State laws being what they are, it didn't take him very far. "My son Greg runs a little cheese and gourmet shop over on Broadway," Mr. Tredenari said. "I help him out from time to time and I'd love to get my wine in there, but the hassle with the state would be just too much."

Tredenari wines ferment in 30-gallon oak barrels right there on 103rd Street, then are transferred into five-gallon glass jugs. Then, eventually, into gallons and fifths. A small portion is left for longer aging in the wood. He keeps a couple of bottles from each vintage and still has at least one from 1967, his first year as a *maître de chais*, or cellar master.

Mr. Tredenari still takes an occasional free-lance assignment, doing commercials or a documentary film, but he had decided not to go back to the world just yet.

"I know this is all relatively unimportant," he says, still talking about his winemaking, "But there is something honest and rewarding about it that you don't get in other things. I love my work but I love this too. In a way, I think I'm lucky to have such choices."

The 1972 Vintage—Much Maligned

IT WAS THE CLERK in a liquor store who started it. "The '72 Bordeaux," he said, "are not fit to drink. We wouldn't have them in the shop."

And sure enough, he didn't. Nor did any of several other places in the same area. Could they really be that bad? It was not a great harvest in Bordeaux, that year, but it was better than some. The summer was grey and cold and often wet, but it was followed by six weeks of glorious autumn weather.

The grapes never had time to ripen the way they did in 1970, but they came through, thanks to the dry autumn, without the rot that plagued the 1969's. The 1972's could be expected to turn out somewhat thin, perhaps short on fruit, and maybe a bit long on acid because the lack of sun that summer did not provide the sugar needed for perfectly balanced wine.

But "not fit to drink"? The 1963 and 1965 vintages were very, very poor, but even the most skeptical enthusiast will recall a couple of good bottles from those vintages. Surely there are a few good 1972's around. The late Frank Schoonmaker said there had not been a bad vintage in Bordeaux since 1968 and Alexis Lichine has said recently that there were many good 1972's.

Of course, these fellows sell wine. Surprisingly, wine people can be remarkably dispassionate in judging the product they purvey, but still it seemed like a good idea to try some. Supplies of the 1972's are spotty in the metropolitan area, not because of any universal trade judgment on their quality, but because there are still a lot of other wines around.

Even so, it was not difficult to come up with a reasonable cross-section of wines of the 1972 vintage, ranging from Château Lafite-Rothschild to Pontet-Latour, a minor shipper's blend.

It can be said at the outset that the wines ranged from poor to very good. There were some remarkably fine, velvety wines, far better than anyone would have expected, given the bad name the vintage seems to have acquired.

Here are the wines tasted in two sessions over the past two weeks:

From St.-Emilion, Châteaus Haut-Corbin, Laroque, Ripeau, Canon, Figeac, Belgrave, and l'Angelus; from the Graves, Château Le Garde; from St.-Julien, Château Gloria, Lagrange, and Ducru-Beaucaillou; from Margaux, Lascombes, Prieuré-Lichine, and Rauzan-Gassies;

from Pauillac, Châteaus Lafite-Rothschild, Grand-Puy-Lacoste, Pichon Lalande, Pichon Baron, and Pontet-Canet; from St.-Estèphe, Château Les-Ormes-de-Pez; from Pomerol, Châteaus Pétrus, Vieux-Château-Certan, and La Pointe. Pontet Latour and La Cour Pavillon, two shippers blends with château-like names also were tried.

No attempt has been made in this list to separate the famous names from the not-so-famous. Both Pétrus and La Pointe are Pomerols, but Pétrus is one of the greatest wines of France. It showed better than others, of course. The question is this: Is it as good a value as some of the others?

Not unexpectedly, the Lafite and the Pétrus were the outstanding wines of the group. While 1972 may not be a vintage to hold, the Lafite was not ready to drink. It was a wine with excellent, deep color, and a beautiful bouquet. It was a wine to keep for another two or three years, perhaps more. At about $11 a bottle (1977), it is a good buy, if only to give people who might never be able to afford a Lafite an idea of what it can be like. It is certainly a better buy than the 1968 Lafite which was being hawked around in 1976 at $4 and $5.

The Pétrus was a soft, rounded wine, ready to drink right now. This is a typical Pomerol and a very good one though Pétrus can be a much bigger wine in better years. Still, it is a good chance to taste a really first class Bordeaux, one classed with Lafite and Mouton, at a reasonable price: about $10.

Vieux-Château-Certan was uncharacteristically hard and green for a Pomerol; not because it was bad but because it was not ready. This is always a good wine and there was every indication that in a year or two, the 1972 will come around nicely. No bargain at $6.50 but not a bad price either.

The La Pointe was thin and tart, not only for a Pomerol, but for any Bordeaux. Not recommended. Neither is Château Pichon Baron, probably one of the more disappointing wines in the tasting. It had an unpleasant nose, and a harsh, vegetable taste. A second bottle was just the same, indicating that the wine was poorly made, not that we had a bad bottle.

Pichon Lalande, at about $6.50, proved to be a rather elegant wine with nice body, color, and bouquet, if a bit thin. The Grand-Puy-Lacoste at about $5 was much the same—it had the same characteristic elegance of a good Pauillac—and it is probably a better buy. Pontet-Canet was very sharp and acidic when first opened. It softened up later, but was basically an undistinguished wine compared with the other Pauillacs. It sells for around $5.40.

Two of the St.-Juliens showed well: Ducru-Beaucalliou and Gloria.

The Ducru had as much finesse and style as any wine in the tasting. It also had more fruit and body than most. It is not cheap—$7—but it is a good wine. One looks for a chance to be hard on Château Gloria, just to counteract the ridiculously overblown praise it has been getting recently. But the 1972 turned out quite well. It had good body and color and probably could use another year in the bottle. Not a bad buy at around $4 although word is that it will go up soon.

The Château Lagrange was an unbalanced wine with too much acid. It was also too tannic and hard.

Among the Margaux, both the Prieuré-Lichine and Château Lascombes showed fairly well although Lascombes probably had the edge. It had a good Cabernet Sauvignon taste, nice color, and more fruit than most. Prieuré was medium-bodied, nicely balanced, and ready to drink. Lascombes at about $5 and Prieure at about $4.50 are reasonably priced wines. Rauzan-Gassies is a wine that swings from poor to good rather wildly, apparently because of the way it is vinified and not because of the vintage. This was not one of the best, even among the 1972's.

The 1972 Vintage—Much Maligned

The single St.-Estèphe, Les-Ormes-de-Pez, turned out to be a pleasant wine, indeed. It was much softer and supple than normally could be expected from a four-year-old St.-Estèphe. It had body and color and was enjoyable to drink. It should sell for around $4 and is worth it. The sole Graves, Château La Garde, had good color, was fairly soft, and had a pleasant nose but the chances are few experts would ever identify it as a Graves. It was just a pleasant, undistinguished Bordeaux.

The St.-Emilions, as they often are, were the hit of the tasting. They were soft, full wines, with good deep color and rich, pleasant texture. Not deep-bodied wines like the 1970's or even the 1971's, but definitely good drinking wines. Except for one: supposedly the best of the lot, Château Figeac. It had a stemmy, vegetal nose, an acrid tobacco taste, and a brownish hue. Again, a second bottle proved to be just the same.

The lesser St.-Emilions were the ones to drink and—when they become more widely available in a few months—to buy. L'Angelus, a popular wine here, was somewhat bland and flat, but it was soft and had a nice bouquet. At $5, though, it is no steal. Château Ripeau was soft and fruity, a typical St.-Emilion. Château Haut-Corbin was slow to open up but after an hour or so in the air it became an attractive wine with deep color, good body, and a good nose. Château Canon was much the same: left open for an hour or so, it became an extremely attractive wine. These last three should sell for around $3 and at that level are good buys.

Of the two shipper's blends, the La Cour Pavillon was the best. In France they would call it a "correct" wine. Which means there is nothing particularly bad about it or good either. The Pontet Latour was a thin wine, almost a *rosé* in color and body, with nothing distinguished about it. These are wines to be produced in large quantities and sold to wine beginners who want consistency in style with none of the problems of trying to figure out regions, château names, and the like. At $3.99 for the La Cour Pavillon and $2.99 for the Pontet Latour, they are overpriced.

Bear in mind that not all wines are available at every shop or even in every city. But there are hundreds of different Bordeaux around and all are worthy of a try. Prices vary, of course, but prices on Bordeaux wines have been depressed for several years and are now beginning to go up again. There is a chance that the prices of the 1972 vintage will hold for a while so there may be some bargains in the $2.50 to $3.50 class for the rest of this year.

St.-Emilion

IT'S ONLY 20 miles from Bordeaux and the route is direct enough, but I always get lost when I drive to St.-Emilion. Could it be the Bordeaux traffic? It would disorient anyone. Or could it be something less easy to define—something having to do with the psychological distance between the two—than the brief trip along Route 89?

St.-Emilion is part of the Bordeaux wine region. In fact it was a wine-growing area probably before there was a Bordeaux. But it is a world apart from the Médoc, the area most of us think of when we think of Bordeaux.

There is a bleak beauty to the Médoc, with its endless rows of vines and limitless sky. But it is a man-made beauty, with nature bowing to form and purpose. In the Médoc, man tries incessantly to bend the earth and the rain to his whim. Now and then he succeeds and it has made him proud and arrogant.

St.-Emilion is breathtakingly beautiful by itself. Men tend the vines and make great wine, but in concert with nature, not in opposition.

The grand *seignieurs* of the Médoc smile icily across the river in the direction of St.-Emilion and the farmers of St.-Emilion laugh heartily back. Have you been invited to lunch in the Médoc? The butler will show you in. A whiskey to start perhaps? The china is Limoges, the crystal Baccarat, the service impeccable.

Ah, but lunch in St.-Emilion is something else again. The table is in the vast kitchen and the pots bubble before your eyes. There may be some old bottles or there may not. Have some more bread. Send those dogs out of the house. Have another tumbler of wine.

This is farm country—picture book France—and the people are proud of their country ways. To be sure, there are famous names here and elegant homes. The Manoncourts at Figeac, the Malet de Roqueforts at La Gaffelière, the Moueix family at various châteaus. But the spirit of St.-Emilion guides them, too. Black-tie dinners are rare in this corner of the world.

Alain Querre may be the quintessential St.-Emilionnais. Sporting western-style boots and a ten-gallon hat, picked up on some trip to the American southwest, he races tirelessly around the country roads promoting the wines of St.-Emilion. His own property, Château Monbousquet, will never produce one of the great St.-Emilion wines. It is too far down the slope from the town where, if anything, the soil is too good. But the owners of far more famous properties look to Alain for guidance in promoting and selling their own wines. "I want the whole world to know our wines," he says.

Not a few lovers of Bordeaux wines started with the wines of St.-Emilion. Like the people who make them, they are warm, open, and easy to like, where the wines of the Médoc are more austere, subtle, and elegant. The wines of St.-Emilion mature faster than the wines of the Médoc. Only a very few improve after eight years; most are ready to drink in four or five.

The best place to see St.-Emilion from is the wide veranda of the charming Hostellerie de Plaisance, which is built over the dome of a church hollowed out of the rock in the 9th century.

Food at the Hostellerie is more than acceptable and, as might be expected, the wine list is excellent. From the terrace, the view includes Tour du Roi dating from the 12th century, the ruins of the Cloître de Cordeliers, an ancient monastery, and, far into the distance, the vines.

There are two groups of châteaus in St.-Emilion: those on the plain and those on the slope spreading in either direction from the town. The most famous château on the plain, right up against the border of neighboring Pomerol, is Cheval Blanc, said to be named for a horse of Henry of Navarre. Best known of the properties on the slope is Château Ausone which may or may not be built on the site of a summer home owned by the Roman poet and statesman Ausonius some 1600 years ago.

Ausone was once said to make the best wine. Presently Cheval Blanc is said to be first. The prices of both wines are astronomical, but Cheval Blanc is invariably higher. Cheval Blanc, about four kilometers from town is a handome property but Ausone, whose cellars are carved from the rock underlying St.-Emilion is far more dramatic. A tasting in that cellar is unforgettable.

When the wines of St.-Emilion were classified by the French Government in 1955, 12 first great growths were named, with Cheval Blanc and Ausone in a special category at the top of the list, and about 70 great growths. My own favorites are La Gaffelière, just down the slope from Ausone, and Figeac, a lovely place on the old road into Libourne, once the shipping port on the Dordogne River for most St.-Emilion wines.

But I have a special favorite, too. It is a small property in the Montagne-St.-Emilion district called Château Belair-Montaiguillon and it is owned by an ex-Philadelphian named David Park. Mr. Park, like many people before him beginning back around the time of Ausonius,

Appellation St-Emilion 1ᵉʳ Grand Crû Classé Contrôlée

PREMIER GRAND CRU CLASSÉ

Château Pavie

SAINT-EMILION

1967

MÉDAILLES D'OR
Expositions Universelles
PARIS 1867 - 1889 - 1900
DIPLOMES D'HONNEUR
LIÈGE 1905, LONDRES 1908
HORS-CONCOURS BORDEAUX 1907

VALETTE, PROPRIÉTAIRES A SAINT-ÉMILION (GIRONDE)

fell in love with the valley of the Dordogne. Coming from a family who owned a supermarket chain, but uninterested in the grocery business, Mr. Park decided to take his money and invest it in a vineyard. The fact that neither he nor his wife knew one grape from another did not deter him.

By a great stroke of luck, he got to know Alain Querre and through Alain, many of his neighbors, most of them third- and fourth-generation winegrowers. In a display of friendliness and generosity rare almost anywhere else in the world, the French families, none of whom spoke much English, taught grape growing and winemaking to David Park who, for a long time, spoke no French.

"They simply couldn't figure us out at first," he told me. "There was even a rumor that we were with the C.I.A." The Parks had a few rough years, particularly in the depressed wine market of 1973 and 1974, but that is past now. They are veteran *vignerons* and their little château—just a handsome country house, really—is accepted by some of the most critical winemakers in the world, their St.-Emilion neighbors.

After the bustle of Bordeaux, St.-Emilion is a perfect stopping-off place for wine lovers. The town is tiny—most of it can be encompassed in 30 minutes—and it is not difficult to set up a tour of some of the neighboring vineyards and cellars.

Near the church, the ancient Cloître des Cordeliers, it is still possible to see the cell where Saint Emilion himself was supposed to have lived in the 8th century. In those days, St. Emilion was on the route—well, almost on the route—south to the shrine of Santiago de Compostela in Spain (from whence, apropos of nothing at all, we derive the name for Coquille St. Jacques). Why Saint Emilion, whose name was Aemilianus then, decided to pack it in short of his goal, or whether he settled in on his way back, is unclear. So, for that matter, is almost everything else about him other than his present value to the tour guides. Since the wine business already was at least five centuries old in the 8th century, it's amusing to speculate that he may have stayed to be close to the principal local product.

Tourism is certainly St.-Emilion's second industry, if that is the proper word for a town so small, but, as yet, the tourists do not come in overwhelming numbers. If they ever do there might not be enough macaroons. Yes, macaroons. For reasons no one seems to be able to explain plausibly, St.-Emilion is noted for its macaroons. No one leaves without a box and they are very good indeed. Just don't try to mix them with a bottle of St.-Emilion. It can be stated fairly authoritatively that no wine goes with macaroons.

What's in a Vintage?

SOMEONE recently asked Brother Timothy, famed cellar master for the Christian Brothers' wineries, if and when he planned to list vintage dates on Christian Brothers wines. "Never," he replied. "At least, not while I'm around."

But what is this—some kind of heresy? Brother Timothy has been making wine for almost 40 years. He is well aware of the significance of vintage dating. The fact is, he takes great pride in his ability to blend wines and he feels that he can best achieve the combinations he wants by reserving the right to use wines from several vintages.

By Federal law, a vintage American wine may contain no more than five percent of the wine of another year. Thus, a wine from a year when the growing conditions produced a high acid content, if it is to be a vintage wine, cannot be blended with another, softer, less acidy wine from another year.

A small producer of premium wines expects this and prices his wines accordingly. Some famous California Pinot Chardonnays, for instance, cost $15 and $20 a bottle. The Christian Brothers also produce a Pinot Chardonnay—at $3.85 (1974)—and they produce it in considerable quantity. This wine is a blend, nonvintage, and it has startled some experts with its quality.

Which brings up the whole business of vintages. How important are they? How good a guide are they to the quality of the wine in the bottle?

Well, for one thing, they don't always mean what you might think they mean. In Germany, a vintage wine can contain up to 25 percent of the wine of another year. In France, there is not *supposed* to be any other year's wine in a vintage dated bottle, but most American vintners believe 20 percent would not be an exaggeration.

Vintages became popular in the 17th century when corks and bottles first made it possible to keep wine. They served as a rudimentary kind of consumer protection because so many years were bad years in the French wine business. The vintners had no control over the weather—which was and still is often terrible in France and Germany. And they had even less control over insects and plant disease. In the 20 years from 1801 to 1820, for instance, only three Bordeaux vintages rated more than a "good."

Today, more vintages are good than are bad. There are still poor years, of course, such as 1963, 1965, and 1968 in Bordeaux. A wine drinker relying on a vintage chart would have avoided all three—and he could have missed some delightful wines at unbelievably low prices. True, they only lasted a few years and there were only a handful of them, but they were good drinking wines. No vintage chart ever explained that.

The statement "1970 was better than 1969," derived from a mistaken faith in numbers is going to cause problems. It was a better year in Bordeaux, but in Burgundy, 1969 was better. And what about great years that are not ready to be drunk? Many newcomers to wine, reading that 1970 was good, buy a bottle of 1970, drink it, and go back to birch beer. The chart said 1970 was good; it did not say that the wine needs three years or more in the bottle. There are 1945's that are not yet ready to drink even though the charts list it as a great year.

In climates where there is always ample sun, a vintage chart is even less important. There are bad years in warm climates, too, but they are rare. For Italian, Californian, and good Spanish wines, the vintage is useful only if you plan to store the wine for years, or if you want to buy a wine with a certain amount of bottle age. The vintage date simply tells you how old the wine is.

One California vintner produces both premium vintage and non-vintage wines. "If we decided to vintage date all our wines," said Samuel Sebastiani, of the Sebastiani Vineyards in Sonoma, north of San Francisco, "there would be some from every harvest that for one reason or another could not really stand on their own, or at least we would not be sufficiently pleased with them to put our family name on the labels." By blending with another year, the Sebastiani's may achieve a wine that meets their standards.

"When a wine's color and balance can't be improved upon by blending," Mr. Sebastiani said, "it probably will be vintage dated." These wines require longer aging and, Mr. Sebastiani said, must be priced accordingly. A Sebastiani Cabernet Sauvignon, for instance, is aged three to three and a half years in redwood casks, six months to a year in oak barrels, and a year or two in the bottle before it is released from the Sebastiani cellars.

Some winemakers who blend one year's wine with another and produce nonvintage wines, single out their best bottles by putting on them the number of the specific blend, such as Bin 15 or Cask 36. Of course, there is only the vintner's word that Bin 15 really is better than 14 or 16.

There are wine experts who predict that nonvintage premium wines eventually will disappear in this country. Most wineries now make superior wines almost every year, they argue, and besides, the consumer feels more at home with a vintage-dated bottle.

Perhaps so. In the meantime, there are some good buys in nonvintage California varietals (wines whose names come from the grape from which they are made). And they are priced well below most of the vintage-dated wines of the same varieties.

A Martha's Vineyard Vineyard

THERE REALLY IS a vineyard on Martha's Vineyard; and not a little backyard operation, either. It is a full-scale, no-nonsense professional operation, and one of these days you are going to see the wine in your local store. Well, maybe not in *every* local store, but in some stores along the Eastern seaboard.

This unusual venture is called Chicama Vineyards and it is the handiwork of George Mathiesen, a 50-odd-year-old dropout from the business world who moved to Martha's Vineyard in 1971 to go into the wine business.

The Mathiesens, George, his wife Catherine, and their six children, had been summer visitors to this island off the Massachusetts coast since 1965. "We first came here on our boat," Mr. Mathiesen said, "and we fell in love with the place."

The Mathiesens still have a boat, but more and more, their time is taken up by their vines and by their winery. What's more, as the operation grows there will be even less time for sailing and other island pursuits.

Right now, the Mathiesens have about 15 of their 75 acres in vines. Eventually, they hope to have 45 acres in vine cultivation. Also, they are trying to interest other Vineyard people in growing grapes. Their winery can handle far more grapes than they themselves will ever want to produce. If the product catches on, it may be necessary to have other growers to meet the demand.

Demand for Chicama Vineyards wine is purely hypothetical at this point. On one sharp brilliant fall day in 1974, the only Chicama wine around was in a couple of five-gallon jugs and a few small barrels in the cellar of the Mathiesen barn. But out in the vineyard, the Mathiesens and a few of their friends were picking the grapes that will become the first real Chicama Vineyards vintage—1974.

Neither George nor Cathy Mathiesen were born to the wine business or any other kind of farming. They got interested in wine in California and gradually it dawned on them that it could provide the kind of life they had been seeking for many years. To learn about grape growing and winemaking, they apprenticed themselves to the crusty old master of New York's Finger Lakes region, Dr. Konstantin Frank.

Dr. Frank is the stubborn genius whose single goal in life is to prove that *vinifera* vines, the famous vines of the European and California vineyards, can be grown successfully in the harsh climate of the Northeast.

"We lived in California for many years," George Mathiesen said, "and we had come to believe the myth of *vinifera*. But we didn't want to plant Lambrusco (the common wine grape of the Northeast) or the hybrids (special crosses of various vines that have succeeded in cold climates). So we called Dr. Frank and he invited us up." Dr. Frank's Vinifera Wine Cellars are high above the shores of Lake Keuka, ten miles north of Hammondsport, the capital of the New York State wine industry.

Cathy Mathiesen took up the story. "We were there to watch and learn," she said, "but on our second day, Dr. Frank—who is now in his seventies—fell and broke his foot. So we brought in the 1971 harvest. He hobbled around with his cast, not missing a thing. You just couldn't buy the knowledge he gave us."

The Mathiesens, imbued with some of Dr. Frank's fervor, have planted nothing but *vinifera* vines: Chardonnay and Riesling, mostly, but also Cabernet Sauvignon, Merlot, Chenin Blanc, Pinot Noir, Pinot Gris, Gamay, Gewürztraminer, and a Russian white wine variety called Rkazetelli.

Eventually, some of the lesser varieties will be dropped. It depends on how they thrive in the Martha's Vineyard soil and climate. Since no one has ever tried to grow *vinifera* grapes here, no one knows how these will turn out.

What is known is that the sandy soil should be ideal and that the climate may be one of the best in the country for these kinds of grapes. In fact, studies of the weather here indicate that the growing season is very similar to the Burgundy district of France and possibly better than some of the prime wine grape regions of California. The proximity of the sea tends to moderate both very hot and very cold weather.

So far, the Mathiesens have spent about $150,000 on their vineyard and winery, exclusive of land. After spring frosts damaged a large portion of their first, experimental crop in 1971, they installed an expensive sprinkler system among the vines. When birds gobbled their way through a later crop, they tried hanging pie plates on strings and eventually bought an electronic gadget that drives off the birds with loud shrieks. High wire fences were installed to frustrate the deer.

The Mathiesen's winery is located temporarily in a handsome little barn they built near the entrance to their property in West Tisbury.

Eventually, they hope to build a much bigger plant, using the huge collection of boulders they acquired when they cleared their land for planting.

There are three stainless steel fermentation tanks in the barn basement, each of which can hold about 1,000 gallons of wine. In the next few years, another eight tanks will be added. Recently, one of the tanks held 750 gallons of fermenting juice from about a ton of California Zinfandel grapes George Mathiesen had bought in Boston. If all goes well, this will be the first wine sold commercially under the Chicama Vineyards label. The Zinfandel was something of a trial run, Mr. Mathiesen said, and also a chance to get the label into a few commercial channels.

The label, incidentally, was designed by the Mathiesen's daughter Lynn, a graduate of Pratt Institute who works in a New York City wine and liquor store when she isn't up here tending vines. The label uses a seagull motif to express the closeness of the sea.

A second tank in the Chicama winery holds about 600 gallons of fermenting Chardonnay grape juice. The grapes were picked earlier this month and crushed in the Mathiesen's brand-new automatic press from France. Still to come are about 200 gallons of Riesling from grapes scheduled to be picked soon.

The Mathiesens have not yet decided how to age these wines—whether they should spend time in oak barrels or be aged only in the steel tanks and later in bottles. These white wines should be ready for the market in about 18 months.

"Next year," said George Mathiesen, "we expect to crush about 18 or 20 tons of grapes and produce 3,000 gallons of wine. We hope to double the figure every year after that until we can do 30,000 gallons annually."

Whatever the climate and soil may provide, Martha's Vineyard is not an easy place to make wine. Every tank, every pump, every bottle, and cork must be ferried over from the mainland. "Even so," George Mathiesen said, "we concluded that of all places in the East, this was most likely to produce the kind of wine we wanted to make. Martha's Vineyard has three important assets for us: the kind of living we enjoy, the right climate for our wine, and strangely enough, a market."

The Mathiesens reason that the Vineyard's 40,000 summer visitors are a ready-made market of sophisticated people willing and eager to buy up most of what they can make. "And what better advertising could we have than those people going home in the fall, all over the country, and telling their friends about Chicama Vineyards?" Mr. Mathiesen asked.

The Mathiesens are not unknown on the island as it is. Last year they sold table grapes from several stands and at the island's popular Farmer's Market. They also sold Cathy Mathiesen's cheesecakes and crusty sourdough French bread.

At the end of the summer season, they decided to hold an open house for all the local people who had asked questions about Chicama Vineyards. "We were amazed," George Mathiesen said; "we got 500 or 600 people.

"We think this operation is unique," he said later, while cleaning crushed grape skins from his press, "because we are trying to do it all ourselves. My wife has always been interested in growing and I learned something about finance and management in the corporate world. A lot of farmers set up legal partnerships with their wives for business reasons. We have a partnership in fact."

George Mathiesen left a pretty good job with the Westinghouse Corporation to take up the life of a *vigneron*. A visitor, watching him juggle pumps and hoses with rough, powerful hands not usually seen at sales meetings, asked if he had any regrets about leaving the corporate jungle four years ago. Brushing aside one of the late-summer bees attracted by the sweet grape juice, he grinned and said: "Man, not one."

Julia Likes Wine, Too

THERE IS a picture around somewhere of Julia Child, in the course of one of her television programs, enthusiastically swigging from a wine bottle. She's lucky she's Julia Child. Why, the Chevaliers du Tastevin have been known to put a man alone in a room with a pistol for less.

Mrs. Child meant no harm. She and her husband love wine; they drink a lot of it. But they are not about to be carried away by the wine mystique.

They are not collectors of ancient Bordeaux. They make no unnecessary ritual of the simple business of serving a bottle. "Would you like this '73 Beaujolais," Paul Child asked, "or a '67 Côte Rôtie?"

First there was a quiche accompanied by a 1971 Niersteiner Domtal, a favorite of Paul Child who got to know German wines while stationed there during his State Department days. The Rhines and Mosels turned out to be a fortuitous find for him. He is just now (1975) recovering from some serious heart surgery and, for reasons known only to the surgeons, he came through the operation almost completely bereft of a lifelong ability to enjoy wine. "It's coming back—damn slowly," he said with evident impatience. "Thank God I can ejoy a couple of these Rhines and Mosels."

The big Côte Rôtie was served with what Mrs. Child dismissed as "just a pick-up meal": some leftover filet of beef with a madeira sauce, sautéed artichokes forestière, and an avocado salad.

Dinner was served at the oilcloth covered table in the center of the big, old-fashioned Child kitchen, a formidable arena in which the chef moves swiftly from cutting board to refrigerator to the oversized commercial gas range.

The arrangement allows Mrs. Child to chop, cut, peel, sauté, and do whatever else she has in mind while missing none of the conversation, which on this occasion was mostly about wine.

More accurately, it was about people and wine—a German winemaker on whose front door the Childs once rapped simply because they had enjoyed his product at home, the Frenchman who makes a superb Beaujolais not far from their second home in the south of France, the outrageous prices charged for wine by some restaurants.

The Child cellar is not large but it is fairly select. There are good clarets from the 1950's, good Burgundies from the 1960's, and a representative selection of German wines, attesting to Paul Child's long interest in them, not to his postoperative problem with French reds.

Because they spend time in France every year, and their home here is closed, the Childs are wary about keeping expensive wines around. "There have been quite a few break-ins," Mrs. Child said. "I hope you won't give anyone the idea that we have an extraordinary cellar here."

Not extraordinary, perhaps, but certainly unusual, is Paul Child's method for keeping track of his wines. The traditional way is to keep a cellar book with pages for purchases, comments on first tastings, later tastings, all that sort of thing.

Some collectors keep a simple file of three-by-five cards; one card for each wine, price, date, and tasting notes. Some collectors are too lazy to use anything. They end up with no idea of what is in the cellar. This has its good points actually. "Look at this 1961 Pétrus I just found stuck in with some Valpolicella!"

Paul Child's system is different. He uses a large composition board about two feet by two feet. Every wine he owns is listed on the board with the number of bottles marked next to it, this way:

Château Inconnu 1959: 1 2 3 4 5 6 7 8 9 10 11 12

As each bottle is consumed, he erases a number. Thus he always is able to tell at a glance exactly what wines remain in the cellar and how many bottles of each. When the Inconnu is gone, he simply erases the name and writes in whatever he buys next. If the board gets too grubby, he can throw it out and start another.

It really is a good idea to keep track of what wines are on hand, even if there are only a couple of dozen bottles. It is even better to note down when the wine is drunk and who drank it. The late publisher Alfred A. Knopf had cellar books going back almost half a century. Besides being a catalogue of some great wine buys they are also a record of what must have been some brilliant dinner parties.

Mr. Knopf loved to look back over the old books, to recall what he paid for some of the memorable wines of the century (often under $2 a bottle) and to see who shared them with him. Then he feigns outrage. "What," he exclaims, "I wasted that wine on *him*!"

A Sommelier Manqué

A SOMMELIER is a man who has spent a lifetime learning wines. The vineyards of the world, the thousands of labels, the good vintage years, the proper wine for every occasion at the best price: these are stuff of which good sommeliers are made. Right?

Not according to Jeffrey Pogash. Who is Jeffrey Pogash and how does he know these things? Jeffrey is a 23-year-old graduate student at Rutgers University who lives with his parents in Maplewood, New Jersey, where he was born. But he is also a former sommelier.

WINE TALK

And not at some pretentious steak joint in Westchester that tried wine when the go-go dancers bombed. He was a full-fledged wine steward at Fouquet's on the Champs Elysées in Paris. And if what he says is true, the sommelier business—like so many other things—just is not what it's cracked up to be.

"Anybody can be a sommelier at Fouquet's," he said. A fact, by the way, of which he is living proof. "An opening comes up," Mr. Pogash said, "and one of the waiters calls his cousin who is out of work or tired of clerking in a drugstore. The fellow comes around and is hired.

"Most of the fellows knew nothing about wine and weren't interested in learning," Mr. Pogash went on. "It was just another job."

The young American worked at Fouquet's through June, July, and half of August. "I had gone to France after college to study and to learn the language," he said. "I took a course in wine tasting while I was studying at the University of Paris and a whole new world opened up to me."

An American friend who was learning the wine business in a Paris retail shop told him of the opening at Fouquet's. He quit his classes at the University of Paris, applied for the job, and was hired.

"I started as the *caviste*," he said. The *caviste* is, literally, the man who works in the cave, which is *cellar* in French. He wrestles the cases of wine, fills the bins from which sommeliers select bottles, and sweeps up. Had Jeffrey Pogash been a *caviste* at Fouquet's a few years ago, he would have bottled wine, too. Fouquet's has its Beaujolais and Aligoté bottled privately, but used to buy the casks and bottle under its own label in its own cellar. The Pré Catalan, owned by the same family as Fouquet's, still does.

Luckily, for the young American, someone quit. So, instead of spending his summer in a damp basement, he found himself in the austere black waistcoat, black apron, and bow tie of a Fouquet's wine steward, serving customers at one of the best-known restaurants in the world.

"It was a 13-hour day," he said. "I began at 11 A.M. and finished around midnight—if I was lucky. The métro shuts down at 1 A.M. and there were times I had to sprint to get the last train home."

At the corner of the Champs Elysées and Avenue Georges V, Fouquet's is in the heart of the fashionable tourist area and a short taxi ride for many people in business, publishing, and the arts. It rates one star in the *Guide Michelin*—no mean accomplishment for a place of its size. There are dining rooms on two floors, facilities for large parties, and huge terraces on both streets.

"I'd work lunch and dinner in the dining rooms," Mr. Pogash said, "and patrol the terraces in between." A sommelier at Fouquet's, he explained, is also a strolling bartender. "If someone ordered a Brandy Alexander, I went to the bar, made the drink myself, brought it back, and served it."

Wine actually was the least of his problems. "Mostly we sold Beaujolais," he said; "endless quantities of Beaujolais. If people ordered carafes, we opened the bottles and poured it out. If they wanted it in the bottle we served the bottle."

Mr. Pogash said he soon found his interest in wine was not shared by his fellow sommeliers. "I enjoyed talking with the customers and helping them with their selections," he said. "The others—Fouquet's had seven sommeliers—just went through the motions, unless we were told to push something."

During one period, he recounted, the head sommelier ordered his crew to urge 1973 Brouilly on the customers because they were over-stocked. "He told us that if we were asked for something else to say we were out of it." Brouilly is a higher classification of Beaujolais.

Mr. Pogash said he never thought the head sommelier accepted him. "He was convinced that he knew everything about wine, that no one else knew anything, and that as an American I could never learn anything about it."

For his efforts, Mr. Pogash was paid 50 francs a day, about $12, less than $1 an hour at the current exchange rate (1975). He also averaged about 40 francs a day in tips but, as the new man, still in his apprenticeship, the tips went to the head sommelier and were split up among the other wine stewards. On an average day, the sommelier from New Jersey sold about 80 or 90 bottles of wine.

"About 90 percent of our customers were French," he said. "Another 5 percent were Germans and the rest were Americans and Mexicans and Japanese. The Americans mostly ordered their wine in carafes."

A carafe of Beaujolais went for 25 francs ($6) at Fouquet's, and a bottle of Brouilly for 40 francs ($10). After that, Mr. Pogash said, the prices climbed into the stratosphere, as they do in most Parisian restaurants. The most expensive wines Jeffrey remembers serving were a 1955 Château Grand-Puy-Lacoste, a 1964 Château Mouton Rothschild, and a 1962 Château Ausone. Not an impressive list, but perhaps not unexpected at Paris prices.

"Businessmen, including the American director of the Chase Manhattan Bank in Paris, were the best customers," Mr. Pogash said. Pierre Salinger sipped an apéritif on the terrace now and then, and Arthur Rubinstein never drank wine with his meals, only Johnny Walker Scotch and Perrier.

Mr. Pogash was disappointed that his confreres at Fouquet's did not share his youthful enthusiasm for wine, but insists they failed to dampen his spirits. On the other hand, they did manage to rid him of any interest he might have had in the restaurant business. When he completes work on a degree in French literature later this academic year, he plans to devote his energies to becoming, of all extraordinary things, a wine writer.

Philippe, Toujours Philippe

"THERE IS an old tale of how seven years of fat cows are followed by seven years of lean cows. I hope we are not coming into a period of lean cows."

The speaker was Baron Philippe de Rothschild. The subject, as it usually is with him, was the wine of Bordeaux. He was in the United States for a few weeks while his wife, Baroness Pauline underwent treatment at Peter Bent Brigham Hospital (1975).

Philippe de Rothschild is known principally for his world-famous Château Mouton Rothschild, one of the five great growths of Bordeaux. His holdings are far more extensive. He owns two other prominent châteaus: Clerc-Milon and Château Baron Philippe, and his company, La Bergerie, is the largest single importer of Bordeaux into this country, mostly the popular Mouton-Cadet.

Baron Philippe, who has spent 52 years in the Médoc, had some glum words about the economics of wine, at the moment, some caustic words for the French government, some sober comments about the hapless Cruses, and a few guardedly optimistic thoughts about the future.

"Wine prices have been ridiculous, obscene, immoral," he said. "And now we are all paying the price. The cellars in Bordeaux are choked with wine. The people with capital will survive, of course, but the small fellow with a house and a car—he is suffering terribly now.

"Still, it isn't as bad as it was in the 1920's and 30's. There are a lot of kids who came into the business after the war and they said 'Oh, we're so smart. Everything we do makes money.'

"Well, the poor blokes. Now they're going to understand what it's like to be in front of difficulties. Why in the old days we were lucky if one out of two vintages were even usable."

Baron Philippe leaned across the table in the nearly deserted Ritz Carlton restaurant and ticked off vintages on his fingers:

"Take the thirties," he said: "1930, 1931, and 1932 were totally erased. In 1933 about two-thirds of the harvest was usable; 1934 was good. In '35 and '36 only a very small percentage of the crop was usable. The '37 was good, but in 1938 and 1939 we could use only a tiny percentage of the crop again.

"Economic conditions in those days were terrifying. After the war, the United States market was closed by Prohibition and later by the Depression. Russia, a major market for a century, was a closed door. The Germans wanted guns, not butter, and Austria was split into pieces. Bordeaux lives by exports and there were no exports whatsoever.

"As bad as things are now," Baron Philippe went on, "they are better than in those days. Obviously, there is more investment. America is buying, Germany is buying. So are Sweden, Norway, and Japan, markets that didn't exist 50 years ago.

"The most important thing for us is quality—the honesty of what's in the bottle. If it says Bordeaux, it must be Bordeaux; if it says St.-Emilion, it must be St.-Emilion."

Which led, naturally, to the recent conviction of two partners in the house of Cruse, a major Bordeaux wine company, of falsifying records and illegally raising the classification of cheap wine.

"I have known the Cruse family through several generations," Baron Philippe said, "and it is a tragedy for them. But I really think they created their own problem by refusing to let the tax inspectors into their cellars.

"As for the theory that the whole thing was politically motivated, I don't believe that for a moment."

A fashionable explanation of what was behind the Bordeaux wine scandal had Valéry Giscard d'Estaing, then Minister of Finance, concentrating his inspectors on the Cruses to embarrass his chief rival in the presidential campaign, Jacques Chaban-Delmas, Mayor of Bordeaux, a friend of the Cruses and, to some, a symbol of the wealthy wine industry of the Gironde.

"I am sorry for the Cruses," the owner of Château Mouton said, "but we've been inspected many times. There can be no exceptions for Cruse."

Baron Philippe grumbled that one reason for the present parlous state of the Bordeaux wine industry was the indifference of the bureaucracy in Paris. "In 15 years," he said, "there have been nine or ten ministers of agriculture. Each comes in with his gang and when he goes, they all go.

"One is worried about whether the Common Market should move to Brussels. The next is concerned about the price of artichokes, and the third about the way veals—what do you call them—calfs, suck their mothers.

"There must be stricter and stricter laws for the production of wine and the government must enforce them," Baron Philippe said, adding: "The C.I.V.B. (Conseil Interprofessional du Vin de Bordeaux—the promotional and professional organization of the Bordeaux wine industry) is good only for publicity. The moment they attempt to enforce a rule of any kind, everyone pulls out.

"True, all professions organize. But we are different. We can't be expected to police ourselves. The I.N.A.O. (Institut National des Appellations d'Origine—a nationwide organization which makes the rules for each region) can do it, but only if the government tells them to."

Sheepishly, Philippe de Rothschild admits that some of the red ink on the current ledger at Mouton is his own fault. "For years," he said, "I wanted to close a road through the property. Do you know what it means to close a road in France? I have spent a lifetime dealing with the French bureaucracy but this was all new. Well, the work was delayed and prices went up. You know the rest.

"The balance sheet is in the red," he said, "but what worries me more is that I can't be developing, building. I do hope we will all be able to have fun again at Mouton. Not only for myself but because what we do there amuses everyone. After all, we have 20,000 guests a year."

With that he rose. It was time for a swim. A few minutes later he was in a taxi on his way to the Boston Y.M.C.A. for his daily 400 meters. "With flippers," he said. "At my age, they make it easier."

The Los Angeles County Fair—A Reporter's Notebook

CUT UP AN APPLE, take a bite. Then write 100 words or so describing what you just tasted. Do the same thing with a pear, then write another 100 words describing the differences between the apple and the pear. Take my word for it, it will not be easy. There is nothing tougher than trying to describe a taste.

Which is why, in spite of jokes and understandable misconceptions, wine tasting is hard work. Ideally, a conscientious wine taster should prepare for the job by being in good physical condition and by getting plenty of rest. Few do, of course, which only makes the task tougher.

The Los Angeles County Fair, held in Pomona every year in the late summer, is the heavyweight championship of wine tasting in this country. Each year, the number of wine entries grows. In 1977 there were 824 wines from 83 different California wineries. There were 22 judges, some from the wine industry and some knowledgeable consumers. They were charged with tasting all 824 wines in three days, picking the best, ranking them, and bestowing on them, gold, silver, and bronze medals, as well as honorable-mention citations.

Each judge has a table, a notepad, judging sheets, a glass of water, some cheese and crackers to neutralize the wine, and—very necessary —a spittoon. Anyone who swallows all that wine will be looped within an hour. Tasters quickly learn that accurate tasting doesn't mean swallowing.

To a layman, the sight of 45 glasses of wine on a table is overwhelming and that task of differentiating among them an impossibility. The sight is formidable to the experienced wine taster, too, but he knows how to handle it.

First, the wines are divided into about a dozen more manageable groups. Then the taster goes through the first group, checking just for smell. Is the wine pleasant and aromatic, or does it have an off-smell such as, a cabbage or geraniums or caramel odor? In any group of wines, usually a third can be eliminated just on smell. It makes one wonder what the winemaker could have been thinking when he bottled the stuff.

Color used to be a more important factor in wine judging than it is now. The industry has made rapid strides in this area in recent years and almost all wines made in this country have good color. Still, a wine that is too old or a wine that has been attacked by air will take on a brownish tinge that makes it a good candidate for elimination.

Finally, it is time to taste the wines. Each judge has his own prejudices and looks for different things in the glass: fruitiness, complexity, good body, freshness—yes, even in aged wines—finish, the length of time the taste lingers. All are qualities experienced judges look for.

Off-tastes, like off-smells, are relatively easy to spot. Usually they come from spoilage that went undetected during the winemaking process. Some come from improper handling of the wine when it was being made, some come from wines being made in a dirty winery.

Some judges, stymied by the age-old problem of describing tastes, resort to literary fancies. One wine writer once likened a Champagne to "a young girl in a long white dress in a summer garden." Another, more succinct, but just as imaginative, pondered a wine for a moment then pronounced: "It has broad shoulders but very narrow hips." Still others resort to arcane flummery such as, "It starts well and has a pleasant finish, but it dies on the middle palate."

Actually, to another judge, this silly language actually may mean something. When three or four people are sitting around straining to come up with some relevant description of what they have just tasted, any words may help. "Coconut," said one of the red-wine panel members at the Los Angeles Fair tasting, "I get a taste of coconut."

"You know," said one of the other judges, "you're right. I get it, too." And in fact, they were right. This hint of coconut comes from certain oak barrels used in aging red wines.

More often than not, analogies will be made to other fruits if the wine is good: apricots, raspberrys, even apples and pears. Bad wines often make tasters think of vegetables or flowers. Wines with too much flavor from oak barrels often have a vanilla taste.

Mint or eucalyptus are characteristic smells in Cabernet Sauvignon wines and "raisiny" is the word often used to describe wines from hot climates such as California's Central Valley. And why not? A raisin is a grape left to shrivel in the sun. If a wine has that taste, it usually means it was made from grapes grown in hot sun. Some tasters will refer to a "hot" taste or a "valley" taste and mean the same thing.

Somehow, in spite of the problems of articulating impressions of taste, there is usually a great deal of unanimity in this kind of judging. Most experienced judges will agree—within limits—which are the good wines in a batch, even if they cannot say exactly why.

Then, too, certain types of wines are easier to judge than others: fruit wines, for instance, or dessert wines. Red table wines are probably the most difficult because the best of them are the most complex, the most subtle of all wines.

In a group of 45 Zinfandels, for instance, it is relatively easy to eliminate 30 wines for off-smells and tastes, but then what? How does one rank the remaining 15? Is wine X really better than wine W but not as good as wine Y?

There is where the tasters must concentrate. This is where every nuance of the wine must be savored and judged and this is where the job really gets tough. After all, someone put an enormous amount of effort into each of these wines and was proud enough of it to submit it for judging.

Ideally, the large groups of wines should be judged early in the day when the judges are still fresh. By late afternoon a taster's palate begins to loose its sensitivity and one wine begins to resemble another. Then, too, each group should be judged by two separate panels. With 824 wines, however, this was virtually impossible, unless another 20 judges can be recruited or the tasting can be stretched to six days or more.

In one case, this year, the chairman of the judging, Beverly Hills lawyer Nathan Chroman did order another panel to taste the 45 Zindandels after the red-wine panel had finished. Mr. Chroman thought the red-wine panel had dismissed some excellent wines. In fact, the second group concurred in almost every decision of the first panel.

The red-wine panel, of which I was a member, fared less well with one particular Cabernet Sauvignon that Mr. Chroman admired. He asked us to retaste that one wine. The second time around, it got a gold medal. We had been wrong.

By the end of a long day of tasting—the Cabernet Sauvignons alone took four hours—the most pleasant thing to contemplate is a cold beer. Nothing wipes out the furry taste, caused by tannin, that comes from tasting so much wine. And, in fact, most serious wine judges can do little more than fall into bed exhausted after a full day of tasting.

The wine judging is over at the 1977 Los Angeles County Fair. Somehow, in three days, 22 of us got through 824 California wines. Those of us on the red-wine panel worked through 31 Pinot Noirs, 44 Zinfandels, 39 Cabernet Sauvignons, and 23 Petite Sirahs. Along with them went dozens of other things called Chianti, Vino Rosso, Claret, Gamay Beaujolais, Gamay, Grignolino, Carignane, Barbera, and Charbono.

It could be worse. One panel concentrated entirely on fruit wines and had to go through apricot, strawberry, raspberry, and even an honest-to-goodness coconut wine in an attempt to find something worth giving a medal to.

Alas, at this point, not even the judges know who won what. It takes almost ten days to match up the winning wines, which come to the judges in glasses marked A through, in one case, RR. Even then, the winning wineries are notified before the judges. What's more, the names of those who win nothing are never divulged—unless by an outraged vintner who thinks his loganberry wine should have taken a gold medal.

The results will be divulged later this week—all except one, which can be divulged right now. In the sweepstakes—the judging to determine the best of all the wines in the fair—there will be no winner.

Winning the sweepstakes, as all the judges are aware, can be the making of some small winery struggling for recognition and cash flow. Even a large winery is not about to turn down this kind of award. Three wines were submitted. We on the red-wine panel offered a Petite Sirah which, we thought, stood out more in its class than any of the other wines we tasted. The white-wine panel offered a spicy, full-bodied Gewürztraminer and a rich, heavy late-harvest Riesling that resembled an Auslese from the Mosel region of Germany. (An Auslese is wine made from grapes that have been left longer than usual on the vine until their juice and flavor is concentrated.)

In no case did the full judging panel decide that one of the wines was worth the grand prize. I supported my own panel's choice of the Petite Sirah but I was more interested in seeing the Riesling win. At first, it seemed gaggingly sweet and heavy. But we had just finished three days of tasting dry, tannic reds. After an hour, the Riesling's real complexity came out. It had an overpowering Riesling bouquet and a lingering aftertaste that put it in the class of the best wines of this type.

It lacked acid, which is needed in sweet wines to provide balance to the sugar. Without the acid, the wine becomes too soft and characterless. Some tasters say the acid provides "structure" or the "skeleton" for the wine. None of the three wines was chosen as a sweepstakes winner but since they all were awarded gold medals, their names will be disclosed later this week when the full results of the judging becomes known.

The red-wine panel at the Los Angeles Fair consisted of myself; Dr. Richard Peterson, a noted enologist and the President of Monterey Vineyards; Narsai David, a Berkeley, California restaurateur with more than 20 years' experience in tasting, selecting, and even making wine; and Dr. Bernard Rhodes, a physician who has planted and owned some of this state's most famous vineyards and who is also a partner in one of the newest premium wineries, Rutherford Hill.

The group has remained intact for two years, which means judging close to 400 wines. There are always arguments over certain wines but the degree of unanimity over the best and the worst in each class is considerable. "I try to keep a panel together for as many years as possible," says Nathan Chroman, the Beverly Hills lawyer who conducts the judging each year for the fair. "It takes several years for a group to begin to really work together and for me to be comfortable with their ability to taste." Some of the judges at the Los Angeles Fair have been returning annually for 15 years or more. Others, each year, are freshmen, just learning the system.

Sonoma Vineyards, a premium winery in Sonoma County, ran away with the honors at the 1977 Los Angeles County Fair. The winery took 13 medals or awards, including one for a wine it is content to call "Adequate Red."

"I can't say it doesn't make you feel good," says Rodney Strong, the founder of Sonoma Vineyards and the winemaker responsible for each of the winners.

The Los Angeles Fair is the biggest wine-judging event in the country. In this, the 42nd year of wine competition, 824 different California wines were entered, including everything from Champagne and tawny Port to Grignolino and coconut wine.

In the prestigious varietal table wine categories, literally hundreds of wines were entered, including 45 different Zinfandels and 39 Cabernet Sauvignons. Sonoma Vineyards scored highly in most of these categories.

In the top-level Cabernet Sauvignons, Sonoma Vineyards' Alexander's Crown 1974 was a gold medal winner. Alexander's Crown is a 61-acre vineyard on a knoll overlooking the Alexander Valley in northern Sonoma County. It is exclusively a Cabernet vineyard and all its grapes go into a special bottling. It is sold as one of Sonoma's special, reserve wines with a gold label.

Sonoma's regular 1975 Zinfandel won a gold medal in that category, competing with wines that in some cases cost twice as much. Other medals picked up by the Windsor, California winery included silvers for Petite Sirah, Pinot Noir and Johannisberg Riesling, and a bronze for Ruby Cabernet, a wine made from a grape that is a cross between the Cabernet Sauvignon and the Carignane grapes. "Adequate Red," an inexpensive table wine made in large quantities, took a first in a special category that has no medal awards.

Most of the awards at the fair this year went to small premium wineries, some of which have only been in business for a few years. This fits a pattern. Frequently, new wineries will enter the competition, win a few awards, then drop out, having used the fair to gain important publicity. For example, the heretofore almost unknown Fortino Winery, in Gilroy, California, came away from the fair with gold medals for its Barbera, Carignane, Petite Sirah, and Charbono, along with silvers for its Ruby Cabernet and Burgundy. The Fortino Winery was opened in 1970 but even some of the most extensively stocked wine shops in the San Francisco Bay Area still do not stock its wines. Needless to say, they are unknown in the East.

The other gold medal winners in the Cabernet Sauvignon class were Ridge Vineyards, a consistent winner at the fair with its powerful, inky-dark wines; Dry Creek Vineyards; and Villa Mt. Eden. Silver medals went to Veedercrest, Edmeades, Freemark Abbey, Burgess Cellars, Silver Oak Cellars, and Parducci Cellars. Most of these wines are available in the better stores in the East, but in limited quantities.

In the Zinfandel group, other gold medals went to Sherrill Cellars, a new winery in Woodside, south of San Francisco, to Edmeades Vineyards in Mendocino, to the P. and M. Staiger Winery, another new name in the lists, and to Dry Creek, which is small but fairly well-known and highly regarded.

Silver medals in the Zinfandel category went to Round Hill, Monterey Peninsula, Fetzer Vineyards, Davis Bynum Winery, and Montclair Vineyards. Round Hill also won a silver medal in the Pinot Noir group, which is amusing because there is no Round Hill. It is the label of an enterprising retailer in the San Francisco area who, from time to time, buys from wineries that have excess gallonage and bottles it— actually they bottle it for him—under the Round Hill label. It is a pretty safe guess that some of the Round Hill wines are actually from Sonoma Vineyards and others are from Souverain Cellars, both wineries that had more wine than they knew what to do with a year or so ago.

The top white wine in any tasting or judging is the Pinot Chardonnay. It is to white wine what Cabernet Sauvignon is to the reds. This year's gold medal winners in the Chardonnay category were Sebastiani Vineyards, Freemark Abbey, and Sterling Vineyards, the winery just sold to the Coca-Cola Company.

Silvers went to Château St. Jean and Hacienda Wine Cellars, both Sonoma wineries. Château St. Jean, which prides itself on its white wines, took gold medals for its Johannisberg Riesling, Gewürztraminer, and its late-harvest Gewürztraminer.

Château St. Jean's late-harvest Riesling got a silver medal as did its Auslese Riesling, an even richer, more select late-harvest wine. Other winners in the Johannisberg Riesling group were Hacienda Cellars, a gold medal, and San Martin Winery, a silver.

Felton-Empire Vineyards took the only gold medal in the late-harvest Riesling group. A silver medal went to Veedercrest Vineyard, along with Château St. Jean in this category. Raymond Vineyards, another newcomer to this list, took the gold medal in the Auslese Riesling group.

Geyser Peak Winery took a gold medal in the Gamay group, and Sterling Vineyards and Davis Bynum Winery took golds in the Merlot category.

Is it really possible for 22 people to taste 824 wines and render honest, accurate judgments on them? Honest, yes. Completely accurate, no. But until some better system is devised, judgings such as the one at the Los Angeles County Fair will continue. Chemists can test for residual sugar, sodium, and other constituents, but no machine has yet been devised that can come up with a printout that reads: "Now, there is one hell of a great wine!"

The Domecqs—First Family of Sherry

THEY TELL THE STORY in Jerez, Spain about the time Henry Ford was entertained by the Domecqs, the great Sherry family, who live a baronial lifestyle undreamed of in Grosse Point. The auto magnate was reputed to have told his host, polo-playing Don José Ignacio Domecq: "I have more money than you, but you have a better way of life." Don José Ignacio readily agreed about his life but observed after his guest had left that Mr. Ford was wrong about having more money.

The substance of the story is probably correct but it seems unlikely that Don José Ignacio would ever make any public utterances about his money. Here in rugged Andalusia there is simply no question about the Domecq's wealth.

WINE TALK

The Domecqs, whose best-known product in the United States is La Ina Sherry, all but overwhelm this small city. Their *palacios* are everywhere; streets are named after them; statues honor their ancestors; and, of course, the endless Domecq warehouses (*bodegas*)—157 of them, blazing white in the relentless Mediterranean sun—seem to comprise half of Jerez's buildings. (Actually they occupy only about a fifth of the city's real estate.)

Beyond the city walls some 7,000 acres of the chalky soil are given over to Domecq vineyards. Still further out are the nine family ranches—*ganaderías*—where they raise cattle, thoroughbred Arabian horses, and fighting bulls. Closer in, along the shores of the Atlantic at Puerto de Santa María and Sanlúcar there are weekend retreats for the Domecqs who occasionally prefer the sea to the saddle.

In the north of Spain, in the Rioja region, the Domecqs have eight other *bodegas* and 3,000 acres more of vineyards that produce table wines and brandy. In Mexico and South America they own five more wineries and distilleries producing tequila and more brandy.

But the brandy and the table wines and the tequila are sidelines. Sherry is what Domecq is all about. Sherry—the name is a corruption of the name of the city, which the Spanish pronounce as hair-eth—has been made here for some 3,000 years, starting with the Phoenicians. The Greeks took over, then the Romans, and eventually the Moors, who called the place Sheres. The wars that raged on the Iberian Peninsula devastated the Andalusian landscape and ruined the export business. One of those who restored it was a Basque Frenchman who arrived in 1730, married into one of the local Sherry families, and began building the business up again. His name still graces the family label: Pedro Domecq.

Today there are, by various counts, some 450 Domecqs, thanks in part to big families—Don José Ignacio has 12 children and 15 is not extraordinary—and to considerable intermarriage. "It is not unusual," one Domecq matron is reported to have said, "for a girl's husband to be both her cousin and her uncle."

The family is divided into five branches descended from Pedro Jacinto Domecq, who died in 1894. They are the Domecq-Riveiro, Domecq-La Riva, Soto-Domecq, Domecq-Diez, and Domecq-Gonzalez, which is Don José Ignacio's branch.

No branch has more control over the family-owned business than any other and José Ignacio Domecq is the only member of the corporate board who also has executive responsibilities in the firm. In fact, only eight Domecqs presently work in the huge company. "They are called to serve here only if they are worthy of it," Don José Ignacio says.

One-mile rows of vineyards, straight due East, at the Paul
Masson Pinnacles Vineyard in the Salinas Valley.

Two of the top executives of the firm are outsiders and they are
undoubtedly harbingers of the future. Even José Ignacio Domecq has
admitted that it is probably only a matter of time before the firm sells
shares to the public to raise capital. Moreover, modern-day Spain has
introduced a note of uncertainty into Domecq's operations that would
have been undreamed of in the past.

Jerez is a paternal—some might say feudal—community. Most
Sherry workers live in free housing, purchase their needs at low-
priced company stores, and retire with pensions equal to their wages.
Since the death of Franco, however, there have been constant strikes
in the *bodegas* and vineyards and rampant inflation hurts everyone.

On the surface, however, life in Jerez goes on as it must have 200
years ago. Favored guests of the Domecqs are quartered in the
Palacio Domecq, an astonishing late-17th century mansion near the

center of the city where liveried footmen appear at the press of a button and where 300 people can be entertained by flamenco dancers on the roof garden at a couple of hours' notice.

Each September, at the time of the harvest, or *vendimia*, thousands of guests descend on the city to consume rivers of pale, Fino Sherry, served ice-cold, and to consume what seems like half the seafood in the ocean. There are bullfights, horse races, carriage races, balls, parties, parades, and polo games for a week, and the whole show traditionally is dedicated to some area targeted for Sherry sales.

There are commercial overtones to the gaiety—overseas distributors and journalists are hauled in by the planeload—but the Sherry barons insist that they enjoy the uproar. "Life can be rather dull in Jerez," said one Domecq who manages to spend most of his time in cosmopolitan Madrid. "We actually look forward to the vendimia."

More than anything else, the Domecqs and the other Sherry houses, such as Gonzalez-Byass and Williams & Humbert, would love to see the United States become more of a Sherry-consuming country. Their Sherry, that is. At present we buy only about three percent of what Jerez produces, compared with the British, who drink up almost forty percent. We drink more California Sherry than we do the real stuff.

After a few bad years, Sherry drinking—imported Sherry—has shown a slight increase in this country but, overall, the consumption of all dessert wines has shown a steady decline since the 1960's. The big wine boom has been a table wine boom. Which may be why the Domecqs currently are in the process of introducing their Rioja wines here.

One problem with selling Sherry in the United States, according to the Domecqs and other Jerez firms, is our conception of it. We tend to treat it as a little-old-lady apéritif to sip before dinner. Frank Gifford quaffing Dry Sack in television commercials is one not-too-subtle approach to that problem.

The Jerezanos would like us to drink Sherry with our meals, as they do. Working through a mountain of lobster and other seafood at Venta Millan, a favorite fish place a few miles from Jerez, Manuel de Domecq Zorita pours ice-cold La Ina continuously.

"We would really like to see American restaurants serve Fino chilled in half bottles, and with the meal," Manuel Domecq said, "rather than just by the glass, but we are not having much success."

A visitor, thinking of the 18 percent alcohol in Sherry, protests—mildly. "It's not a problem," Manuel Domecq insists. "Sherry is only a little stronger than table wine and if you pace yourself, you will never even feel it."

As a matter of fact, he was right—that time. But how can you take the advice of a Domecq on drinking? After all they are all fond of quoting these lines, attributed to another Sherry man:

> I must have a drink at eleven;
> It's a duty that must be done.
> If I don't have a drink at eleven,
> Then I must have eleven at one.

California—A Little History

STEVEN SPURRIER is a young Englishman who sells wine in Paris. His little shop is in an ancient street a few steps from the Church of the Madeleine in the center of the city. Next door is a small bar where Mr. Spurrier gives courses in wine appreciation.

Last year, after a trip to California—his first—Mr. Spurrier resolved to have a tasting at his school. It would include some of the extraordinary wines he had discovered in America and some of the very best wines produced in France.

What happened around the little bar in Mr. Spurrier's Académie du Vin is now history. In a single stroke, he proved that American wines had come of age. His tasters included some of the most famous figures in the French wine world: restaurant owners, writers, and critics of wine, and government wine experts.

When the smoke cleared, the French experts were astonished and more than a little embarrassed. They had chosen two of the American wines as the best in the tasting.

The results of the Spurrier tasting were electrifying to wine enthusiasts everywhere—except in northern California. There, winemakers and wine drinkers had been saying for a decade that they were beginning to produce wines equal to anything in the world.

Nor were they particularly premature in making such claims. In the late 19th century and in the first decade of the 20th, California wines —along with wines from New York and even Missouri and Ohio— won awards in judgings all over the world.

Prohibition called a halt to all that. What's more, the mad rush to get back into the wine business after Repeal in 1933 was probably as harmful to the business as Prohibition had been. The first wines produced were so bad that they set the California wine business back 50 years.

It was not until after World War II that the impetus to produce truly fine wines really began to be felt in California. And it was not until the 1950's that really extraordinary wines began to appear in any quantity.

Today, the great wines of that era, the wines from Inglenook and Beaulieu Vineyards among others, command small fortunes in wine shops and restaurants. But it was really the affluence of the 1960's that marked the acceptance of California wines as being among the best produced anywhere in the world.

Unfortunately, what was happening in the Napa and Sonoma Valleys in those days went unnoticed by the general public—even by the growing wine drinking public. California wine enthusiasts routinely snapped up every bottle the best of the California wineries could turn out.

While the rest of the country automatically paid homage to Burgundy and Bordeaux and patronized American wines, the Californians quietly smiled and went on buying. They knew something the rest of us didn't: that America had emerged as an important producer of fine wines.

Connoisseurs elsewhere in the nation had begun to catch on to what was happening in California long before the Paris tasting. Still, it took an Englishman to bring home to a lot of us what a good thing we had right in our own backyard.

Mr. Spurrier put the California reds against Bordeaux reds. That's because both California and Bordeaux make their best red wines from the same grape, the Cabernet Sauvignon. He put the best California whites against Burgundy whites for the same reason. Both are made from the Pinot Chardonnay grape.

The French panel chose a Cabernet Sauvignon of the 1973 vintage from an obscure Napa Valley winery called Stag's Leap Wine Cellars over such superstars as Château Mouton Rothschild 1970 and Château Haut-Brion 1970. They chose, too, a 1973 Chardonnay from the equally unknown Château Montelena, also in the Napa Valley, over a

STONEGATE

Napa Valley
CHARDONNAY
1975
ESTATE BOTTLED

Produced and bottled by
Stonegate Winery, Calistoga, Napa Valley, California
Alcohol 13.8% by volume

raft of famous Burgundy whites including a 1973 Bâtard-Montrachet, one of the greatest of all French wines.

There were a lot of things wrong with the tasting. Most significant, the Bordeaux reds were far too young to go against the early-maturing California wines. Also, the Burgundy whites were not of the best vintages.

But then, no tasting is perfect. In fact, most tastings are highly imperfect. Give the same panel the same wines a day later and see what happens. The results will differ. Not a lot, but enough to make one wonder about tastings.

Even so, the Paris tasting, if it did nothing else, served notice on the world that we are beginning to produce excellent wines in this country. And, if I can borrow a line from the late Al Jolson, "You ain't seen nothing yet."

Our best wines are produced in an area that begins about 40 miles north of San Francisco and stretches another hundred miles north into Mendocino County where vines and giant redwoods thrive in close proximity. The climate in Napa and in Sonoma Counties often resembles the climate of Algiers or Spain more than it does the best wine-growing regions of Europe. Scientists continue to discover even better places to produce grapes than we already have. Some are in the counties where the best wines are made now. Others—many others—are in tiny pockets of perfect weather as far south as San Diego and as far north as the Yakima Valley in Washington.

In the late 1960's and early 1970's, giant corporations became interested in the wine business. They bought out old-line wineries and created new ones of their own. Recession-spawned setbacks in wine consumption and a couple of years in which nature refused to cooperate with corporate goals soured big business on wine.

Even today, if you talk to the acquisition experts on Wall Street or to the loan officers at big California banks, the word on wine is "forget it." At the same time, young people with a spirit of adventure and a distaste for routine living continue to open new wineries and to produce fine wine.

At 1976's Los Angeles County Fair, this writer tasted—and did his best to evaluate—more than 40 Zinfandels, more than 30 Cabernet Sauvignons, and more than 20 Petite Sirahs, many of them submitted by small wineries eager for accolades and recognition.

Some of these adventurers will fail, but some will not. They will add to the already vast array of fine wines produced in this country. Some of them, if they persevere, may one day become as well-known to wine enthusiasts as the château names of Bordeaux and the vineyard names of Burgundy.

The major problem for many California vintners is distribution. The finest wines in the world are of no importance if they cannot be sold in the shops. There are liquor stores around the country that offer more than 200 different California wines, but there are others which sell none.

It's all very well to read about an extraordinary new California Cabernet or Chardonnay, but if the wine is not for sale it is soon forgotten. Until recently, this was often the case almost everywhere outside of California. Today, more and more wineries realize that, even though Californians will buy up every bottle they can produce, their future lies in national distribution, no matter how limited.

Americans are drinking more and more wine, but we hardly classify as a wine drinking nation. In fact, we rank 30th in the world, with a per capita consumption of about two gallons a year (Portugal, Italy, and France rank first, second and third, in that order). Eight of every ten bottles we drink are domestic wine and seven of the eight come from California.

Most of the California wine is inexpensive wine. We usually drink it as jug wine. Which is not to denigrate it in any way. Europeans, particularly the French, are constantly amazed at the quality of our

jug wines and anyone who has sampled the "vin ordinaire" in a French café realizes instantly how much better our cheap wines are.

Moreover, the jug wines have been getting even better in recent years, thanks to the abundance of quality grapes. At one time, most jug wines were made from heavy-bearing, low-quality grapes grown in the hot San Joaquin Valley. Recently, however more high quality grapes have been harvested than the smaller, premium wineries could use. So the big wineries have been buying them for their jug wines.

Probably the most popular of all jug wines are Hearty Burgundy and Chablis Blanc, both made by Gallo. The Gallo Winery, incidentally, is probably the largest winery in the world. The Gallos dominate the American wine market, producing about a third of all the wine we drink.

Millions of gallons of Gallo wines are consumed by people who are unaware that they are drinking Gallo wine. Carlo Rossi wines are made by Gallo; so are Paisano wines and Boone's Farm wines. Where a famous château in Bordeaux may produce 25,000 cases of wine from each vintage, Gallo bottles 100,000 cases of wine every day.

Italian Swiss Colony and Guild, a cooperative that bottles under various labels including Cribari, Tavola, and Roma are two other

[171]

California giants. Nor is it an accident that so many of the names connected with jug wines are Italian. The big wineries were founded by Italian immigrants or their children to supply wine to other Italian-Americans.

One of the most interesting recent trends in the wine world has been the production of relatively inexpensive wine by some of the premium wineries. Several years ago, the Robert Mondavi Winery in Napa Valley led the way with a line called, simply, Mondavi Red Table Wine and Mondavi White Table Wine. Traditionally, inexpensive California wines such as Gallo's have been vinified in a style called "mellow." That means soft and easy to drink. Usually sugar is added after fermentation to achieve mellowness. The Mondavi line was a new departure: inexpensive wines fermented dry, with the acidity of the best premium wines.

Sterling Vineyards, another premium Napa winery, followed suit, producing a fine dry wine it calls Sterling Red and a somewhat less dry white called, naturally, Sterling White. One of the most attractive of these new wines is produced by Fetzer Vineyards in California's Mendocino County. Fetzer's Mendocino Red is aged in small oak casks which impart the style and flavor of far more expensive wines.

These second lines of the premium wineries are, to some extent, also the result of the overly large grape crops in recent years. There is no indication, however, that they will disappear, in short crop years. "We will find the grapes," says Robert Mondavi.

These wines which sell for about $2 to $2.50 a bottle are not only great wines for everyday drinking; they also afford many thousands of people who might otherwise never taste a really fine California wine an opportunity to get to know the style and taste of the premium wines.

These wines are interesting for another reason: They do away with the old generic names such as Burgundy, Chablis, and Chianti. The fact is that a California Burgundy bears absolutely no resemblance to a true French Burgundy except that they are both red and wet.

The use of generic names, still very much in evidence on the jug wine labels, started out as a way to sell California wine to recent immigrants. There was a time when even the best California Cabernet Sauvignons had to be sold as claret.

Today, the name of the producer is coupled with the type of grape from which the wine is made to indicate both the kind of wine and its quality. Some premium winemakers go much further. For example, Freemark Abbey, one of the finest Napa Valley wineries, even puts the name of the vineyard from which the grapes were picked on its best Cabernet Sauvignon.

NET CONTENTS
750 ML (25.4 FL OZ)

ALCOHOL 12%
BY VOLUME

CHANDON

Blanc de Noirs

NAPA VALLEY SPARKLING WINE
Produced and bottled by Domaine Chandon, Yountville, California

Ridge Vineyard indicates on its bottles the region and in some cases the specific vineyard where its Zinfandel grapes were picked. Thus in any given vintage year there may be four or five different Ridge Zinfandels, all the same grape and all from the same winery, but distinctively different wines because of the varying soil and climate conditions in the various vineyards.

The most controversial use of a generic name in this country is the case of American Champagne. Rightfully, of course, Champagne is the wine of the Champagne region of France. By law, no sparkling wine made anywhere else in France can be called Champagne and the French have gone to court successfully to prevent the use of the word on Spanish, Italian, German, and Canadian sparkling wine.

They ignored the American sparkling wine business so long that they realized it was too late to try to stop the use of the word Champagne in this country. Big American producers maintain that Champagne long ago came to be a name for a type of wine as well as the name of a section of France. Since they make that type of wine, they say, they are entitled to use the word, and they do.

Now comes the Domaine Chandon. This is a new winery at Yountville in the Napa Valley, built by Moët-Hennessey, the huge French holding company that controls Moët et Chandon, the largest producer of Champagne in France, Hennessey Cognac, and the House of Christian Dior, among other things.

After five years of preparation, Domaine Chandon released its first sparkling wine in December 1976—2000 cases. It is called Napa Valley Brut. Nowhere is the word Champagne mentioned. "Champagne can be made only in the Champagne region of France," says John Wright, the president of M. & H. Vineyards, the Moët subsidiary that runs Domaine Chandon.

Most premium winemakers predict that generic names will ultimately disappear completely from American wines. "We no longer have to depend on European names or European standards," says August Sebastiani. "We've come well beyond all that in this country." Actually, Mr. Sebastiani, the owner of the phenomenally successful Sebastiani Vineyards in Sonoma County, California, still keeps a Chianti in his line of wines but he insists that he does it "only for sentimental reasons."

Parisians Have to Learn, Too

THEY WERE sitting around a tiny horseshoe shaped bar in a former locksmith's shop in the Cité Berryer, an 18th century shopping arcade near the Place de la Madeleine.

There were four or five Americans, a couple of Canadians, a New Zealand woman, and an Englishman, and they were all trying to learn something about wine. They were students at the Académie du Vin, a unique little school run by two Americans and another Englishman.

The Académie offers a basic course in wine appreciation, an advanced course in Bordeaux wines, and an advanced course in Burgundy wines. There is also a course in wine analysis based on methods developed at the University of Bordeaux.

This was the second session of three in the advanced Bordeaux course. It was a tasting of a group of wines of the 1962 vintage from some of the major *communes* in the Bordeaux region: St.-Emilion, Pomerol, Graves, St.-Julien, Pauillac, and St.-Estèphe. The wines included Châteaus Figeac, Pape Clément, Mouton Rothschild, and Montrose.

Parisians Have to Learn, Too

Patricia Gallagher giving a wine appreciation lesson to American tourists, in Paris.

The instructor was Bernard Bourquin, a chemist who studied at Princeton and a wine lover who is convinced that his fellow Frenchmen know next to nothing about wine. "Even the restaurant people," he said. "It's terrible."

Mr. Bourquin is doing what he can to change that, just as his father, Constant Bourquin, did with his book *Understanding Wine*, some years ago. But so far, most of the Académie's students are foreigners.

"We're up to about 15 percent French, now (1975)," said Steven Spurrier, the trendy, 36-year-old Briton who is the man behind the Académie. Mr. Spurrier created something of a stir a few years back when he opened a wine shop, Caves de la Madeleine, adjacent to what is now the Académie.

It was considered something rash for an Englishman to attempt to sell wine to the French but, after a few poor investments early on, Mr. Spurrier has made a success of his business—so much so that he has now branched out by acquiring some vast *caves* in an old quarry outside of Paris as a warehouse in which to store his customer's wine.

His plans are nothing if not ambitious. He hopes to own some vineyards, back experimental plantings to produce new kinds of wines, and to become a name known for his wine selections, much as Frank Schoonmaker and Alexis Lichine have done.

The Académie du Vin, which he started with Jon Winroth, wine writer for the *International Herald Tribune* and Patricia Gallagher, a 29-year-old oenophile from Newark, Delaware, is another part of his burgeoning little wine world.

In addition to the regular courses, the Académie arranges trips through the wine regions for its students. There, they are hosted by the same people who supply Mr. Spurrier with his wines. Special courses can be arranged for groups interested in specific wines, say Champagne or Chablis, and recently the Académie has started giving lessons to American college girls in France for their year of European study.

In fact, Mr. Spurrier was called away from a lunch and tasting around his marble-topped Napoleon III bar to take a call from one of the girls who wanted a package of wine shipped to her father in Alabama. He came back smiling and shaking his head. "It's going to cost her a fortune," he said, "but money doesn't mean anything to them."

Mr. Spurrier, who admits to having a little money of his own, graduated from the London School of Economics and then went with a major wine company in London. He moved to the south of France, where he still owns some property. He tried selling antiques for a while but got lonesome for the wine business.

He bought his little shop in the Cité Berryer in 1970 but worked as a delivery and stock man for the previous owner first. Meanwhile, Mr. Winroth, 39, had been giving some wine courses on his own around Paris. He first met Mr. Spurrier when he came to write about his shop. It was then Mr. Spurrier bought the old locksmith's shop next door.

The beginner's course at the Académie costs 444 francs or about $100. The advanced courses run 300 francs or about $70. The beginner's course includes about 40 wines. There are fewer in the advanced courses, but, if the 1962's recently were an example, the quality is extraordinary. In their next session, the Bordeaux students will get a tasting of various vintages of Château Figeac in St.-Emilion.

The wines are accompanied by cheeses from what Mr. Spurrier insists is the best cheese store in Paris. The lady from New Zealand must have agreed the other night. Before the group was into its third wine she had finished off a third of a pound of cheese and half a dozen slices of the Académie's stone-ground bread. Perhaps Mr. Spurrier should consider an Académie du Fromage.

A Comeback Story: Sonoma Vineyard

SOMEDAY someone is going to write a novel about the wine country —the American wine country. There have been a few, of course, but they really were stories based on that fundamental theme in American fiction: old-world values in a new land.

This story will be about an American who chooses to make a new life for himself in the vineyards. Not a wealthy man, mind you; rich men have always been attracted to winemaking, but with them, where's the conflict? They can afford to fail.

It can be an exciting book. There will be natural disasters, early success, corporate intrigue, financial failure, exotic settings, in short, the works, fictionally speaking.

To make it easy, I'll even supply a model for the central figure: Rodney D. Strong, to me, one of the more interesting people in the world of wine. People come to wine from many walks of life; Rod Strong must be one of the few who began as a professional dancer. He studied with George Balanchine, Paul Draper, and Martha Graham. In the early 1950's, he lived in Europe, dancing at the Lido in Paris, the Sporting Club in Monte Carlo, and the Casino in Cannes.

Back in the states, he appeared at the Persian Room in New York, the Palmer House in Chicago, and the Caribe Hilton in San Juan, choreographing his own act. He appeared on the *Ed Sullivan Show* several times and eventually made his Broadway debut in Leonard Sillman's *New Faces of 1956*.

Dancers, like all athletes, grow older and Rod Strong decided in 1960 that it was time to move on. His forebears had been winemakers in Germany and, as a boy, he had worked in his grandparents' vineyard on the Rhine. It seemed logical that he and his wife, Charlotte, do something with wine, so they opened a shop in Tiburon, a pretty town with a good tourist trade across the bay from San Francisco.

The Strongs called themselves Tiburon Vintners. They bought bulk wine, bottled it themselves, and sold it over the counter. Soon they were into the mail-order business, shipping wine all over California.

Then came one of those flashes of inspiration that, for better or worse, change people's lives. Rod Strong decided to "customize" his wines. Soon he was shipping hundreds of cases of wine labelled "Bottled expressly for . . .," or "Holiday greetings to . . .," or "From the cellar of . . ."

Rodney Strong at Sonoma Vineyards in California, which he founded and where he is winemaster.

In just two years, the Strongs were able to rent a winery 50 miles north of Tiburon in the heart of the Russian River Valley in Sonoma County. In a short period of time, they controlled Windsor Vineyard and were beginning to think in terms of a national business.

Soon thereafter, Peter Friedman, a merchandising specialist with Doyle Dane Bernbach, the advertising agency, joined the booming young company. He became president, and Rod Strong who, a few years earlier had been a bustling shopkeeper, was now board chairman and chief winemaker of Windsor Vineyards.

It was a heady time in the wine country. The big boom was on. What's more, Americans finally were catching on. The United States, they discovered, could produce wines as good as or better than any in the world.

Windsor Vineyards, just then becoming Sonoma Vineyards, was riding high. A magnificent new winery was built—a dramatic cruciform structure with vaulting ceilings, fountains playing under the entrance ramp, a French restaurant, and a Greek theater.

A Comeback Story: Sonoma Vineyard

A vineyard acquisition plan was begun. By the end of 1973, Sonoma Vineyards had acquired some 5,200 acres of the best—and most expensive—grape-growing land in California. Only huge Almadén among the premium winemakers had more.

Meanwhile, the company had gone public. From $6 a share in 1970, the stock climbed to $41 in 1972. In his ultramodern office under the apex of the wings of his new winery, Rod Strong, the one-time dancer, was literally sitting on top of the wine business.

Then the whole thing began to come apart. For one thing, sales had never really gotten off the ground. And wasn't the whole glorious expansion program predicated on national sales? "We just didn't have the clout," Rod Strong said later. "We couldn't break through the established competition."

Many of the optimistic predictions made in the late 1960's about wine industry expansion turned out to be exaggerated. Demand was growing but, because of the recession, much slower than anyone had expected. In the salad days, Sonoma had paid $4,000 an acre for land that had been worth little more than $1,000 a few years earlier. Now the price was back down again—just when the land had to be sold. By 1975, the business was $26 million in debt and the stock had slid to 75 cents a share.

And yet, through all those dreary times, Rod Strong continued to produce superior wines. His special, estate-bottled 1974 Chardonnay is, I think, one of the best white California wines in recent years. His regular North Coast Chardonnay is not far behind.

Sonoma Vineyards' 1973 North Coast Cabernet Sauvignon is one of the best bargains in premium California wine and several of Rod's late-harvested Johannisberg Rieslings during the past few years were as good as anything the state had produced. "Our financial problems never affected the quality of the wine," he said.

Meanwhile, the winery was on the block. David J. Mahoney, the aggressive boss of Norton Simon Inc. sent three aides to look the place over. When he turned down their recommendation to buy, they quit Norton Simon and joined Sonoma Vineyards as part of a complicated refinancing plan that also brought in the Renfield Corporation, a major wine and liquor distributor and importer. Kenneth Kwit was named board chairman, John W. Anderson became president, and Alin Gruber became senior vice president. Rodney Strong, who started the whole thing 17 years ago, with the little shop in Tiburon, was made vice president. But, more important, he is still the winemaster. "I'm very happy," he said; "I'm doing the job I've always loved best."

You expect people to say things that that, but Rodney Strong probably means it. He's 48 now but is in better shape than men half his age. He also has the aura of confidence and self-assurance that you expect from a man who has been to the top, back down again, and survived.

Come to think of it, there probably is no novel in all this. True, the marketing men came riding out of the East, John Wayne-like in the nick of time. True, the good guys seem to be winning. But there is no denouement, no big finale. Still it's one of my favorite wine stories. It's a real American tale with a lot of naïveté and crazy enthusiasm and, so far, a happy ending.

Sauternes

THE WINEMAKERS of the Sauternes region of France are sure that they make one of the great wines of the world and it vexes them no end that their work goes largely unnoticed by the people who should be their customers.

They have a point. Even connoisseurs will pay homage to the greatness of Château d'Yquem and then neglect to buy any. True, Yquem is quite expensive, but that is not the reason. Yquem is very sweet and we live at a time when dryness seems to be the mark of fine wines.

To try to counter this trend, Alexandre Lur-Saluces, the owner of Château d'Yquem, makes occasional visits to these shores, bearing with him the story of Sauternes and the good wishes of his fellow Sauternes-makers, few of whom can afford the trip as readily as he.

People who know and love the great wines of Sauternes and its neighboring community, Barsac, relish them as superb afterdinner wines, to be sipped sparingly with fresh fruit or a biscuit.

The Comte de Lur-Saluces wants to change all that. He says you can drink the sweet white wines of Sauternes with just about anything. Ever eager for something new, the members of the Wine and

Food Society decided to try the theory out. So, with the affable young proprietor of Yquem on hand, they gave themselves a dinner at the Pierre at which each course was accompanied by a sweet Sauternes or Barsac, or one of the sweet white wines from the adjoining *communes*, Ste.-Croix-du-Mont, Loupiac, and Cerons.

Let's just say that one would really have to be a fanatic about Sauternes to really enjoy it with every course of a meal. One might also say that the Sauternais are not going to do themselves any good trying to convince us that a sweet white wine goes well with everything. They like their wines with fish, for instance. This has got to be a special taste because the natural complement to most fish is the driest of whites, the steely Muscadet of the Loire Valley.

At a special tasting of wines from the Sauternes region the other day, fresh oysters were served with two Yquems, 1967 and 1968. Mr. Lur-Saluces, who was present, seemed to enjoy the combination immensely. He even had a word for it, as the French often do. The oysters and the Yquem connive together, he said. Well, maybe. A number of people present thought the Sauternes completely wiped out the oysters.

More common and worth trying, if only as an experiment, are the Bordeaux customs of serving Sauternes or Barsac with pâté at the start of a meal and with Roquefort cheese at the end. Here are two dishes that can hold their own with the sweetness of the wine. Both combinations are much savored by gourmets in France and here. Whether the Sauternes is superior to a good red wine is something you must decide for yourself.

Bear in mind that none of the foregoing is in any way meant to be a denigration of Sauternes. At their best, there are simply no other wines like them. They are made from grapes picked very late in the season, often weeks after the rest of the harvest in Bordeaux is over. So late, in fact, that the growers run serious risks of losing their crop to frost—and in some years they do.

The real secret of Sauternes and Barsac is not the late picking, although this ripens the grapes to an extraordinary sweetness never found in earlier pickings. It is the noble rot, the mold engendered by the soft, wet mists of the region that gives the Sauternes grapes their unmatched quality.

The rot, known more elegantly as *pourriture noble*, attacks the skins of the grapes, causing holes through which the water in the pulp evaporates, leaving only the most concentrated juice.

Not all vines are attacked by the mold, and not all grapes on a vine or in a bunch. Thus the usable grapes must be picked by hand, one by one. This is why Château d'Yquem makes an average of 10,000 or so bottles a year while a château in Graves or the Médoc a few miles to the north may make 10,000 cases from the same sized property.

Obviously, the cost to make such wine is high. But, surprisingly, the prices in New York do not correspond. There are a dozen Sauternes and Barsacs in the stores in the $5 and $6 range (1974). Some are even less, from time to time. Yquem, needless to say, is not among them.

Every wine drinker should experience a good Sauternes or Barsac. At the outset, though, it might be wise to try one with a pear. Later you can try it with the fish.

Some Nice Little Wines

MOST chauvinistic wine arguments take on the aura of the old "my father can lick your father" challenge. Which means that they involve a great deal of heat and very little light.

Is Stag's Leap Cabernet Sauvignon really better than Lafite-Rothschild? Is our Chateau Montelena Chardonnay really better than their Bâtard-Montrachet? Whatever the answer, it is nice to see both sides rolling around on the floor together, battling it out.

The only problem is: For most wine drinkers the discussion, as well as the outcome, has little bearing on reality. Few us have ever drunk those wines; some of us never will.

Still the competitive urge persists; my old man can lick your old man. Are our wines really better? What about the everyday wines many of us drink. How do we fare in that category?

It has been said that American *vin de consommation courante*—wine for drinking now—is the best in the world. Prompted by some recent promotion for imported wines aimed at the lower end of the market, we decided to make a small test. We went to several Manhattan retail shops and bought a dozen or so wines—some European, some American, and set up a small personal tasting.

Some Nice Little Wines

The wines were not our jug wines versus their jug wines. We went one level higher, at least in price, to the wines that are supposed to have some individual distinction beyond the pleasant but neutral contents served up in the jugs. There was one exception: We included a jug generally reputed to be far superior to others of its class.

Here are the wines, in fifths unless noted, with prices (1978):

Sebastiani Mountain Burgundy, half gallon	$3.89
Barengo California Burgundy	2.99
Fetzer Mendocino Premium Red	2.10
Gouriet Rouge, 1976	3.29
Premiat Pinot Noir	1.99
Pedroncelli Sonoma County Burgundy	2.49
Inglenook Navalle Burgundy	2.15
Robert Mondavi Red Table Wine	2.49
Saturnin Panisse, Rouge Panisse, 1975, one liter	2.79
Beaulieu Vineyards Napa Valley Burgundy, 1973	3.29
C.K. Mondavi Burgundy, half gallon ·	3.29
Ecu Royal French Country Red, half gallon	3.99
Alexis Lichine Red Table Wine (France)	3.29
Chantfleur Vin Rouge (France)	2.99

The reputedly excellent jug was the C.K. Mondavi Burgundy. The C.K. stands for Charles Krug, the winery that makes, or at least bottles, the wine. Krug is owned by one branch of the Mondavi family. The wine may do well against other jugs. In this group it was heavy and sweet.

The other branch of the Mondavi clan, headed by Robert Mondavi, is responsible for the Robert Mondavi Red Table Wine. It is a clean, dry red that will never intrude on your meal or cheese. It has little character to remember.

For its price the Inglenook Navalle was a good buy, but not as good as the Fetzer which, while heavier, has far more character. It is okay, solid, and assertive. Hardly a delicate wine, but a fine everyday companion.

The Sebastiani did not stand out in this company. Neither did the Barengo. The Beaulieu Vineyards 1973 was easily the best of the California wines, but then it was also the most expensive.

Among the European wines, the Premiat, which comes from Rumania and which has been enjoying some popularity, showed very little promise. It was a heavy, unsophisticated wine with a cooked smell. The Gouriet Rouge is billed as a George Lang selection. Mr. Lang, a restaurateur and man of the world, might do well to take his name off this product. It simply does not fit in with his reputation for style and excellence.

The Chantfleur is a small wine with some body and a pleasant bouquet; the Ecu Royal is a completely indifferent wine. The Lichine is an excellent red wine with what seems to be a generous helping of Merlot grapes in the blend. The Rouge Panisse is another good wine, soft, rounded, and full of flavor. Moreover, at $2.79 for a full liter, it is a good buy.

In overall ranking, I'd put the Beaulieu Burgundy first, the Fetzer Mendocino Premium Red second, the Rouge Panisse third, the Lichine Red Table Wine fourth, and the Robert Mondavi Red fifth.

Bear in mind that this was a small sampling based on the wines available in a couple of New York stores. There are dozens of other so-called California Burgundies and even more simple table wines in France, Italy, and in Rumania.

If you are a jug wine enthusiast, you might consider the next step up, generic wines such as those discussed here. You might find one of these to your liking or you might find some others to be far more appealing. In any event, these wines are the threshold to the great wines of the world, something the jugs almost never can be.

Compare by taste, then compare by price. Just remember that in California, the word Burgundy can mean almost anything—except a really great wine. Serious winemakers who try to emulate the great wines of the real Burgundy in France call their efforts Pinot Noir. Pinot Noir is the grape that goes into all great French Burgundies and into the best California versions of the French Burgundies.

Watch That Clerk

IT HAS BEEN said before and it will be said again: The kindly old wine merchant with only your best interests at heart is a character out of Dickens. That is, fictional.

Which is not to knock your neighborhood wine man. He has to make a living, too. Still, some of the stories that come to my attention are, well, extraordinary.

In 1974, for instance, a woman who lives on the upper east side of Manhattan told of buying a 1969 Bordeaux for $4 at a neighborhood shop. She brought it home, found the cork wet and loose in the neck of the bottle, and the wine, once the cork was removed, decidedly not to her taste.

She recorked the bottle and, since it was Saturday, waited until Monday to make her way back to the store. But why not let her tell her own story?

"The young man who had sold me the bottle," she wrote, "heard my complaint and referred me to the owner. I explained that the cork had been wet and he said that wines perspired in warm weather and a wet cork was not uncommon.

"When I said the cork sank into the neck, upon application of the corkscrew, he said he was not responsible for the way people opened bottles of wine. I have been opening bottles of wine for 12 years and rarely have broken a cork or spilled more than a few drops.

"He then *drank a slug from the bottle* and said it tasted fine to him and that there was nothing wrong with it, and pushed it across the counter to me. I said I was astonished and that I didn't want it back.

"As I turned to leave the store, I heard him tell the young man to throw it out. I stopped and turned around and told him that if he thought it was so good, why didn't he keep it and drink it. He said nothing and I left.

"I hardly know how to tell you that I am not an aggressive or overbearing woman; I did not make a scene or raise my voice—and there were no other customers in the store. But from the moment this man heard he had a complaint on his hands, he was unsmiling, unpleasant, and completely on the defensive.

"This shop has not lost a large customer although, certainly, I would have gone back for more of the same wine had I liked it. However, one likes to browse and chat with a wine merchant and this I will never be able to do in that place."

[185]

WINE TALK

It is really too bad there were no other customers around. The sight of a wine merchant swigging on the bottle and declaring it sound is something that should be shared. Better yet, everyone in the store could have had a swig followed by an intense discussion and several fist fights. Eventually the whole group could have adjourned to the local police precinct and, finally, have ended up on *Eyewitness News*.

Of course, this is much too flippant a treatment of the situation the woman was kind enough to commit to paper and send to me. The fact is, that wine buying is a high-risk activity. Wine, thank goodness, is not entirely a mass-produced product. It is subject to the vagaries of the individual producers and to the conscientiousness of the shippers, importers, and retailers through whose hands it must pass before the consumer can buy it.

A container holding a thousand cases of Scotch can sit on a blazing hot pier for days with impunity. A container of wine cannot. But not all longshoremen know this. And that is only one of the hazards a bottle of wine must face.

In this case, the woman had bought a single bottle of a classified St.-Estèphe. She paid a bargain price. Which means she took a chance.

Americans are taught to expect uniformity in quality and taste—or money cheerfully refunded. Some wine merchants go along with this. But it is provided for in their markup. Just as it is at restaurants that obligingly replace a bottle rejected by a customer.

Suppose the bottle was perfectly good, despite the loose cork? Should the dealer or the distributor be obliged to foot the cost of the wine simply because the woman decided she did not like it? After all, 1969 was not much of a year in Bordeaux.

There are no pat answers. The alternative to the confusion and aggravation of wine buying is a limited selection of homogenized, unchanging, brand-name wines, whose purchase requires neither discernment, skill, or experience.

On the other hand, with that kind of wine, it is unlikely that your friendly local wine man would drink from your bottle to show you up.

Clos de Vougeot

VOUGEOT, a little Burgundian village, is not much more than a wide spot in the road, halfway between Beaune and Dijon. But it is in the center of what is probably the greatest wine region of France, and on certain nights of the year it is a mecca for the wine lovers of the world: the nights when the Chevaliers du Tastevin gather here to do honor to the wines of Burgundy.

In the fall of 1972, 560 members and friends of the La Confrérie des Chevaliers du Tastevin—the Brotherhood of the Knights of the Tastevin—came here to the Château du Clos de Vougeot for the 417th such evening, the Chapitre Extraordinaire d'Automne.

Most of the black-tie crowd was made up of Frenchmen, but almost every country on the continent was represented, as was the United States and South America. One Washington banker arrived, exhausted, directly from Kinshasha, in Zaire, the former Belgian Congo, where he had been on a business trip.

The Château du Clos de Vougeot was built by Cistercian monks in 1551. The Cistercians had owned the Clos, a walled vineyard, itself and tended its vines since the 12th century. The property remained in church hands until 1790 when, following the revolution, church properties were confiscated and broken up. Over the years there have been many owners. Since 1944, the château has been owned by the Confrérie, while the vineyards, totalling some 125 acres, are owned by about 60 different growers.

A *tastevin*—literally, a wine taster—is the small silver cup that sommeliers dangle around their necks. Each new member of the Confrérie is presented with his own *tastevin*, suspended from a brilliant orange and yellow ribbon which he wears around his neck at, as one member's wife said, "the slightest provocation."

Tastevin dinners and tastings are held in many cities, including New York, but few members would argue that they compare with the parties here at Clos de Vougeot. The château lies about halfway up the vineyard slope from Highway N-74 and is reached by a narrow road through the town of Vougeot. On the night of a *chapitre* it can be seen from the highway, its sand-colored, ancient walls and every window ablaze with light. The vast inner courtyard where monks once walked in prayer is a sea of color, with elegant gowns competing with the medieval robes of the officers of the Confrérie.

Promptly at 8 P.M., the throng is summoned to table in the great hall by trumpeters in scarlet-coated hunting garb. From that point until precisely midnight, the eating, drinking, singing, and speech-making never stop. The spirit is lighthearted and, on my visit, the gaiety never flagged.

The first order of business is a series of comic speeches emphasizing the importance of wine drinking and the unimportance of most other earthly endeavors. Then, to much applause, the Cadets de Bourgogne march in and begin to sing. The Cadets are a group of about 20 local men, ranging in age from 21 to about 78, with a vast repertoire of songs about drinking, lovemaking, and, of course, Burgundy. Half the audience knows the songs by heart and joins in. Each new speech and each course of the meal are announced by trumpeters in medieval dress, and the evening ends with the investiture of new members and the award of special honors to several old members.

In November, 1972, the guests of honor were Jean Amadou, a French comedian, and Benson E.L. Timmons III, former U.S. Ambassador to Haiti and Deputy Director General of the Office of Economic Cooperation and Development in Paris.

The Brotherhood of the Knights of the Tastevin, for all its trappings of the Middle Ages, dates only from 1934. Hard times had hit the vineyards of the Côte d'Or and local people were seeking ways to promote Burgundy wines. The Confrérie turned out to be an eminently successful venture. Today there are imitations of it celebrating the virtues—and pushing the sales—of many wines, and public relations men are busy thinking up new "commanderies" and "confréries" all the time.

But the Chevaliers du Tastevin claim theirs is the most successful of all. If the *chapitres* here at Clos de Vougeot are any indication, they may be right. There are about 15 parties here a year and the $30 tickets (1972) are usually sold out well in advance.

Naturally, not everyone is impressed. A veteran New York wine merchant scoffs at the whole thing. "A lot of people dressing up in silly clothes to eat mediocre food and drink indifferent wine," he said with a snort.

The wines were not extraordinary vintages. But then, the French are not nearly as concerned with drinking super-rare and super-expensive wines as are Americans. (Selling them to Americans is, of course, another matter.) The meal? Well, it wasn't the Grand Véfour, but a couple of the courses, notably the trout and the duck, were pretty good and so was the service. Besides, where else are you going to see 500 pounds of lemon sherbet shaped into a giant Burgundian snail and carried into the room to the accompaniment of 17th century trumpet fanfares?

Berry Brothers & Rudd

BERRY BROTHERS & RUDD, a liquor store at 3 St. James's Street in London, is probably one of the oldest establishments of its kind in the world. It goes back at least to 1699. The firm originated and still owns Cutty Sark Scotch. Princes, statesmen, poets, and American gangsters have been among its customers. And yet, for some reason, the store is most widely known for its peculiar practice of weighing people.

Not just anybody, of course. You have to be a good customer. But for several hundred years, being weighed at Number 3, like receiving the Order of the British Empire, has signified acceptance and accomplishment to many an Englishman.

Berry Brothers & Rudd was founded as Bourne's Italian Warehouse around the end of the 17th century. William Pickering married the Widow Bourne's daughter in 1703 or 1704 and soon was in charge of the business. At the time it was also known as The Old Coffee Mill and a replica of a coffee mill still hangs above the front door.

The first Berry came to work at Number 3 in 1803 and the managing director today is Anthony A. Berry, his direct descendant.

The low-ceilinged salesroom with its wooden floor, high desks, and comfortable old chairs is more club-like than businesslike. The only bottles visibile are tucked away in breakfronts and are obviously not for sale. The room is, in fact, much the same as it was in the 18th century when Frederick, the Duke of York, was a steady customer. Indeed, the old books show that he weighed himself some 50 times on the huge scale that still dominates the shop.

Frederick, a son of King George III, last stepped on the scales at Number 3 in 1800 when he weighed a hefty 14 stone 8½, or 204½ pounds. He died 27 years later, deep in debt, which may explain why he is not listed in the firm's books in his last years.

Frederick's younger brother, William, the Duke of Clarence, later to become William IV, was also a regular at the shop. A rough and tumble naval officer much of his life, William made no bones about his affection for wine. According to one anecdote in Berry Brothers' archives, William was entertaining King Leopold of the Belgians at Windsor Castle when he shouted across the table to Leopold: "What's that you're drinking, sir? God damn it, why don't you drink wine? I never allow anybody to drink water at my table!"

Perhaps one of the lightest customers was the writer Charles Lamb, who stepped on the big scale in 1814. He tipped them at 129 pounds. The heaviest? In 1825, a famous race track figure of the time, Thomas Thornhill, weighed in at 334½ pounds. An Irish wrestler topped that in 1950 with 371.

Anyone who suffered through the recent film *Lady Caroline Lamb* might have come away with the idea that Lord Byron looked something like Richard Chamberlain. Actually, he was quite short and had an alarming tendency to run to fat. On his first visit to Number 3 as a 17-year-old student at Trinity College, Cambridge, the poet weighed 13 stone 12, or 194 pounds. That was on January 4, 1806. Two years later he was down to 153 and although he crept up a stone or so over the next few years, by 1811, the year before the publication of *Childe Harolde*, he was down to a svelte 9 stone 11½, or 137½ pounds.

William Pitt, Charles Fox, and Sir Robert Peel are just a few of the famous men who were customers of Berry Brothers & Rudd and who stopped by to have themselves weighed on the shop's scales.

Here in London, where wine has become everyman's drink far more rapidly than it has in New York, Berry Brothers, with its elegant Georgian facade and Regency prints on the panelled walls is something of an anachronism. "Perhaps," said James Anderson, an aide to Anthony Berry, "but the feeling is that there will always be a need for true wine merchants, men who taste wines at lunch every day right here in the boardroom as their fathers and grandfathers did before them. Men who visit the vineyards and who offer very personal service to their customers."

One of the strangest customers ever to receive Berry Brothers & Rudd service was Jack "Legs" Diamond who, according to old hands at Number 3, turned up one day in the 1920's with two tough-looking companions and ordered a substantial quantity of Scotch, all of which was carried away by a fleet of taxis the next day. "Perhaps it was as well that we could turn a blind eye on its final destination," said a Berry Brothers' publication.

In those days, during Prohibition in the United States, whiskey was purchased legitimately here in Britain and shipped to Nassau, from whence it found its way to the States just a few miles away. The late H. Warner Allen wrote: ". . . though Number 3 was careful to keep its fingers clean from dabbling in illegality and bootlegging . . . the legal demand for its wares in the Bahamas was vast, and the label of Berry Bros. & Co. was becoming more and more an accepted guarantee of quality and honesty in a country hagridden with adulterated imitations." This may also have been the beginning of the popularity of Cutty Sark in the United States.

Perhaps the most poignant visit to the little shop on St. James's Street was made during World War II when wine, like every other commodity on this fortress island, was in pitifully scarce supply. Some time after the occupation of France, a French officer entered the shop and asked if there were any of the 1933 Château Mouton available. A clerk was explaining that whatever wine the store had was reserved for old customers, when H. Warner Allen, who was working in the shop at the time, recognized the officer: It was Baron Philippe de Rothschild, the owner of Mouton which was then in the hands of the Germans. Whatever 1933 Mouton could be rounded up was shared with the *proprietaire* in exile.

There Is Only One Way to Learn

MOST LETTERS from readers deal with practical matters. "Can I make my fortune from this old bottle I discovered in my aunt's attic?" "My liquor dealer says the wine you praised last week doesn't exist." "Should I drink the Champagne I won at the church bazaar in 1968?" That sort of thing.

Once in a while, however, something unusually interesting comes along. Such a letter showed not long ago. It was both valuable and depressing. But here, read it—slightly edited for space:

"Recently, while planning a dinner party, I noticed ads in *The Times* for wine sales. Using vintage charts and Alexis Lichine's suggested Bordeaux classification printed in Peter Sichel and Judy Ley's *Which Wine?*, I found a bargain.

"For about $7.50 the fifth (1977), I could and did buy Château Brane-Cantenac 1966. Now this château is a second growth by historical designation and an exceptional growth according to Lichine. At the same time that my bargain was advertised I noticed that Château Ducru-Beaucaillou, also a second growth, was being sold for several dollars more the bottle. I was pleased with my find. Pleased that is till we drank it. Awful. What did I do wrong?

[191]

"I know that the better a wine, the more aging it requires, and that a '66 probably is not yet quite ready to drink. Yet '66 is the oldest I can afford on any regular basis. I know that wines from St.-Estèphe mature more slowly than wines from St.-Emilion because I read that in your column, but I know nothing about wines from Cantenac Margaux.

"How am I supposed to learn? The general advice is to deal with a knowledgeable dealer. Who are they? The clerks I see up and down Madison Avenue do not appear any more knowledgeable than I. Was there some cataclysm in Cantenac-Margaux or, more particularly, at Brane-Cantenac that season?

"If so, how am I supposed to learn that except by trial and error? Was the fact that each bottle, though bought from the same store, had a different importer's label a clue? Are there certain stores that carry damaged goods? If so, how am I to know? Would I have been better off with a lesser growth of '66 or even a '70 on the theory that it would have matured more rapidly?

"All in all," the woman concludes, "it was not a good evening for claret. . . . If you answer that my palate was at fault, it's possible. I had as a dinner guest, however, a greater maven than I . . . and he too thought my Brane-Cantenac was faulty."

And here, all this time, these pieces have advanced the doctrine that discussing, buying, and drinking wine is fun. If this poor woman is hopelessly entangled in her books and charts and vintage dates, it is safe to assume that there are many more around like her. Good heavens! If this is the sort of thing *Wine Talk* has fostered, something is very wrong.

Let's dispense with the specifics first. "I know nothing about the wines from Cantenac Margaux." If it really matters, check the wine books. They all have long sections on Margaux and most of them cover Cantenac, the little *commune* just south of Margaux, separately.

"Where are the knowledgeable wine dealers?" They are scarce, very scarce. So are good plumbers, editors, and butchers. And no matter how good the fellow is, how is he to know what is in your particular bottle of Brane-Cantenac?

"Was there a cataclysm in Cantenac in 1966?" That's easy. No.

"If so, how am I supposed to learn except by trial and error?" No one has ever devised a better way.

"Was the fact that each bottle, though bought from the same store, had a different importer's label a clue?" Not really. Who knows what adventures your Brane-Cantenac experienced over which the importer had no control whatsoever?

"Are there certain stores that carry damaged goods?" As a regular practice, no. All of them get some bad stuff now and then, most of which seems to disappear down the customers' throats with nary a complaint. Many stores treat their wine cavalierly but most of the places specializing in wine, at least in New York, make an effort to see that none of the first growths are stacked against the oil burner.

"Would I have been better off with a lesser growth of '66 or even '70 on the theory that it would have matured more rapidly?" Who says your Brane-Cantenac was not matured?

Somehow this woman has managed to take something that should be fun and turn it into joyless drudgery and classic bourgeois one-upmanship. The 1966 on the bottle has become like the green and red stripe on a suitcase.

Nowhere in this letter is there any mention of taste or color or past bottles well remembered. Would this party have been such a disaster if everyone had relaxed over a lot of bottles of a nice Côtes du Rhône and forgotten about 1966 and Cantenac and all that?

The lady seems to have picked up a bad bottle. So what? Wine is not Campbell's soup. That particular 75 centiliters of wine went into that particular bottle back in 1968. The lady who served it has undoubtedly been through a lot since 1968; the rest of us certainly have. Why not the wine, too?

That's one of the fine things about good wine: it stubbornly resists our efforts to reduce it to a standard formula: '66's are superb, '70's are not ready yet, and all the rest. One simply cannot learn all there is to learn—or even a small part of it—from books and vintage charts and wine columns. There simply is no substitute for pulling corks.

Expensive? No more than tennis lessons. Moreover, there is no conceivable reason why anyone has to go for the glamour vintages before they have a good grounding in lesser wines.

Côtes du Rhône would have made a good dinner for this woman but that may be the opposite extreme. There are half a dozen Rhône wines that would have graced her table at less cost than her 1966 Bordeaux: Hermitage, for example, or Châteauneuf-du-pape or Gigondas.

There are plenty of really beautiful Burgundies from the early 1970's, selling for under $5; 1972 Chassagne-Montrachet, 1972 Auxey-Durreses, 1973 Savigny-les-Beaune and 1973 Aloxe-Corton among them. There are plenty of delightful 1967 Bordeaux around for less than that ill-fated 1966 and, yes, there are some very nice little 1970's clarets around, too, ready to be drunk now. Which ones? Pick up a couple in your shop. Try them and decide for yourself.

WINE TALK

The world of wine is a vast one. It is there for anyone who cares to explore. But there are no magic formulas designed to produce superb old bottles at a snap of the fingers. There are risks and there are pitfalls. There is also the day when you open a bottle you found yourself, sit back and say: "Now that is really good!"

But no book or chart is going to do that for you. You have to do it yourself.

Chablis—Or Is It?

THE TREND to lighter drinks and the phenomenal success of white wine has been well documented by now. "A glass of white wine" is as common a phrase around bars now as "scotch on the rocks."

Many people go a step farther. They say "A glass of Chablis." In fact there are still quite a few menus that list Chablis along with Burgundy as the house wines, to be sold in carafes or by the glass. Of course, it is not really Chablis. No one in his right mind would sell genuine Chablis by the glass.

It is a California wine, or possibly a New York State wine, which has been given the generic name of Chablis and which is actually a blend of various wines made from usually inexpensive local grapes.

One of the recent wine books notes that Americans call this generic white wine Chablis because it has the qualities and style of genuine Chablis. Wrong on two counts. First the local so-called Chablis barely resemble the French product, if at all. The American wines are soft and pleasant; the French wine is sharp and can take your breath away. The Americans gave their wine the French name because it was familiar, easy to remember, and could cover any one of a dozen different blends of wine.

Gallo Chablis Blanc, the bar wine in hundreds of restaurants, is a blend of various grapes including probably the Thompson Seedless and Chenin Blanc. True Chablis is made only from the Pinot Chardonnay grape, the classic white wine grape of Burgundy.

Chablis—Or Is It?

The town of Chablis and the Chablis region surrounding it are usually considered part of Burgundy. Actually it is a separate region some 75 miles north of Beaune, the center of the Burgundy wine region. In fact Chablis is about halfway between Beaune and Paris.

Only Champagne is further north than Chablis among the wine-growing regions and there is an austerity, a hardness in both wines, that sets them apart from other French wines and reflects the shorter summers and paler sun that are their lot. Long, hot summers produce big, rich wines. Cooler, shorter hot seasons produce more acidy wines —such as Chablis.

Chablis was once a far more popular white wine in this country than it is now. For one thing, our tastes in food have changed. Chablis is a superb wine to go with oysters and we don't eat oysters the way Diamond Jim Brady did. Then, too, we have discovered the wines of the Loire: Muscadet, Sancerre, and Quincy. Muscadet, particularly, is a fresh, sharp white wine that goes very well with seafood—and until recently at half the price of Chablis. Sancerre, a favorite in some of the best Paris bistros, has more body and style than Muscadet. So does Quincy, which is usually harder to find in the shops or on wine lists.

Americans in recent years have shown a marked preference for the white wines of Burgundy itself and for the wines of the Mâcon region, south of Burgundy: Mâcon, St.-Véran, and Pouilly-Fuissé. In fact, in New York restaurants, Pouilly-Fuissé is often the most popular of all imported wines.

All these wines, like Chablis, are made from the Chardonnay grape. Because they are produced in more southerly regions, however, they are softer and easier on the palate. As a wine to drink with seafood, however, not even the best Sancerre is a match for a *grand cru* Chablis. The best Chablis have a magnificent dryness, a unique bouquet, a pale straw color tinged with green, and what some experts describe as a steely or a flinty taste. Like everything else in Europe, Chablis is divided up into classes. There are three that count: simple Chablis, *premier cru* Chablis, and *grand cru* Chablis.

There are seven *grand cru* vineyards: Vaudésir, Preuses, Les Clos, Grenouilles, Bougros, Valmur, and Blanchots. In any normal harvest, the *grand cru* vineyards will produce around 27,000 gallons of wine, or far less than some small wineries in northern California.

The *grand crus* vines must be cropped back so severely under French law that only 310 gallons, or about 150 cases of wine, can be produced per acre. The alcoholic content must be 11 percent. This can be raised to about 13 by the legal addition of sugar during the fermentation process. In poor years—and Chablis has more than its share because of its northern weather—wine from *grand cru* vine-yards can be dropped down into the next category, *premier cru.*

Here there are 24 specific vineyards. All the *grand cru* are within the borders of the town of Chablis. The *premier cru* are there, too, and also in half a dozen surrounding little villages.

The *premier cru* rules call for a maximum of 356 gallons per acre and a minimum alcohol strength of 10.5 degrees. The average harvest produces about 205,000 gallons. Much of the Chablis that comes to this country is *premier cru.*

The next classification is just Chablis. It must have at least 10 degrees of alcohol and the annual harvest produces about 215,000 gallons. Incidentally, all these wines are whites. Some reds are made in the area but none can bear the name Chablis.

There is a fourth classification called Petit Chablis but little of it ever gets to these shores. If anything, this country gets more than its share of good Chablis, including *grand cru*, because the fashion for the wine has dropped off. This means there are some good buys around.

Chablis is made and sold in the Burgundian style—that is, a lot of small proprietors, some of whom make, bottle, and sell their own wine under their own names; and some of whom make their wine and sell it to a large shipper. The shipper then blends it with other wine of the same classification—we hope—and sells it under his own label.

It can get rather confusing. Take three hypothetical portions of the Vaudésir Vineyard. One is owned by a man who bottles his own wine and sells it under his own name. Another is owned by a man who sells the wine to a shipper who blends it with wine he buys from a couple of other men who own pieces of the vineyard. The third portion is owned by the shipper, who bottles it separately and sells it as his own estate-bottled wine.

Thus there are three bottles of Chablis Grand Cru Vaudésir; all from the same vineyard, two from the same shipper, but all different, and all from an area not much bigger than a soccer field.

One thing to remember about Chablis, genuine Chablis that is: It will last. More than that, it will improve in the bottle. Our colleague, Terry Robards, writes of tasting a 1928 in 1973 and finding it still good. Hugh Johnson says of Chablis: "A strange and delicious sort of sour taste enters into it at ten years or so, and its golden green eye flashes meaningfully."

This assumes, of course, that the wine has been stored well during those years. Few wines get the respect they deserve in this country, especially from the distributors and retailers, so it would be risky to buy an old Chablis unless you were absolutely certain of its history since leaving the vineyard.

Better to buy a few, if you have a decent cellar, and lay them away for a few years, although not necessarily 45 years as in the case of that 1928.

A Question of Temperature

THE BASIC RULES about the temperature of wine are really simple: Reds are best at room temperature and whites are best when chilled.

How could anyone quarrel with that? Well, the truth of the matter is that wine enthusiasts argue about temperature almost as much as they do about the wine itself. They pounce on innocent terms like "room temperature" and even "red wine" like courtroom prosecutors. Room temperature? Whose room? Red wine? Which red wine?

Let it be stated at the outset that the haggling of experts often generates more heat than light and often serves more to confuse and mystify than to explain. The fact is, red wines really should be served at room temperature and whites should be chilled—unless you like them some other way.

A few years ago, there was a lot of smirking over published reports that Frank Sinatra enjoyed his red wine chilled at lunch time. Recently a fellow turned up in New York City who makes Beaujolais in a wide spot in the road near Lyon called Le Breuil. Comte Henri de Rambuteau confessed that not only does he drink his Beaujolais chilled—he even puts ice in it on hot summer days.

Red wines such as Beaujolais and the lesser blends from California that are called Burgundy and claret may actually be improved by chilling. They have a sweet finish that is nicely cut when the wines are served slightly cold.

What Mr. Sinatra does with his best wines was not recorded for posterity, but Mr. Rambuteau made it clear that he does not drink the finer wines of Beaujolais—Moulin-à-Vent, Morgon, St.-Amour, and the rest—with ice cubes. The only red wines that benefit from chilling are the lesser ones.

Unhappily, this is a point lost on some of our restaurateurs, mostly Italian. Given that the climate in much of Italy cries out for cool drinks. Given that much Italian wine is inexpensive stuff that cannot be hurt by chilling. There is still no excuse for taking good Chianti Classico and practically freezing it.

A few days ago, at a pleasant little restaurant in Albany, New York, of all places, the wine card disclosed a great buy: a Verrazzano Chianti Classico 1969 for $6. It came to the table icy cold and required 30 minutes of hand-warming before any of the considerable taste and bouquet became apparent.

Similarly, a new little place on Ninth Avenue in Manhattan, Mama Mia, came up with a Bardolino from Bolla the other day, thoroughly chilled. True, Bardolino is almost a *rosé* but still it should not have been chilled.

The business of room temperature is often argued by wine lovers who like to point out that the rules were made by people who never heard of central heating. Consequently, they say, fine wines should be served at temperatures five or ten degrees below what we think of as comfortable.

In practice it is almost impossible to find anyone who does this. Bottles that come from a chilly cellar invariably are up to room temperature by the time the wine is consumed. Moreover, a five degree difference between the room temperature and the temperature of the wine usually will seem to be much greater, interfering with the taste and the nose of a fine wine.

Of white wines, Hugh Johnson has written: "I do not think that there is a right temperature for white wines." He goes on to observe that some people like them cool, some icy, some just chilled. "I think they are usually served much too cold in the United States," Mr. Johnson, obviously an Englishman, writes, "but then, so is the water, the beer, and even the salad."

Mr. Johnson can keep his tepid water, warm beer, and wilted greens, but he probably is right about our tendency to bring white wines down toward the freezing point. At most American dinners where the white wine is supposed to be remarked upon, it is necessary to let it sit in the glass for 30 minutes just to find out what it tastes like. Just as with the reds, excess chilling serves to mask all the bouquet and flavor of the wine.

There is an elaborate chart around somewhere that purports to show what temperatures are appropriate for most wines. It puts young dry reds, such as Beaujolais, at around 55 degrees, aged dry whites at about the same temperature, and young dry whites, which are the whites most people drink, at around 47 degrees. Champagnes and other sparkling wines are said to be best at around 42 degrees and the sweet white wines, such as Sauternes, as just above freezing.

It is the fashion in France to serve very old Sauternes extremely cold, at times with the bottle encased in ice. Mr. Johnson, again, demurs. To ice great wines, he maintains, is to waste them. For Champagne, he recommends "the temperature of a deep cellar: distinctly cool, perfectly refreshing, but not searingly cold in the throat like a can of lager straight out of the icebox."

German and Alsatian wines all should be served chilled. Again, though, it can be and often is overdone. The chilling is to enhance the wine, not to mask its qualities.

Most white wines can be properly chilled by being placed in a refrigerator for two or three hours before they are to be used. An hour in the freezer compartment will do the same job, but the best method is to use an ice bucket. This need not be something from Tiffany's with an elegant stand. In the *Signet Book of Wine*, Alexis Bespaloff suggests:

"Empty one or two ice trays in your biggest cooking pot, fill it with water and put in the bottle. It should be cool in 15 or 20 minutes."

Own Your Own Vine

WOULD YOU LIKE to own your own grapevines in a producing vineyard? Would you like to assist in the development of the Hudson Valley as an important wine region—the way it was early in the country's history? And would you like to be entitled to a case of wine each year produced from the vineyards of which you are a part owner?

[199]

Then you might consider joining the Société des Vignerons here at Benmarl Vineyards, a few miles north of Newburgh, New York. The Société is the creation of Mark Miller, once a prominent magazine illustrator and now, for almost two decades, a dedicated winemaker, grapegrower, and champion of the Hudson Valley as a premium wine grape region in the United States.

Mr. Miller is also a tireless promoter, not only for his region but for his winery and for other small wineries throughout the state. Fittingly, he was present in Albany in 1976, when Governor Carey signed into law a "small winery" bill that Mr. Miller and others had fought for for many years. Among other things, the law will adjust annual winery license fees to the size of the operation—Benmarl will pay about $125 a year instead of about $1500—and will permit small wineries to sell a large part of their production at the winery.

"These hills were covered with vines a hundred years ago," Mr. Miller said in 1976, looking out from Benmarl towards the Hudson and the hazy line of the Connecticut hills off to the east. "I would like to see them that way again."

There is a sense of urgency about Mr. Miller's dream. Tacky urbanism, in the form of budget housing development, is creeping slowly but inexorably up the valley from New York City, 60 miles to the south.

"A lot of the younger people around here gave up their fruit trees because it was no longer economically worthwhile for them to put in the work," Mr. Miller said. "But I think grapes, good grapes, could be a profitable crop for them." He said he had convinced a few of his neighbors to plant small vineyards and hoped to bring in even more full-time and part-time farmers. "This is still basically an agricultural economy," he said, "and I'd like to keep it that way."

The Benmarl Vineyards cover about 35 acres, rising steeply from Route 9 to the Miller home and the Benmarl winery. At one time, the vines reached almost to the river, down from the east side of the highway, much of which is now in fruit trees. Mr. Miller leases an area on that side of the highway for use as a nursery and experimental vineyard.

Most of the Benmarl vineyards are planted in what are known as French hybrid grapes—crosses between different kinds of grapes that are bred to withstand the cold winters of the eastern part of this country. Seyval Blanc, and Baco Noir are the principal hybrids, but Auror, Maréchal Foch, Chancelor, Chelois, and Verdelet also are grown.

Benmarl also grows and makes wine from the famous *vinifera* grapes which produce the finest wines in Europe and California:

Mark Miller, the owner of Benmarl, checking grapes.

Chardonnay and Johannisberg Riesling, and in small quantities, Cabernet Sauvignon and Pinot Noir.

Mark Miller and his son Eric, now the winemaker at Benmarl, are experimenting with various strains of *vinifera* to learn which adapts best to the soil and climate of the Hudson Valley; but they are strong defenders of the hybrids as excellent grapes for the area. "The hybrids have produced wines with a distinctive regional character," Mr. Miller said. "The slatey soil, the hard winters, and the long Hudson River summers have combined to develop wines unlike any produced from these grapes anywhere else in the world."

Benmarl's red wines include the Baco Noir and Baco Clair, a lighter wine from the same Baco grape, and Domaine Rouge, a blend of various red-wine grapes. The whites include Seyval Blanc, l'Aurore, a soft wine made in small quantities, Chardonnay, and the blend, Domaine Blanc.

The Benmarl wines are available at serious wine shops in the New York area and at a number of restaurants with good American wine lists, including The Four Seasons. Eventually they will also be available at the winery itself.

A portion of Benmarl's production is unavailable to the public. It is reserved exclusively for the members of the Société des Vignerons and is known as the Cuvée du Vigneron. Membership in the Société, including dues and first year initiation fee, costs $130 (1976). This includes a "vineright" representing two vines of a variety chosen by the member. Each vineright holder is entitled to 12 bottles of wine each year, which is about the amount of wine two vines will produce.

There are two types of vinerights: bearing and nonbearing. The bearing vineright entitles its holder to 12 bottles of wine free each year. The nonbearing vinerights do not yield any wine until the vines have completed their fourth year in the vineyard. Nonbearing rights, designed to underwrite new vineyards, are available only to members already holding a bearing vineright.

At harvest time, the members of the society often come to Benmarl to help in the picking. They return, too, at bottling time to choose the blend from which they want their 12 bottles to come. After all the rights have been exercised, the remaining wine in that cuvée is sold exclusively to the members of the Société.

In addition to the initial vineright purchase and initiation fee, each member of the society pays an annual fee of $30, the estimated cost of the upkeep of the two vines. Société members can buy as many vinerights as they wish.

Vinerights are permanent holdings. They can be assigned to heirs and successors. There are about 350 members in the Société at present; the Millers would like to have 2,000. "That would give us the kind of capital we need to continue our experimental work," Mr. Miller said. "Also it gives us a market for our wines and a host of loyal supporters and promoters."

The Millers, who lived for many years in the Burgundy region of France, hope someday to see Benmarl as the center of a thriving wine region much the same as Burgundy is in France. They feel the passage of the small-winery bill is a step towards realization of that dream.

Wine in the Sky

SOME YEARS BACK, before wine really meant anything to the airlines, I had occasion to fly to San Francisco. Fate gave me one of those middle seats—no window, no aisle. I forget who had the window seat but I'll never forget the chap who came on just before the doors shut and plunked into the space on my right.

He was a rough-looking type wearing work pants, a plaid wool shirt, and a canvas windbreaker. He buried his crew-cut head in a newspaper and had nothing to say to anyone until the stewardess inquired about drinks. He took a blended whiskey on the rocks. Only one. But miracle of miracles, his glass was never empty.

We must have been over Pittsburgh before I figured out what he was up to. He had a pint in his jacket pocket and, with the agility of a shell-game master, he slipped that bottle out, topped off his drink and put the bottle back. He deplaned, as the airlines like to say, in San Francisco and strode out of that terminal like a sturdy teetotaller.

I only mention this bit of aviation history by way of illustrating the fact that one of the more pleasant ways to drink on a plane, scandalous though it may be, is to bring your own. It is necessary to add immediately that this practice is frowned upon, if only because few of us have the capacity of that rugged fellow on the coast-to-coast flight. It is also necessary to add immediately that I am talking now about wine. Anyone who lubricates his way across the nation with a pint or two of sour mash bourbon is obviously asking for trouble. But it is no feat at all to sip good wines from sea to shining sea.

In fact, thanks to some tough airline competition in California, it is now possible to do just that. It seems that, a few years ago, an upstart airline in California called Pacific Southern Airlines began carrying people between Los Angeles and San Francisco at incredibly low prices. Being an intrastate carrier, they cared not a whit about the Civil Aeronautics Board and their rules about fares.

To compete, the major airlines also lowered fares and, from time to time, offered other inducements to lure away PSA customers. At one point, United Airlines came up with unlimited wine—after you purchased the first glass. (Actually, Western Airlines had been offering a better deal for years—free Champagne.)

Somehow, the idea spread. Now thanks to stiff competition on cross-country flights, it is possible to buy a glass of wine for a dollar shortly after lift-off and get unlimited refills for the next 3000 miles. "You can drink the wing tanks dry," is the way one airline aide rather indelicately put it.

"It is not unusual for 60 passengers (in economy class) to run through 30 bottles on a transcontinental trip," said Creighton Churchill, wine writer and consultant to American Airlines. "What's more," he said, "no money is lost on the deal and it's possible that a little is made."

Sixty into 30 comes to a half-bottle apiece, and as any wine lover knows, no one is going to get drunk on that. But, of course, there are those passengers who take the first glass and no more and there are those who don't even take the first glass. Which means a lot of wine for a small coterie of aficionados.

"Even so," said one airline food specialist. "You never see anyone out of hand. Or almost never. The cabin staff has control of who drinks what and they usually can spot the guy—or girl—who has gone too far. They cut him off. Believe me, wine is far less of a problem than hard liquor."

Both American and United offer unlimited refills after the initial $1 purchase of a glass or in the case of United, a combination pack that includes a split of wine and a specially designed plastic glass. Unlimited wine has always been a feature of first-class airline service.

Wine itself has been a part of airline service almost since the days when cabin meals consisted of box lunches. In recent years, with the enormous increase in interest in wine, the airlines have been quick to cater to their client's developing palates.

When Concorde service was established between Washington and London and France in 1976 the first reports of supersonic flight for the public rarely failed to mention the fact that such wines as Château Haut-Brion and Dom Pérignon Champagne were poured generously at Mach 1.2.

In fact, since the planes are all pretty much the same and the schedules equally similar, it is entirely possible to conceive of flying according to the *carte des vins*. If, for example, you happen to be flying from New York to either Los Angeles or San Francisco, you might like to know what will be available, winewise.

On American, in first class, you will be offered one of two whites and one of two reds. The whites, Sonoma Vineyards Chardonnay 1975 and Ste. Michelle Vintners Chenin Blanc 1976. The reds: Mirassou Vineyards Cabernet Sauvignon 1972 and Monterey Vineyards Zinfandel 1975. Economy class passengers will be offered Sonoma Vineyards French Colombard 1977 and Wente Brothers Zinfandel 1974.

Wine in the Sky

United Airlines, on its coast-to-coast flights, will be pouring Mirassou's 1976 White Burgundy and Beringer Brothers 1974 Cabernet Sauvignon in first class, and those little combination bottle and glass packages in economy. One of them will be Pinot Noir.

TWA features Paul Masson Pinot Chardonnay of a recent vintage and Louis Martini Cabernet Sauvignon 1973. To keep both coasts happy, the Champagne may be either Almadén or Korbel from California or Great Western from New York.

The only passenger who is wine-pampered more than the transcontinental traveller, is the trans-Atlantic traveller who is wooed by half-a-dozen carriers for any given flight. I have a friend who passed the long night between Kennedy and Geneva on a Swissair flight by consuming all or part of 17 half-bottles. Moreover, he insists that he was in excellent condition when the flight ended.

Flying overseas is an ethnic experience. Carmel wines on El Al, fine Chiantis and old Barolos on Alitalia, great clarets on British Airways (well, they owned Bordeaux for 300 years didn't they?), and superb German vintages on Lufthansa, including the lovely Wiltingener Scharzhofberg Kabinett 1975 and the 1976 Eltviller Sonnenberg 1976 from Freiherr Langwerth von Simmern.

Air France, which should be second to none when it comes to wines, does itself proud in first class: Perrier-Jouët Blason de France Champagne, Château Pichon Lalande 1970, and Clos de la Roche 1969 from the Côte de Beaune. There is Puligny-Montrachet and Clos de Vougeot and the whole list is a perfect reason for bringing back the great liner *France* because who has time to enjoy these wines during an airplane trip?

Economy class can be risky on Air France which may be why some passengers, no names please, bring their own. Air France crews, God bless them, find nothing *outré* in all this. In fact, they readily provide extra bread and cheese. Or so I am told.

Nebbiolo—Your Basic Italian Grape

ONE WAY to make sense out of the complex subject of wine is to break it down into components. Bordeaux, for example, would be a component of the wines of France. The Médoc would be a component of Bordeaux, and St.-Julien, say, would be a component of the Médoc. Disassembled that way, the subject begins to make sense.

Italy has always been a tougher nut to crack because the geographical breakdown does not work as well. The regions are not as well-known and there are some wines whose names, while famous, have nothing whatever to do with geography. Barolo, for example, is the name of a village; Barbera is the name of a grape.

Recently, Peter Morrell, a New York retailer, looking for a way to promote various Italian wines in his stock, came up with an interesting component of his own: the Nebbiolo grape. The Nebbiolo grape is the common denominator of a whole batch of interesting Italian wines that otherwise might be difficult to categorize, among them: Barolo, Barbaresco, Gattinara, Spanna, Inferno, Grumello, Ghemme, Sassella, and Valgella.

But those are only the better-known products of the ubiquitous Nebbiolo. There are a dozen other Nebbiolo-based wines—rarely seen outside of the regions where they are produced—including Boca, Fara, Sizzano, Lessona, Camiglione, Bricherasio, and Frossasco.

The name of the grape comes from the Italian word for fog, *nebbia*. Indeed the best Nebbiolo wines come from the northern regions of Italy where the fog clings to the hillsides on September mornings, much as it does in Burgundy. Piedmont and northern Lombardy are the greatest Nebbiolo-producing areas.

The best Nebbiolos—the Barolos, Barbarescos, and Gattinaras—are long-lived wines that may not reach their peak until ten years after fermentation. The lesser wines, including those simply listed as Nebbiolos, are usually at their best two or three years beyond the vintage date. Sometimes the lower-quality Nebbiolo grapes end up as sparkling wine which is rarely seen in this country. Often, lesser Nebbiolo wines are actually blends. Ghemme, for instance, may contain as much as 30 percent of the Vespolina grape and up to 15 percent of a grape called Bonarda Novarese. The best Ghemmes, however, will contain 80 or 85 percent Nebbiolo.

The finest of the Nebbiolo wines is almost certainly Barolo, which comes from the town of that name and several neighboring *com-*

ALCOHOL BY VOL. ~~12%~~ 11,5%
750 ML. (25.4 FL. OZ.)

ESTATE
BOTTLED

DOLCETTO D'ALBA

DENOMINAZIONE D'ORIGINE CONTROLLATA

PRODUCE
OF ITALY

PIEDMONT
RED WINE

CONF. DEPOSITATA

IMBOTTIGLIATO NELLA ZONA DI ORIGINE DA

BERSANO

ANTICO PODERE CONTI DELLA CREMOSINA
E CASTELLO DI BARBARESCO S.P.A.
SEDE IN NIZZA MONFERRATO (ITALIA)

Bottiglia numerata № 76472   383/AT

Otho Bensou

munes in the province of Cuneo in the Piedmont. This is a big, intense wine that not only needs long aging in wood and glass but which usually needs considerable aeration after the bottle has been opened.

The wine must have two years in wood and a year in the bottle before it can be sold. A Barolo Riserva must have four years' aging and a Riserva Speciale must have five.

Barbaresco, which is produced in several *communes* adjacent to the Barolo area, is also a 100 percent Nebbiolo wine. It is a rounder, softer wine than the Barolo and takes fewer years to age. The aging requirements are less stringent: two years for the regular Barbaresco, three for the Riserva, and four for the Riserva Speciale.

There are devotees of Italian wine who insist that the finest of all Italian wines is not Barolo (which was first produced by a Frenchman in the 19th century) or the legendary Brunello di Montalcino, but Gattinara, from a town of the same name north of the autostrada that connects Milan and Turin in the province of Vercelli.

In fact, even the older Barolos have a lack of finesse, for this writer, that keeps them out of the Pantheon of really great wines. There is a subtlety to some Gattinaras, however, that hints at a greatness other Italian wines may not always have. The wine must be four years old before it can be sold and two of those years must be spent aging in wood.

Gattinara also must be made from grapes grown on hillsides.

[207]

Grapes from the lower slopes and valley floors must bear a different name. In the case of the wines lower down the slopes from the Gattinara vines, the grapes and the wine they produce is called Spanna. Spanna (which, incidentally, is just another name for the Nebbiolo grape) appears now and then on some of the more enterprising Italian wine lists and it can be one of the best Italian wine buys available.

In Lombardy, the Nebbiolo grape produces such wines as Grumello, Inferno, and Sassella, produced in the Valtellina region. Grumello is probably the best although the Sassella producers are said to get the superior grapes. All three wines can be found in this country, though in limited quantities.

There are 12-year-old Barolos in the shops for under five dollars a bottle and Spannas of the same age for under $3.75 (1978). It is not impossible to still find 1955 Spannas for $12 and 1966 Barbarescos for $6 or less. Because Italian regulations make it imperative that these wines be properly aged, most are ready to drink when purchased but most of them will last much longer if properly stored. There can be considerable disparity in price, even within a vintage. Thus, a 1970 Gattinara under the Sogno di Baco label may sell for $4.75 while the same vintage under the Antoniolo label will be $5.98 and the 1967 under the Brugo label only $4.99.

The enthusiast will try several. One might be best for drinking immediately; one for holding for a few months or years. This fact is clear: in no other group of wines are there as many bargains as in the lesser-known Italian wines. How long this situation will last is difficult to predict. As French wines become more scarce, many wine lovers will turn to Italy.

A Day on the Mosel

EXCEPT ON WEEKENDS, the summer crush of tourists has ended in Bernkastel, this storybook little city on the Mosel River. Consequently, few people are yet aware of the extraordinary thing that has

happened in 1976 on the hills that climb dizzily up from Bernkastel's narrow cobblestone streets and tilted medieval buildings. It has been, simply, one of the greatest vintages of the last 100 years.

To understand something of what has happened it is necessary to know a little about German wines. They are rated by sugar content. The sweetest are the best. Sugar in grapes comes from the sun. Sunshine is a prized commodity in these steep, northern river valleys and, more than in any other wine region, success is measured in days, even hours, of warm sunlight.

To get as much of the precious warmth of the sun as possible, German vintners leave their grapes on the wines far into autumn. Some vintages have not been picked fully until December.

The bulk of German wine goes, as it does in most wine countries, into table wine for domestic consumption. Kabinett wines, with higher sugar concentrations, are the first level to qualify for export. Next come the Spätlese wines—deeper, richer, with still more sugar. Then there are Auslese wines, made not from bunches but from separate grapes selected for their richness in sugar.

Beerenauslese wines come from grapes that have been attacked by *botrytis cinerea*, a mold known as noble rot in English, *pourriture noble* in French and *edelfäule* here in Germany. The mold eats through the grapeskin, releases water in the fruit and leaves only concentrated juice.

At the top of this vineyard hagiography is the Trockenbeerenauslese, a special nectar produced in rare years where minute quantities of grapes achieve phenomenal levels of sugar content. The wine is complex, heavy, and possesses a bouquet that fills a room when a bottle is opened. A price of $60 a bottle is not unusual.

The quality of the 1976 vintage is so high that some vintners have more Trockenbeerenauslese than they do Kabinett wine. "I don't think we are going to make anything lower than Auslese," said Karl-Heinz Lauerburg, a prominent producer here and one of three owners of Germany's most famous vineyard, the Bernkasteler Doktor. In fact, Mr. Lauerburg, like other premium wine producers, may downgrade some of his wine, selling Beerenauslese as Auslese and Auslese as Spätlese.

At Schloss Schönborn, one of the famous wineries of the Rheingau, the quality of the grape "must"—unfermented juice—last week was unprecedented. The quantity of sugar is a measurement of specific gravity and is called the Oechsle rating. According to government figures, the highest Oechsle ratings for the 1911 vintage, a legendary one, were 99.5. In 1921 they reached 105.4. At Schloss Schönborn in Hattenheim, on the Rhine, last week, they reached 168 in one vineyard and 175 in another.

The minimum Oechsle grade for Auslese in the Rheingau, the region where Schloss Schönborn is located, is 95. This year, according to the estate manager, Robert Englert, nothing less than 110 Oechsle will be used. The minimum for Trockenbeerenauslese in the Rheingau is 150 Oechsle; Schloss Schönborn brought in grapes from the Erbacher Marcobrunn vineyard, of which they own a part, at 186.

Quality is down somewhat in the Rhine and Mosel Valleys, but that does not worry the wine producers. They are more concerned with selling the high quality wines they are producing. "Ordinarily, we would sell our highest quality wines at premium prices," one Rheingau vintner said, "but with everyone making these extraordinary wines, the shippers are going to hit us with low prices.

"Anyone who has the money to finance his crop and the space to store his own wines can hold on to these 1976's. In a few years they will make his fortune. But most of us will have to sell and it will be the shippers who will make the profits on these extraordinary wines.

"We could live ten years on this crop if we had the space and the money," said Mr. Lauerburg.

Actually, the excitement over the current vintage is no guarantee

BOTTLED BY

J. Lauerburg

WEINGUT — BERNKASTEL-MOSEL

PRODUCT OF GERMANY

1973
BERNKASTELER BADSTUBE
WHITE WINE
QUALITÄTSWEIN   MOSEL-SAAR-RUWER
Shipped by **H. SICHEL SÖHNE**, MAINZ
CONTENTS: A. P. Nr. 2576146014/74   ALCOHOL
1 PINT 7 FL. OZS.   9,5% BY VOL.

Schieffelin & Co.—New York
IMPORTERS SINCE 1794   SOLE U.S. DISTRIBUTORS

that the wines will live up to their expectations. Many things can happen between the picking and the drinking. One problem is always the balance between sugar and acid. High sugar content with low acid means a flabby, soft wine. Balance is everything.

In the Rheinhessen, the wine region south of Mainz and the Rheingau, the sugar contents are equally high, but the acid levels are low. The low-acid wines will have the beautiful natural sweetness expected of German wines, but they will lack the character of the more elegant wines of the Rheingau where the acid content is high. As a rule, units of acidity in German wine should amount to a tenth of the sugar density: 70 Oechsle should have at least 7.0 acidity.

One 1976 Lauerburg wine, an Auslese from the Badstube vineyard, had an Oechsle grade of over 110 and an acidity of about 10.0—an excellent balance. But a number of wines in the Rheinhessen were showing an acidity of 5.6 or lower.

German law does not require that a label show the sugar and acid content of a wine. Thus it is a good idea to stick to famous names from the Rheingau and the Mosel when buying German wines. There are, alas, dozens of them. Hopefully, a good wine merchant can help. Finding a good wine merchant is another problem.

Ironically, the unusual 1976 vintage in Germany comes right after the 1975 vintage which was also extremely good. The best of the 1975's, from the best vineyards of the Mosel and from the Rheingau, will not be released for another six months or so. But many of the lesser wines already are reaching the market, here in Germany and in the United States. They are beautifully balanced wines with great style. That is, they have excellent color and bouquet without being cloyingly sweet on one hand, or overly sharp and steely on the other. They are wines that will improve with age—even the Kabinett wines can use another year in the bottle—but can be drunk now and enjoyed. The 1975 German wines are classic: balanced, fruity, correct for light foods, and as apéritifs, except, of course, for the very highest quality wines which will be available to only a very few people at best.

The 1976's are something entirely different. It is as if General Motors took an advertisement in the newspaper tomorrow to announce that in 1977 only Cadillacs will be built and sold. More Cadillacs does not necessarily mean cheaper Cadillacs.

Tasting the '61s at Château Latour

SERENE AND ELEGANT, Château Latour stands in a tiny park surrounded by vineyards. To the east, the vines march in perfect rows down to the wide, muddy Gironde, the river that carries Bordeaux wines to the sea and the world beyond. The vines and the river are framed by the windows in the ornate, Victorian dining room.

It is a classic Bordeaux scene and the perfect setting for a tasting of classic Bordeaux wines. Not many years ago, five château owners and managers, a wine broker, and a journalist met around the burnished circular dining table in that room for a tasting of what generally is recognized as one of the great Bordeaux vintages of our time: 1961.

Tastings of this order are serious affairs in the United States, as indeed they often are here in France. Talking is frowned on except for a few words in hushed tones. Brows are furrowed and stares fixed.

Tasting the '61s at Château Latour

Noses are buried in glasses seeking to sniff out the mysteries of the grape. Wine is sipped, slurped, and spit out, lest an expert become inebriated and, consequently, less expert. Notes are scribbled, erased, and scribbled again. In short, a most serious business. And a hard one. Attempting to fathom the qualities of a wine and somehow to articulate the senses of taste and smell is no easy task.

The Latour tasting was cognizant of all these things but it was like no serious tasting this writer had ever attended previously.

To begin with, the tasting was part of a full-course meal. The first four wines came with the first course, a magnificent jambon de bayonne. The second four wines came with the main course, a filet of beef; and the last three were served with the cheese. "There is no reason why we should not enjoy ourselves," said Henri Martin, a director of Latour, owner of Château Gloria, Mayor of St. Julien-Beychevelle, and organizer of the tasting.

Each group of wines was removed before the next group was poured, but the cellar master of Latour, who served them would pour any of the 11 for anyone interested in back-tasting. There was no spitting and, since the wines were mostly excellent, quite a bit was consumed. "We are happy," said Jean-Eugene Borie, "but we are certainly not drunk." No, but it was a good thing we ate the meal while we were tasting.

At the end of the meal, or at least before the soufflé and Sauternes, the names of the wines were revealed: Châteaus Gloria, Haut-Batailley, Lynch-Bages, Beychevelle, Ducru-Beaucaillou, Pétrus, and the five first growths, Haut-Brion, Lafite-Rothschild, Latour, Margaux, and Mouton Rothschild. The first four served were: Gloria, Haut-Batailley, Lynch-Bages, and Beychevelle. Next came Ducru, Mouton, Margaux, and Haut-Brion. Finally Pétrus, Lafite, and Latour.

By universal agreement, Château Pétrus was the best. It had depth and power—all the best wines did—but it was rounder and more pleasing than the others. It was easily the wine among the best ones in the tasting most ready to drink.

Château Latour was second. Most of the tasters felt it had really not yet developed—that it might be five years before it was ready to drink. It was the hardest of the wines and had the least forthright bouquet.

The disappointment of the tasting was Château Beychevelle which often manages to compete with the biggest name wines. In this case it was really the poorest wine in the lot. It was brown, thin, and sharp. In short, far over the hill. Château Gloria did not fare too well at this tasting. It, too, was past its prime.

Almost without exception, the first growths got the highest ratings in the tastings, although not everyone ranked them the same way. This writer's ranking went like this: Pétrus, Lafite, Haut-Brion, Latour, Margaux, Mouton, Ducru-Beaucaillou, Lynch-Bages, Haut-Batailley, Gloria, Beychevelle.

Later someone said that Beychevelle was going through a bad period in the early 1960's and that the vineyard has been considerably replanted since then. Short-lived Merlot grapes were replaced by Cabernet Sauvignon. Most of the wines of the great châteaus are blends of Cabernet and Merlot. In Pomerol where Pétrus is located, and in St.-Emilion, Merlot predominates. In the Médoc and the Graves, Cabernet is more important.

No tasting is completely fair to the wines involved if only because of the limitations of the tasters. The 1961 tasting, by presenting the wines in an ascending order of prominence, undoubtedly favored the first growths served near the end. They may even have benefitted by being drunk with the cheese.

No matter. It was a memorable occasion. No wine enthusiasts would quibble about the conditions when offered an opportunity to sample 11 great 1961 Bordeaux.

The tasters, in addition to Mr. Martin, Mr. Borie, who owns Haut-Batailley and Ducru-Beaucaillou, and this writer, were Jean-Paul Gardere, the managing director of Château Latour, Jean-Louis Mandrau, his chief assistant, John-Louis Triaud, Mr. Martin's assistant at Château Gloria, and Bernard Haramboure, a *courtier en vins*, or wine broker, in Pauillac.

A Little Vodka, Maestro

THE WORLD LOVES Gary Graffman for his Rachmaninoff; his friends love him for his tangerine vodka. This may be because so many of his friends also play the piano. Or, it may be because his tangerine vodka is something quite exceptional. But then, so is his lime vodka and his lemon vodka, not to mention his grapefruit vodka and his chili pepper vodka.

Grapefruit vodka? Gary Graffman? Why is a renowned pianist peeling grapefruit when he could be playing a Transcendental Etude? "It's a hobby," he explains. "A pastime. Everyone seems to like it so I keep doing it."

Flavored vodka is like one of Schumann's "Kinderscenen" to Mr. Graffman. As a boy here in New York in the 1930's, he sampled the vodka his Russian-born parents drank—and found it good. "They dropped a lemon peel in the bottle to flavor it," he said. "When I got to thinking about it, I said: 'If lemon, why not lime? If lime, why not orange?' "

The freezer compartment in the Graffman's bar refrigerator holds the answers to these questions: a collection of various flavored vodkas, all prepared by the master's hand. They are served ice-cold in tiny, stemmed silver glasses from Pakistan, souvenirs of Gary and Naomi Graffman's ceaseless wanderings over the globe.

Vodka—plain vodka—is nothing more than distilled neutral grain spirits. Cheap vodka—and most vodka is cheap vodka—has a powerful medicinal smell and a raw taste in the back of the mouth. There is a natural tendency to ameliorate the effects of this stuff with orange juice, tomato juice, or anything else at hand.

The Russians and the Poles learned long ago that doctoring vodka was not such a bad idea. Zubrovka, vodka flavored with buffalo grass, and Pertsovka, vodka flavored with pepper, are old favorites in Eastern Europe. They are even made commercially and imported to the United States.

Perched on a stool behind the bar in his cavernous midtown apartment the other day, Mr. Graffman served a commercial Pertsovka he had carried home from the Ukraine, along with a pepper vodka he had made himself.

There was no comparison. His was a big, strong, fiery mouthful that tasted more like concentrated peppercorns than something flavored with pepper. The Russian concoction was pale and weak. "Think of this with smoked salmon," Mr. Graffman exclaimed. "You put pepper on the salmon anyway. Why not have it in the apéritif?"

Mr. Graffman favors a mixture of peppers, his being from Hediard, the elegant gourmet shop that competes with Fauchon on the Place de la Madeleine. It is a mixture of black, grey, and Jamaican pepper. "I try to get the peppercorns," he said, "but last week they were out. I had to take a bottle of crushed pepper."

Gary Graffman is one of the busiest musicians in the world. He plays a staggering schedule of concerts, flying more than 100,000 miles a year. ("Some day I want to do an article on airline food," he said with a grim smile.) Because they spend so much of their time in jets and motels, Gary and Naomi Graffman devote much of their precious spare time to good food and drink.

"Naomi is the serious cook," Mr. Graffman said. "I do ducks and chickens on the spit in the fireplace."

The Graffmans are enthusiastic and knowledgeable wine drinkers, but they find it difficult to drink anything but vodka as an apéritif. "Everyone asks for it," he said.

The tangerine vodka is probably the most popular. Like all the fruit-flavored vodkas, it is made by immersing the fruit peel in a half-gallon of a name-brand domestic vodka, usually Smirnoff.

"You look for a good, fresh piece of fruit," Mr. Graffman said, "one with plenty of oil in the skin." He prowls the Ninth Avenue markets for his, when he isn't bringing strange fruits or seeds home as trophies from one of his concert trips.

"You need the zest—the peel—of about four fruits for a gallon of vodka," he said. "I leave it in a closet, at room temperature, for about 72 hours. But that's the beauty of this thing—you can make it as strong or as light as you like."

Mr. Graffman shakes up his vodka jugs every 12 hours, then, after three days, strains the vodka through a sieve into a clean bottle or into several bottles. In Russia, vodka lovers flavor their spirits with tea, cherry pits, anise, even ginger. Mr. Graffman once used the peel of loranges, a combination of lemons and oranges grown near Livermore in California.

There used to be a store near 105th Street on Broadway that carried imported Russian buffalo grass but it is out of business now and Gary Graffman has no new source. He still has about a quart of homemade Zubrovka with the long stalks of buffalo grass in the bottle. It has a unique, almost vanilla-like flavor.

For his pepper vodka, he adds a bottlecap-full of peppercorns, or crushed pepper to a half-gallon of vodka. The pepper throws a brownish-green deposit which must be filtered out. Like the fruit vodkas, it takes about three days to reach the strength that the Graffmans like.

To make his own aquavit, he adds about a capful of caraway seeds, a few sprigs of fennel, and a bit of lemon peel to the half-gallon of vodka. "It goes beautifully with herring," Mr. Graffman said.

An experimental Pertsovka, made with hot Mexican peppers—one pepper is left in the bottle—tasted like the perfect companion for furnace-like Mexican food. The Graffman lime-flavored vodka had an artificial lime bouquet but a pure, fresh lime taste. The grapefruit vodka had a true grapefruit taste but lacked the intensity of some other flavors. Mr. Graffman does not take his success with vodka-flavoring too seriously. "I never use a really good imported vodka," he said. "It seems sort of a waste."

Counting Our Blessings, Winewise

HAVEN'T PICKED OUT your wine for Thanksgiving dinner? Well, don't look here for help. If you were hoping for yet another red-with-the-meat, white-with-the-fish lecture, forget it. This is an unabashed, heart-on-the-sleeve Thanksgiving story.

Let's face it: Thanksgiving is a peculiarly American, heart-on-the-sleeve kind of day. We do have a lot to be thankful for and, while it sounds a bit presumptuous, wine enthusiasts may actually have more to be thankful for than many others.

The simple fact is that we constitute the most favored wine drinking community in the world. True, we rank only about 31st among the nations in the amount of wine we consume, but we probably drink more good wine than any other nation in the world. And not just in terms of price though, heaven knows, we can probably afford to spend more on wine than anyone else.

No, we simply have more good wine available than anyone else and that goes for the French and the Italians who annually drink more than 15 times as much wine as we do. For all their vast production, neither country provides its wine drinking population with anything to match our inexpensive jug wines.

Not long ago, a Bordeaux château owner seriously proposed that France's vin ordinaire be abandoned for a wine-type product made from water and flavorings. "That part of our market," he told me, "is so completely mired in bureaucratic muddling, politics, and corruption that the best thing we could do would be to switch the vineyards of the Midi over to grazing land or some other crop and start from scratch with the wine market."

Our own wine industry has had its own problems with fraud and corruption but they have been minuscule compared to Europe. Even at the lowest levels, our vintners produce excellent wines. Moreover, there is no ceiling whatsoever on quality. As vineyards mature and as our collective taste improves, our wines will improve, too.

Twenty years ago, Petite Sirah and Carignane were indifferent blending grapes. Today, thanks to the growing skill of both the winemakers and the grape growers, both varieties produce fine wines. Even more recently, the idea that California or New York could produce a great Chardonnay or Riesling was considered naïve. Today, they rival some of their European counterparts.

California remains the verdant font from which most of our wine blessings flow, but each day, it seems, some surprising new wine appears in New York or Michigan or Virginia or even Rhode Island or Massachusetts. The definitive book on American wines, Leon Adams' *The Wines of America*, remained definitive about two or three months after it was published a few years back. Mr. Adams has to run just to stay in place. New wineries open up almost faster than he can list them, and certainly faster than he can revise his book.

But it is not just American wines that overflow our larder. Even the most plastic shopping centers in mid-America contain liquor stores with wine selections unobtainable anywhere else in the world. It is not unusual to read an advertisement in a newspaper placed by a shop boasting of its selection of more than a thousand different wines.

For several hundred years, the British have prided themselves on the catholicity of their wine tastes. "We don't make our own wines," they were fond of saying, "so we have become connoisseur of everyone else's."

True enough, as far as it goes. They are still tops when it comes to claret. Moreover, the invasion of the British wine world by the big breweries has resulted in modern shops with extensive selections. But there is nothing in Great Britain to match the great wine shops of our big cities. The range of wines available to us, not just among the great wines of the world, but in all price ranges, is incomparable.

What's more, choice to some extent governs price. If Beaujolais soars out of reach, the Parisian has to shrug and buy a Minervois or Corbières, second-rate stuff. The New Yorker can switch to a Rioja from Spain, a Cabernet from Rumania, anyone of a dozen fine Chiantis from Italy, or to any one of an almost endless array of American wines.

Counting Our Blessings, Winewise

Not only does he get a good wine, he affects the price of Beaujolais. When, for several reasons, Americans balked at French wine prices in 1972 and 1973, the market quickly collapsed. It could happen again.

It goes even beyond that. With the choice he has, the American consumer has a great deal to say, however indirectly, about quality. Every few months, some producer in Europe or South America or North Africa launches a new wine in this country in an attempt to cash in on our lucrative market. Five years ago, some rather poor wines gained a foothold on the strength of foreign labels and American inexperience. Most of them are gone now, and new ones that do not measure up quickly fall by the wayside.

Lest this Pollyanna-like mood get out of hand, it is worth noting that there are dangers inherent in some of the best features of our bountiful wine world. The most serious is the real danger that bigness, spurred on by mass marketing will eventually do to wine what it has done to automobiles, television, and frozen food. We will have the ultimate American wine: gaudily packaged, highly praised, and totally lacking in character. Remember the Marmon and the Duesenberg and the Cord? They were, in their own way, Lafites, Moutons, and Haut-Brions.

But this is no time to worry about all that. Or about the fact that there are still controlled states where you must buy your wine from the government, just as there are states where it is impossible to buy a bottle of wine in a grocery store. Let's be thankful for what we have—the best wine environment in the world.

And if you really haven't any idea what wine to buy for Thanksgiving dinner, go out and get some 1976 Beaujolais. Chill it a bit, relax, and enjoy. As Miles Standish may or may not have said: "You never had it so good."

[219]

Master of Wine—Or Mistress?

I HAD, with regrets, just turned down an invitation to a challenging tasting and was idly considering the excellent wines I would miss. Then I saw a line on the invitation that I had not noticed before. It said: "Afternoon Program for the Ladies."

The assumption, obviously, was that most of the women who would come would not be interested in trying the wines. For all I know, the assumption was accurate. I also know of quite a few households where, had I sent off a similar notice, I would be marked for serious bodily harm.

The fact is that women are into wine. There is even a mystique surrounding this new enthusiasm and it goes something like this:

Women have better palates because they are constantly critiquing their own food. They are better than men with bouquets and aromas because they are constantly dabbling in perfumes and colognes, and they are good on wine colors because they are up on interior decorating and clothes.

I have a different theory and it goes like this:

Women are becoming more and more interested in wine for two reasons. First, because they like the taste of it and, second, because they buy most of it, particularly in states where wine can be sold in supermarkets.

If women seem to have more acute sensory perceptions it may be simply because they try harder. Professionals who teach wine courses often say that the women in their classes are more enthusiastic and concentrate more intensely than the men.

All of which brings me to the subject of this piece, Serena Sutcliffe, a London wine consultant and broker and one of two women Masters of Wine in the world. A tall, Katharine Hepburn-ish woman of 32 with great poise and charm, Miss Sutcliffe recently completed a three-week trip around the United States, talking to wine clubs and becoming acquainted with some of our wines and the people who make them.

"I don't think women are really any better equipped than men to appreciate wines," she said, sipping Perrier in an east-side bar. "Oh, perhaps their palates are less abused, but I'm not at all sure about that. I do know that I got good questions from the women at my talks, and usually they constituted half of the audiences."

[220]

Miss Sutcliffe's own introduction to wine began back in the 1960's when she first went to Paris as a translator. "I started buying a bottle or two," she said, "then I started visiting the wine regions on holidays and weekends. I told myself I was going for historical reasons. Finally a friend told me, 'Look here, you're interested in wine, not history,' and, of course, it was true."

Gradually, the tall young Englishwoman began to make friends in the wine country, particularly in Burgundy and the Loire, which are not all that far from Paris. "I began helping out in the vineyards and the cellars," she said, "and all the time, I was talking, tasting, and learning."

Gradually, Miss Sutcliffe began buying wine for her friends in Paris. "I was hooked," she said laughing, "but I didn't realize it until one day I went home to my flat on the Ile de la Cité, opened the door and all the cases tumbled out.

"I decided to find work in the wine trade," she said, "and I knew I had to go back to England to do it. In France they are too area conscious. In Burgundy they know only Burgundy; in Bordeaux only Bordeaux.

"I wrote 12 letters to London firms. All 12 answered, saying they didn't exactly know where to fit me in. Anyway, I got a job with Rutherfords which is part of Martini & Rossi and that's where I began to learn the wine business."

While working in London, Miss Sutcliffe began to work at becoming a Master of Wine. The English wine trade is probably the oldest in the modern world—older certainly than the trade in Paris. The Company of Vintners, the ancient wine guild, traces its origins back to the time of the Norman conquest when ships from Bordeaux and La Rochelle regularly unloaded their cargoes of French wines on the London docks.

The wine trade's standards had always been high but after World War II, it was decided to formalize some of those standards and the title of Master of Wine was created. The title is still limited to people in the wine trade and the course of study has always been long and arduous.

"It can be expensive, too," Miss Sutcliffe said. "Just buying the wines I had to taste cost me a good part of what I earned." She took the long and difficult series of examinations in 1976—and passed. Involved were a variety of written tests not only on oenology and viticulture but on marketing, importing, even retailing. And there were series of blind tastings—reds, whites, sparkling wines, even Ports, and Sherries.

[221]

"I made it," she said proudly. "You're supposed to have been in the trade a minimum of five years. I did it in just a bit under."

With the initials M.W. on her business card, Serena Sutcliffe took two major steps, sequentially. She quit her job at Rutherford's ("I think my boss rather resented my being a Master of Wine, since he wasn't."), and she got married—to David Peppercorn, himself a Master of Wine.

"It caused a sensation in the trade," she said with a grin. "It was all so incestuous. Actually, it was a perfect match because our cellars were so compatible. David had a lot of magnificent old wines he'd inherited from his father and I had all my beautiful 1966's and 1970's."

The Peppercorns, with their wines and a telex machine, inhabit an old townhouse behind Oxford Street not far from the center of London. Both are highly successful wine consultants. David Peppercorn for many years had been a buyer for I.D.V., a vast British combine of breweries, distilleries, and wine operations. He went independent in 1974, two years before his future wife. They were married in 1977.

Miss Sutcliffe travels in Europe, mostly France, for about a week out of every month. "A small grocery chain will say to me: 'Find us a good Mâcon Blanc,' or a mail-order house may need some 1973 small châteaus from Bordeaux. My job is to find them."

Often producers in France or Italy will ask her to find them customers in England. "David and I might work together on that," she said. "He may have a customer for my producer."

Although married only 10 months, Miss Sutcliffe discovered a new love on her recent American trip. "I am absolutely impassioned by the California wine scene," she declared. "If only I had had more time there.

"We had a tasting of California Merlots and St.-Emilions in Los Angeles," she said. "It was great because it wasn't competitive. It was just for general interest and quality evaluation and the California wines showed beautifully." Merlot, by the way, is the principal grape of the St.-Emilion region of Bordeaux. Only recently has it become popular in California.

"I hate the idea that California wines must compete with the French," Miss Sutcliffe said. "Each has a lot to teach the other. Does California really want to be Europe? They must decide what they really want to do. . . ."

All this seems to have strayed from the theme of women and wine. Perhaps that is as it should be. After joining Serena Sutcliffe for a tasting recently, a prominent American wine specialist said:

"Serena, after all, isn't a woman who happens to be a wine expert. She is a first-rate wine expert who happens to be a woman."

A Little British Humor

EVERY TIME another of my articles on French wines appears, a strange rumbling and muttering rolls out of the west—where the Californians have been known to grow a grape or two—and down from the hills of Hammondsport where the New York wine men toil.

Well, it is true. The French have always gotten better than a fair shake. But this is true of most wine writing in this country. A lot of us are hopeless Francophiles and it shows.

Not so the English. They have been around a long time, much of it battling in one way or another with their nearest neighbors on the continent, the French. No matter that they practically invented the Bordeaux wine trade. No matter that they continue to be among the best customers for French wine. Let's just say they have fewer illusions.

As a result, they are much harder on the Frenchmen when they feel they've stepped out of line. Take the case of the recent wine scandals. While we tended to shuffle our feet and look embarrassed, the British tended to be outraged. One way to manifest outrage is in humor. Which is exactly what some fellow named Miles Kington did in *Punch* in a piece called "Where Do Bordeaux Wines Really Come From?" We quote generously herewith.

At the outset, Mr. Kington puts to rest the misconception that the wine situation and the oil crisis have something in common.

"For one thing," he writes, "new sources of Bordeaux wine are being found every day in countries all over the world. For another, ordinary Bordeaux wine has a slightly fruitier taste than oil."

Addressing himself to the question of where wine comes from, Mr. Kington explains: "A really good wine can start life as a rough vintage in Morocco or Australia, travel across the sea to France to become a modest local growth, and end life as one of the finest clarets money can buy.

"But," he warns, "it must be carefully guarded during this process in case it is contaminated by the gaze of the tax inspector or in case it accidentally ends up as a Spanish red."

There are, Mr. Kington tells us, three important wine-growing areas in the Bordeaux region: "A huge mixing vat not far from the city, a lorry depot to the south, and a vast tanker installation near the coast."

His definition of the term "château" should lay that mystery to rest for the foreseeable future. It is, Mr. Kington, explains, "the French word for the little drawing of a castle that many firms like to put on the label to encourage confidence in the wine. Some of these châteaus are very big and important," he goes on to say, "which means more money being spent on the ink for the label. . . ."

Mr. Kington insists that under French law, the word *château* cannot be put on a wine label unless it is spelled correctly.

His notes on winemaking are particularly enlightening, to wit:

"The process of wine-producing starts with the traditional ceremony of treading the invoices. The invoices, import documents, and tax returns are all put into a large vat," Mr. Kington explains, "and there trodden by several accountants until the ink has begun to run a juicy blue colour.

"The documents are then removed and carefully treated so that the wine begins to mature into something much better than the rough Tunisian it may have started as."

Next, according to our author, "comes the long period of fermentation and filtering during which all impure elements must be removed from the label." At this point, he goes on, "the wine is awarded its so-called 'cru.' " *Cru*, in French, means "thought to be," Mr. Kington tells us. "Thus, a *premier cru* is thought to be first class."

Like any conscientious wine writer, Mr. Kington winds up with that essential bit of pedantry, the list of definitions. Here are a few:

Young—the ink on the label is still wet.

Pétillant (French for sparkling)—some lemonade has been added.

Sediment—the accumulation at the bottom of the wine of fragments of torn invoices, twigs, old labels, etc.

Full-bodied—will stain the table indelibly.

Light-bodied—will not stain the table too badly.

Bin—place where they throw unusable wine, ready for blending with usable wine.

Mis en bouteilles—means bottled and is a guarantee that the wine is not in a tank. *Mis en bouteilles au château*—the wine was bottled and labelled at the same time.

Lest Mr. Kington feel he has been too severely plundered here, he should know that he will have completely free access to our monograph on American jug wines, soon to be released. It discusses the significance of the IBM 360 in wine blending, along with the vital roles of the marketing man and the public relations consultant in American viticulture. It will be called "God, Sun, and Soil."

Sebastiani

IT IS 5:30 A.M. On a hill behind the picture book little city of Sonoma, California, a white Chevy pickup comes to life. Behind the wheel is a 65-year-old millionaire who thinks he is a simple farmer. A worn denim jacket buttoned against the predawn chill and Big Boy striped bib overalls cover his ample frame. A rancher's wide-brimmed straw hat only partially obscures his assertive Florentine nose.

August Sebastiani is headed, as he is every morning at this time, for breakfast at the Lazy Dee, a ramshackle hash house a mile or so out of town on Route 12, the main road out of the valley south to San Francisco. Among the farmers, ranch hands, deliverymen, and other early risers at the Lazy Dee, August is one of the crowd, at least during breakfast.

He is, in fact, president and chief operating officer of Sebastiani Vineyards, a one-time unknown supplier of tank-car wine that has, in just a few short years, become the hottest name in the booming California wine business. He is also the patriarch of a vital Italian-American family that has, for half a century, dominated the life of this corner of the California wine country.

August Sebastiani is the son of a poor Italian immigrant, but he himself was never less than well-off. Still, his newfound success is disconcerting. "It scares me," he says, contemplating new sales figures, "it really scares me. I don't know what we're doing, but we must be doing it right."

What the Sebastianis are doing is riding the crest of America's love affair with wine. As recently as 1966, they produced some 30,000 cases of wine a year. This year they are expected to ship up to 2.5-million cases.

"Either by design or accident, the Sebastianis have positioned themselves perfectly for today's market," said an admiring competitor. "Their lower-end wines are perfect for the new drinkers coming off sugary jug wines and their higher-end premium wines, while maybe not the match of some of the best of the 'boutique' wines, are among the best bargains in the fine wine business."

Actually, in tastings, Sebastiani premium wines consistently do as well or better than competitors' wines costing half again as much. In 1976, for instance, at the Los Angeles County Fair, against some of the most famous wineries in the state, Sebastiani wines won more awards than anyone else.

When August Sebastiani says "We must be doing something right," he is using the family we, not the corporate one. There are some 140 employees in the winery—a sprawling collection of tanks and warehouses on the east edge of Sonoma—but the family is always in charge.

Sam, 37, intense and self-assured, is August's eldest son and heir apparent. He is overall manager of winery operations and his father's close confidant. Don, 25, voluble and ebullient, is the second son and key outside man, happy to give talks and tastings anywhere. Fourth man in the tight management group is Richard Cuneo, who is married to August's daughter, Maryann. The Sebastianis say they made Dick their controller because his family came from Genoa, the traditional seat of Italian banking.

In classic Mediterranean style, Sebastiani life centers not on the office, as it does for so many successful American men, but on the home which, for August, is a huge Tuscan-style stone mansion he built a decade ago two hundred yards up the hill from the winery.

The head of the Sebastiani household is Sylvia Sebastiani, 62, a renowned cook and unflappable hostess, who can entertain a dozen wine salesmen on 30 minutes' notice while minding two infant grandchildren and planning a party for 30 relatives.

In an age of corporate subservience, when businessmen see their wives on weekends and are expected to move to another split-level every two years, the Sebastianis represent a return to an earlier ethic, when families stayed close, when emotion was not a weakness, and when to work together, eat well, and celebrate life was not a barrier to success.

The Sebastianis have been very successful. 'One night Sylvia said to me, 'August, what are we worth?' " the head of the family said recently. "I told her, 'Momma, I have no idea.' I hate to even make a guess because if it got out, and anything happened to me, that would be the figure everyone would use. Whether it was right or not."

The Sebastiani label says "Vineyards Established in 1825." Perhaps, but not by them. The Franciscan monks were the first vintners in this region. Sonoma, which is 60 miles north of San Francisco, was the northernmost of the Camino Real—the last Spanish mission in the chain that began in San Diego.

The first Sebastiani in California, August's father Samuele, arrived in Sonoma in 1895, to carve cobblestones for the streets of San Francisco. Born in Farnetta, near Lucca in Tuscany, he had landed in San Francisco, penniless, two years earlier at the age of 14. Within a decade he had saved enough to buy an abandoned winery and start his own business. Some of Samuele's original equipment today stands in a place of honor outside the Sebastiani winery.

Samuele Sebastiani was the complete padrone. When the local theater burned down, he built a new one. It is still there—the Sebastiani Theater. He built a bowling alley, a skating rink, a bus terminal, a hotel, and an apartment building. He built 52 houses for his workers and, as late as World War II, still was renting them out for $18 and $20 a month. He built and paved local streets and at one time had a private water system larger than the city's.

He built a fruit cannery that, when Prohibition closed in, provided jobs for his winery workers and an outlet for the fruit grown by farmers who no longer had any reason to grow grapes. "I thought he was crazy, diversifying," August said. "I wanted him to put everything in the wine business. Had he listened to me, we would have been broke when Prohibition came."

The elder Sebastiani made a lot of money but once he went broke, too. In 1923, he got caught in a wildly fluctuating market, couldn't sell his wine, and couldn't pay his suppliers.

"He actually was bankrupt," his son August recalled. "Only no one knew it except the guys he owed money to. He went to all the farmers he owed and gave them notes. In 1931, he paid the last one off. He was the kind of guy who didn't believe in bankruptcy. His word and his reputation were too valuable to him."

In his later years, Samuele Sebastiani was prosperous enough to tear around the Sonoma Valley in a Cadillac roadster, oblivious of the speed limits, and to hobnob with other well-to-do immigrants, including A.P.Giannini, founder of the Bank of America.

"My dad used to keep a flask of brandy in that roadster," August said, "and the cops used to stop him once in a while so they could all have a drink. Here at the winery, he used to take old man Giannini down to a little private tasting room he had where they'd drink grappa. With all the hollering and yelling, I used to think they were fighting. Hell, they were just having a good time."

Samuele Sebastiani was in the bulk wine business—a profitable trade and an uncomplicated one. "We'd make a million gallons a year," August said, "and most of it was gone before the next crush. We didn't have to tie money up in cooperage (barrels for aging wine) or in aging (while wine is storing it obviously brings in no cash). The money was in the processing."

August began bottling his own wines after his father's death in 1944. According to one story, Sylvia returned from a bridge party one day, extolling the Sherry she had been served. "Why don't you make a Sherry like that," she asked. He recognized the name. "I do make it," he replied, resolving on the spot that henceforth Sebastiani wines would bear the Sebastiani name. In 1953, the first Sebastiani labels appeared, joining the long list of Italian names associated with California wines, from Guasti to Gallo, from Mondavi to Martini, most of them like the Sebastianis, family firms, passed from father to son.

California wineries come in all sizes, from Gallo, with its quarter of a million cases a day, to the few remaining backdoor wineries, where inexpensive jug wines are sold at a counter in the garage, usually by the winemaker's wife.

The Sebastianis, like the Martinis in Napa, the Fetzers in Mendocino, and the Mirassous in Santa Clara, try for the middle road: premium wines in quantities large enough for national distribution, while remaining independent family businesses.

More and more, California vintners, particularly those in the premium wine business, are narrowing their lines to a few items that sell the best. After all, Château Lafite-Rothschild sells one product— an expensive red wine. Sebastiani Vineyards honors an older tradition in California, that of the full line. At the moment, there are 34 different wines under the Sebastiani label, from rare old Cabernet Sauvignons to Vermouths and sparkling wines, made and bottled for them elsewhere.

Much of the present Sebastiani volume—and income—is due to a phenomenally successful group of wines called mountain varietals. These are blends of very good wine from the best grapes and inexpensive wine purchased from bulk producers in less attractive growing areas than the Sonoma Valley. This cheaper line helps to pay the bills; and it makes it possible for the Sebastianis to hold wine for aging without worrying about notes coming due.

There are still thousands of cases of Sebastiani Cabernet Sauvignon of the 1968 vintage in the winery. The Sebastianis dole it out whenever and to whomever they see fit. There are even 1000 cases of the 1941 Cabernet, bottled in 1947, still awaiting August's signal to be released.

August Sebastiani was born and raised in a sprawling California country-style home next door to the winery and a two-minute walk from where he lives now. His sister still lives in the old family home. His wife, Sylvia, née Scarafoni, was born on a dairy farm 100 miles east of Sonoma but grew up, after her family moved, a few doors away from the Sebastiani family home. She and August went to high school together, worked in the Sebastiani cannery together and were married in 1936. He was 23; she was 20.

Most of Sylvia's cooking specialties—well-known Italian dishes with a California flavor—have been collected in a book called *Mangiamo*. It is one of the winery's best promotional tools. Special guests get autographed copies. They contribute nicely to the personal touch the Sebastianis work to impart.

"There is no Mr. Almadén," says Don Sebastiani, "and there hasn't been a Paul Masson for a long time. There is a Mr. Sebastiani, and a Mrs. Sebastiani, and we want people to know it."

From time to time, August wanders through the tasting rooms to hear what the tourists have to say and to keep an eye on the people who serve them. Once in a while, someone recognizes him from the national advertisements showing him in his famous overalls. Mostly, he is unrecognized—at least until he offers a pretty girl a free bottle of wine in exchange for a kiss.

August Sebastiani is a restless, driven man and his energy has taken him beyond the wine business once or twice during his life. He was a cattle rancher and for a time owned a plumbing business. He loves to hunt and keeps a boat for frequent fishing trips, often with journalists whose company he enjoys and whose value to Sebastiani he fully understands.

These days he spends a lot of time on birds. He is a recognized authority on waterfowl and his collection of rare doves is said to be one of the finest in the world. He often supplies unusual birds to zoos who can find no other source. Always in the background at the family home is the cooing and clucking of the hundreds of birds that live in aviaries behind the house, and the occasional screams of the multi-colored peacocks who stroll arrogantly around the lawns and drive-ways. There is also a wildlife preserve at the 500 acre ranch in Schellville, down the road from the Lazy Dee. During the migrating season, August often supplies his winged guests with 250 pounds of feed a day.

The Sebastianis grow some of the grapes for their premium wines, but most come from other farmers in the area. In 1975, when there was a glut of grapes, August bought them when other wineries did not—but at his price. "Sure, grapes were going for $600 a ton in 1973," he said, "but what did that mean in 1975—nothing. I paid $175, take it or leave it. I was being Santa Claus and they said I was hard on them."

The following year, when other wineries were reveling in the fact that grapes were overabundant and cheap, August quietly signed a number of growers to long-term contracts. Prices climbed again dur-ing the California drought, but the Sebastianis were assured of a good supply. "Let's just say that I've been at this a long, long time," August said, grinning.

For the moment, at least, the sky is the limit for the Sebastianis. They have doubled the winery capacity in recent years and there are vague plans for a vast new plant, perhaps on property they own out near the Schellville Ranch. But growth is a mixed blessing. "We're going to have to zip it down, one of these days," August says. "We simply can't accumulate enough capital on our own to keep up with the demand we're getting."

He takes a visitor through the winery tasting room to make his point. Dozens of tourists are lined up at the bar. "We have 18 people working here," he says, "and we need more. I remember when anyone who wanted to see the place had to ring the doorbell. The accountant would put aside the books and show them around. I'm not sure it wasn't more fun then. But what can we do? We have a tiger by the tail."

An official of a large food company with interests in the wine business predicts that the younger Sebastianis will be "more receptive to the realities of corporate life." In other words, that they will sell out to keep the business expanding after their father retires.

Sam and Don say no—never. And there is no indication at the moment that August is about to quit. "I'll never do it," he said flatly. "I even avoid retired friends. You get a guy who was an astute banker a few years ago and now he only wants to tell you about his geraniums."

Ordering a guest into the pickup, he drives out to the Schellville Ranch and stops near some small new vines. "You look at these fellows and worry over them," he said, "and at the same time you're anticipating what kind of wine they will make years from now. It's a wonderful business. I could never give it up. Never."

A Yank in Champagne

THE HIRED CAR pulled in through the gates of Maison Ricciuti, one of the small Champagne firms along the main street of Avenay, a town in the center of France's Champagne region. The driver, a vacationing steelmaker from Birmingham, Alabama, pulled to a stop in the courtyard and hailed the first man he saw. In his few, halting words of French he tried to make it known that he wanted Champagne.

The man outside the car listened for a moment, then broke into a broad grin and said: "Why don't you speak English like everyone else around here?"

"I don't get a chance to do that very often," Albert Ricciuti said over a bottle of Champagne at his kitchen table here one day recently. "Most tourists head for the big Champagne houses in Epernay. They have no idea there is an ex-G.I. making Champagne just a few miles away."

Avenay is about three miles from Epernay but 4,000 miles from Baltimore, where Al Ricciuti was born and raised. He first came to this little town on the banks of the Marne in 1944 when his infantry unit was part of General George S. Patton's Third Army.

"We were bivouacked here three days," he recalled. "A couple of my friends had met some girls and had been invited to dinner. I knew a little French so they asked me along." Not unexpectedly, Mr. Ricciuti met one of the girls and eventually married her. Her family was in the Champagne business and now so is he.

But it wasn't the usual army love story. After the war he returned to

[231]

Baltimore and began a career in the National Guard. From time to time, he corresponded with Paulette Revolte, the girl he had met. "Nothing serious," he says now. Neither of them ever married. Then, in 1962, Mr. Ricciuti returned to France to retrace the Third Army's course through Europe. And he saw Paulette again. They were married. He settled here in the valley of the Marne and became a Champagne maker.

Like father, like son. Albert Ricciuti's father had hardly settled in Baltimore, after emigrating from Italy, before he went to France in 1917 with the American Expeditionary Force. He met a girl in Arles and, after the war, married her and took her to Baltimore.

"That's why I knew some French," Mr. Ricciuti said. "My mother taught me."

Paulette Revolte's family came from the industrial north of France —from Lorraine. Originally they had been in the cheese business. "During the war," Mr. Ricciuti said, "my mother-in-law began buying parcels of vineyard land around here. Now we have about 14.5 acres —five hectares. Not much for a big firm but quite a large holding for a small house like ours."

The Revolte vineyards—no parcel is larger than four acres—are spread around Avenay, none more than two kilometers from the Ricciuti home and—more important—the cellars below it.

Half of each annual harvest of Pinot Noir, Meunier Noir, and Chardonnay grapes is purchased by the giant Champagne firm of Mumm. With the rest, Mr. Ricciuti makes about 20,000 bottles of his own Champagne. Since Champagne is aged at least a year by law, there are never less than 40,000 bottles in the cellars carved from limestone under the Ricciuti home.

"Sometimes I go down there at night just to look at them," Mr. Ricciuti said. "I still find it fascinating. My wife says I'm like a miser gloating over his money."

Except for the occasional tourist (like the man from Alabama), most Ricciuti Champagne is sold to regular customers. About half is shipped in orders of 10 or 12 bottles; the rest is bought by customers who drive out from Paris for the day. Avenay is about 75 miles, an easy trip on the new auto route.

"Sometimes all the people in an office will get together and buy maybe 150 bottles," Mr. Ricciuti said.

The Ricciuti blend—all Champagnes are blends—is a rich, full, unsubtle wine. It has none of the austere elegance of some of the famous labels, but it is a true Champagne with a flowery bouquet that can fill the room when a bottle is opened.

August Sebastiani in the aging cellar of the Sebastiani winery in Sonoma, California. It was established in 1900 by his father, who emigrated from Tuscany. Despite many chances to sell it, Mr. Sebastiani has kept it.

The Ricciuti-Revolte line includes *demi-sec, sec, brut réserve,* and *brut rosé.* The *demi-sec* is really a sweet Champagne. *Sec* is less sweet and *brut* is dry. The *demi-sec* and *sec* cost 22 francs ($4.50), the *brut réserve* is 23 francs ($4.65), and the *rosé* is 28 francs ($5.75) (1978).

Maison Ricciuti is almost entirely a family affair. Al does most of the work himself, assisted by the son of a brother of Paulette (the brother was killed by the Gestapo three days before D-Day). The Ricciutis' son, John Charles, who was 13 years old on Christmas Day, helps out when he is home from a Jesuit boarding school in Reims.

"My boy was born in 1963, just after President Kennedy was killed," Mr. Ricciuti said. "I named him John. My wife said: 'Fine, so long as his second name is Charles—for President de Gaulle.'"

The Ricciutis are solid members of the little Avenay community. She is a member of the City Council in charge of what the French call *embellissement*—beautification of the town. He is the unpaid manager of the local semiprofessional football (soccer) team.

Paulette Ricciuti—unusual in this part of France—is an excellent pizza-maker. Some years ago on one of the couple's biannual trips to the States, Mr. Ricciuti took his wife to the Baltimore tavern and pizzeria where he once worked part time. The owner taught Paulette the secrets of good pizza, secrets she now employs every Friday night for the Ricciuti dinner.

The essence of good pizza is a good tomato sauce. The Ricciutis grow their own tomatoes from American seeds and make their own sauce. Since they have a ready-made bottling line in the cellar they use it—and their Champagne bottles too. So in one corner of Maison Ricciuti, while the bottles resemble all the others, they actually contain tomato purée waiting to recreate Baltimore-style pizzas to be enjoyed with the rough red Italian-style wine Mr. Ricciuti makes—strictly for private consumption—from some of his Champagne grapes.

Does a transplanted Baltimorean ever have second thoughts about his new life?

"I was homesick a bit at first," he said, "but the biggest change was not from one country to another but from a big city to a small town. It would have been pretty much the same, I think, if I had moved to a different town in the States."

Mr. Ricciuti belongs to the American Legion and Veterans of Foreign Wars posts in Paris. He also puts in two weeks a year in Germany serving with the United States Army Reserve.

"I clean out the Post Exchange then," he said. "My freezer is filled with turkeys and bacon I bring back from Germany.

"I do miss some things, though, and I can give them to you in order: My family (his mother, 81, lives in Catonsville, Maryland), the Orioles and the Colts, steamed crabs, and Chesapeake oysters."

A Wine Museum

THERE IS ONE in Beaune, France. There is one at Bully Hill, New York. There are several in Germany and there is the magnificent one at Château Mouton Rothschild. Wine museums, of course. But there are none like the Wine Museum in San Francisco, in the heart of America's wine country, the repository of the Christian Brothers Collection.

The Beaune museum celebrates the lore of Burgundy. Walter Taylor's collection at Bully Hill is mostly a tribute to his father, Greyton H. Taylor, the winemaker, and the extraordinary Mouton assemblage is an expression of the taste and wealth of that extraordinary man, Philippe de Rothschild.

The museum in San Francisco is really a celebration of wine. The collection ranges from an Israeli wine jug that is 2,600 years old to the latest book on the Napa Valley. Except for the museum in Beaune, in the heart of the Burgundy wine country, wine museums can be relatively inaccessible. The San Francisco Museum is at the western terminal of the Hyde Street cable car; and it is safe to say that, while many of them may never have known it was there, almost every tourist to visit San Francisco in the past two years has walked within a few yards of the Wine Museum. The museum is at 633 Beach Street, a few steps from Ghirardelli Square and any wine enthusiast who misses the opportunity to spend a couple of hours in the museum has missed one of the city's brighter attractions.

The Wine Museum is a successful offshoot of the long-standing and happy relationship between the Christian Brothers, a Catholic teaching order, and two German Jewish refugees, Alfred Fromm and his partner, the late Franz W. Sichel. The firm of Fromm and Sichel has acted as distributor of the Christian Brothers' wines for almost 40 years.

Many of the things in the museum's collection belong to the Christian Brothers, but most of them were collected by Mr. Fromm and his wife, his late brother, Norman Fromm, and Mr. Sichel.

In one way, the museum, which is housed in a wing of Fromm and Sichel's headquarters, is an expression of Mr. Fromm's gratitude for the success he and the Christian Brothers have enjoyed together. But even more, perhaps, it is an affirmation of his strong belief in the European cultural tradition he saw threatened at such close hand, the tradition he and so many like him fled to America to preserve.

[235]

Albert Ricciuti is a native Baltimorean turned French Champagne-maker.

While the collection ranges over almost 4,000 years of history, the grouping is not chronological. It is arranged around three themes: the grape and harvest and the vintner at work; wine in mythology; and, finally, the celebration of life and wine.

There is a collection of rare wine books, some from the 16th century, and all available to scholars and serious researchers. There are regular lectures and frequent exhibits. One month will have a showing of Daumier drawings of wine men. Next may be an exhibit about wine in the opera. One of the most popular was called "Thomas Jefferson and Wine in Early America." This included tracing Jefferson's trips through the wine country of France, and his letters recommending the 1784 Bordeaux on the ground that there had been no other good year since 1779.

Always on display are parts of the Franz W. Sichel glass collection, on loan from the Franz W. Sichel Foundation, including drinking vessels that date from the Roman era.

Artists represented at the museum include Thomas Rowlandson, Chagall, Picasso, Kokoschka, and Maillol. Free-standing "readers" offer casual visitors a wide knowledge of the history of wine, wine-making, and of the collection.

The Wine Museum is, in a sense, a long-needed home for the collection it houses. Beginning in 1967, a sampling of the collection toured the country in an exhibit called "500 Years of Wine in the Arts." It visited 20 major museums around the country, finally coming permanently to rest at the museum in San Francisco where it opened in January, 1974.

According to Ernest G. Mittelberger, the museum's director and a longtime California wine man, 175,000 visitors from all 50 states and 11 foreign countries visited the Wine Museum during its first year of operation.

"It's particularly impressive when you bear in mind that there is no wine to be had here," Mr. Mittelberger said.

According to the original plans for the museum, it was to have two purposes: "To be a place where people share and learn about the delight, rituals, history, and folktales of wine and its enjoyment" and "to show the quality and diversity of artistic expressions man has created to record his appreciation of wine from earliest times to the present."

The Wine Museum of San Francisco is open every day except Monday until 5 P.M. It also is closed Good Friday, Easter, Thanksgiving, Christmas and New Year's Day. There are guided tours, although they really are not necessary.

Bristol Cream—What's in a Name?

THERE IS a wall plaque along New York's East River Drive at about 23rd Street, commemorating the fact that parts of the roadway were built on fill from the ruins of bombed-out, wartime Bristol, England.

This grim rubble served as ballast for ships that had brought supplies to embattled Britain and were returning to the United States empty. Now, ships from Bristol to the United States carry far more pleasant cargoes, including ever-increasing amounts of Sherry from, among others, John Harvey & Sons, Ltd., the makers of Harvey's Bristol Cream.

Harvey men feel this is particularly appropriate because that wartime rubble probably included some of the original Harvey headquarters on Denmark Street, Bristol, destroyed by German bombs on November 24, 1940.

A trading port since Roman times, Bristol grew rich on sugar and slaves. Today, its largest industry and export is tobacco. But to most Americans—at least to those who drink—the name is synonymous with Sherry, and one specific Sherry at that.

Bristol Cream, its makers say, is the most popular imported Sherry in the United States—and the most expensive. Its sales in the United States have bucked the trend in that country to drier, lighter wines.

The British are Sherry's best customers. They put away 9 million bottles a year. "It's all part of the British penchant for sweets," said Robin Frost, a Harvey's executive. "We have the worst sweet tooth in Europe—and the biggest dentist's bills."

There is, of course, nothing British at all about Sherry. It comes from the area around Jerez de la Frontera in Spain, and much of what is consumed in the United States is shipped directly. Harvey's originally imported solely for British consumption, blending various Sherries in Bristol to suit the British taste. The fame of those blends made Harvey's an exporter, too. Britain now buys some 60 percent of all Sherry shipped from Spain, and Harvey's ships 70 percent of all that is reexported.

The British began buying wine in Bristol at least as early as 1210, when, records show, King John sought to replenish his cellar here. Sherry was first introduced here in the 16th century and by 1643 the city was known for its own Sherry style, called "Bristol milk."

Bristol Cream—What's in a Name?

Bristol milk is a generic term. Bristol Cream belongs exclusively to Harvey's. The name originated, according to the company's press releases, about 90 years ago when "an aristocratic lady" visited the cellars to taste the company's Bristol milk. Then, invited to sip a lesser-known blend, she exclaimed: "If that be milk, this is the cream."

Whether the name would have stuck had it been uttered by someone less aristocratic is problematical. The fact is, this blend of various old and new wines has become one of the best-known liquor labels in the world.

More than anything else, Sherry, like Champagne, bourbon, and other popular potions, is the result of blending. Thus, the idea of a vintage Sherry is meaningless, other than to note that it was bottled in that year. The point of blending, other than to provide a certain taste, is to insure that the 1972 bottlings are as close as possible to the 1962's and 1952's.

There are some rare, old, bottled Sherries here at Harvey's headquarters and they have, in fact, changed with bottle age. "But," said Michael McWatters, chief of quality control and a great-grandson of the first John Harvey, "they are not Bristol Cream."

Now a branch of Allied Breweries, Ltd., Harvey's long ago moved from the narrow medieval streets of downtown Bristol, where it was founded in 1796, to a modern plant on the outskirts of the city.

There, in the fall of 1972, almost a quarter million cases of various Harvey Ports and Sherries were awaiting shipment. A few weeks earlier double that amount had been on hand. Sherry is a seasonal item, with 60 percent of it sold during the last three months of the year (and some 25 percent consumed in a three- or four-week period around Christmas).

The old Harvey building in the center of Bristol has been restored. It houses some offices, a wine museum, and a restaurant. The museum and the restaurant are located in the vast cellars that originally were the storerooms of an Augustinian monastery founded in 1140.

Harvey's conducts a bustling business in French and German still wines and the cellars house a collection of rare old wines said to be one of the best in England. Many of the bottles are listed on the Harvey restaurant's extensive wine list.

Ordering Wine with No Pain

A FRIEND OF MINE, who necessarily spends a lot of time in Texas, returned from one such foray with the wine list from a small-town café. It read like this:

That has to be the ultimate, no-problem wine list. No sweaty palms when the sommelier approaches in that place. Still, even a Texan must tire of such a selection after a while. Let's face it: Sooner or later there comes a time when each of us must face up to the *carte des vins*.

Until recently, most wine lists seemed to have been designed to be intimidating. Restaurants where lists of wines with unpronounceable names were handed to the innocent diner by a remote sommelier were the norm. The hand of friendship, or of confidence, was rarely extended. But as wine has become more and more a part of everyday life in America, as people have experimented with wines at home and realized that the rules for choosing and serving wines are sensible rather than snobbish, they have learned to relax.

Restaurateurs are waking up, too. The kind of wine list that leads off with very old vintages at very high prices (there to give the list prestige but which the restaurant really does not want to sell—once they're drunk, there goes the prestige) and gives the impression that wine is something esoteric, is gradually disappearing.

I used to eat in a little French place on Eighth Avenue in New York City called the Coq au Vin. It was—and still is, for all I know—a typical west-side bistro with simple but good food and a brief wine list. One night I ordered one of the less popular bottles on the card. "Is this supposed to be good?" asked the young French waitress.

"It should be," I said.

"You know," she went on, "when I was a kid in Brittany (she then looked to be about 18), I thought there were just red and white wines."

Most Europeans do not grow up automatically to be wine experts. They drink the local *vin du pays* and have never concerned themselves with vintages, *appellations*, or which way the slopes of a vineyard face.

The young girl in the Coq au Vin was no different from many of the poker-faced waiters in far more exclusive places. Wherever you are, the chances are excellent that the man or woman confronting you with the big leather book of wine names knows very little more about its contents than you do.

To some extent, brand-names have simplified the ordering of wine. Mouton-Cadet, Grande Marque, Blue Nun, Mateus, Almadén, Christian Brothers—they are easy to pronounce, easy to remember, and, for the most part, easy to drink. Moreover, they are well-distributed in this country. The Mouton-Cadet you order in Portland, Maine, is also available in Portland, Oregon. And it tastes the same, too. As the popularity of these reasonably priced table wines has increased, restaurant owners are reshaping and rewriting their wine lists to attract people, rather than turn them off.

Windows on the World, the restaurant on the 107th floor of the World Trade Center, offers a brief selection of excellent American and European wines at the bottom of its lunch menu—among them, a 1974 Chablis; the Pritchard Hill Chenin Blanc from Chappellet Vineyards in California; Château de la Chaize Brouilly 1976; a Wehlener Sonnenuhr from Prüm; and the Californian Ridge Lytton Springs Zinfandel 1974. Prices range from $4.50 for a good Spanish Rioja to $16 for a 1966 Château Gruaud-Larose from Bordeaux. At dinner, the list is longer but still not intimidating. For connoisseurs and adventurers there is a third, far more complete list.

Frog, a relatively new restaurant in Philadelphia, includes about 100 wines on its list and manages to give a brief description of each as well as a few lines on the country from which each wine comes. There is, too, a list of wine specials and wines in limited quantities. Frog's wine card is fun to read as well as to order from.

Just as picking up a drumstick or a lamb chop bone is socially acceptable, so is ordering wine from the right-hand column. I mean by price. Decide on a price range, then look around for something in that range. Captains at the deluxe Four Seasons, when asked, will usually recommend something in the $15 to $18 range. If you want to pay less, the choice is still wide.

Many restaurants now offer a separate, moderately priced list, which simplifies things immensely. Sardi's, the theater-district landmark, recently revised its wine list completely. The new card has one of the best selections of California and New York State wines in the city and includes a separate list of seven good imported bottles averaging around $7 each (1977).

WINE TALK

Maxwell's Plum and Tavern on the Green, the two extravaganzas created by Warner LeRoy, recently revised their wine lists. Gone are the pretentious old bottles at astronomical prices. Now the lists are capped with a collection of a dozen wines from France, Germany, Spain, and California, the most expensive being a Sancerre for $9.75.

Even elegant Lutèce has a separate, moderately priced list. It is tucked discreetly into the main wine book, which is proffered to each guest. Lutèce's captains, especially Jean, who commands the second floor dining room, are knowledgeable in wine matters and eager to help.

The trick, if that's the proper word, is to know your price range and to have some idea of what you want—a dry, light red, or a medium, sweet white, for example. Consult the waiter or the captain. If he has any training at all, he can tell you whether you have chosen well, or suggest something he thinks may fit your taste better. Just don't be afraid.

There is a way to avoid wine list worries completely. Go to a restaurant that offers a preselected dinner that includes the wine. In New York, on the last Thursday of every month, Le Pont Neuf on East 53rd Street features a menu of wines and food from a particular region of France. The usual cost is $20 per person (1977), exclusive of tips and tax. Each Saturday evening (except during July and August) Marmiton on East 49th Street has a Champagne festival at which $35 covers the cost of the meal (from a limited menu) and a bottle of French Champagne. Occasionally, Le Chambertin, on West 46th Street, offers a fixed-price dinner that includes wine. It is done to move wines that are at their peak or beginning to slide, and is a good deal for the restaurant and a true bargain for its guests. The Cellar in the Sky, a restaurant that is actually part of Windows on the World, nightly offers a full dinner, from Sherry to brandy, for $45.

A recent meal at Cellar began with Wisdom & Warter Pale Fino Sherry from Spain, moved on to Freemark Abbey Chardonnay 1974, from California, and thence to a Bordeaux, Château Lynch-Bages 1962. A Spanish 1970 Rioja from the Marqués de Cáceres was served with the cheese and one of the rarest of fine German wines—take a deep breath—a Weinheimer Sibyllenstein Beerenauslese 1975 came with the orange soufflé.

Bear in mind, all this is arranged in advance by the restaurant. This kind of meal may not tell you everything you wanted to know about wine but was afraid to ask, but it is certainly one of the most pleasant ways yet devised to learn more about wine without even having to cope with a wine list. It is a minicourse in wine and there is no way to flunk.

Come to the Cabernets

EVERY SO OFTEN someone announces that the fashionable wine from California this season will be the Zinfandel or the Petite Sirah or the Merlot. Everyone dutifully hastens to stock up on whatever is supposed to be the one.

As they continue to experiment, the winemakers make better and better wines from all these grapes. Sooner or later though, everyone comes back to Cabernet. Just as in Bordeaux, the Cabernet Sauvignon is the premium red wine grape. Difficult to raise and small in yield, it nevertheless produces the finest of all American wines.

The Cabernet Sauvignon is a late maturing grape in California. Usually it is not picked until late in October when it is touch and go whether the grapes will get all the sun needed to bring up their alcohol content or whether the rains will set in and dilute their sugar content. Rain can also knock the grapes off the vines, barring any extra sugar development when the sun returns.

Because so many of the producers of Cabernet Sauvignon are small wineries, much of it never gets outside California's borders. This is unfortunate for east coast wine lovers, but, in a way, perhaps it is just as well. By one recent count, there are more than 100 Cabernet Sauvignon labels available in California. Add to that the fact there can be three or four vintages available and the picture for the un-sophisticated consumer is one of considerable confusion.

Even so, there are at least 20 excellent California Cabernets available in the east, ranging in price from around $4 to $30 or more for older vintages. Recently (1977), I tasted a group of 19 of them. The wines were from the 1973 and 1974 vintages and the only thing they had in common was the fact that they are all distributed by the same firm. Both 1973 and 1974 were good vintages—yes, they do have vintage years in California—following two rather indifferent years, 1971 which was mediocre and 1972 which was, for most wineries, quite poor. Both vintages, 1971 and 1972, should be drunk soon. They were light wines with little staying power.

The 1973 vintage was a big crop and the growing conditions were ideal in the Napa and Sonoma Valleys, from whence most of our best Cabernet Sauvignons still come. The long summer was fairly cool, giving the grapes a chance to mature slowly. Then there followed some good hot sun that caused the grapes to be both high in acid and high in sugar, the two key constituents in a well-balanced wine.

WINE TALK

The 1973's we tasted were Joseph Phelps Vineyards, Beaulieu Vineyards, Mayacamas, Spring Mountain, Freemark Abbey, Ste. Michelle (from Washington State), Robert Mondavi, Freemark Abbey (Bosché Vineyard), Chappellet, Ridge (Montebello Vineyard), Pedroncelli, and Beau Tour, a second line of Beaulieu.

If the 1973's had an overall characteristic, it was a slight vegetable quality. One of the tasters called it herbaceousness. The Freemark Bosché, made from grapes from a single, highly regarded vineyard, and the Ste. Michelle were disappointing, but there were no bad wines in the entire group.

This writer's favorites were the Spring Mountain, the Mayacamas, and the Ridge, although anyone's enthusiasm for the Ridge would be tempered somewhat by the price. Both the Ridge, which like the Bosché, comes from selected vineyards, and the Spring Mountain can benefit from more time in bottle—particularly the Ridge. Its considerable qualities have only begun to show.

If anything, the 1974's seemed more advanced than the 1973's. Those tasted were Kenwood Vineyards, Clos du Val, Caymus Pedroncelli, Spring Mountain, Robert Mondavi, and Joseph Phelps. In this group, I preferred the Caymus, the Clos du Val, the Mondavi, and the Spring Mountain, roughly in that order.

The surprise was that the Spring Mountain was fourth. In other tastings this had proved to be a magnificent wine. It seemed younger here. The Caymus was a nice find—a big wine, but not harsh, with deep color and flavor. Neither Phelps' wine fared brilliantly in this tasting. Perhaps this is because the winery has only been making red wines for a couple of years. The Phelps' whites, particularly the Johannisberg Riesling, are hard to beat.

Many of the wineries, favored with extra large crops of Cabernet grapes in recent years have put out second lines of wine, such as the Beaulieu Beau Tour. One of the best of these around, although it was not included in this particular tasting, is called Liberty School. It is the second line of Caymus Vineyards.

One of the games California wine enthusiasts play is trying to guess where the wine comes from. In recent years of economic uncertainty in the wine country, some wineries were left with vast stocks of unsold wine. Often this very good wine shows up in second-line labels. Various origins are given for the Liberty School nonvintage Cabernets, but wherever they came from they were treated well at Caymus.

Another of these second lines worth trying is Silverado Cellars, which is put out by Château Montelena, the winery whose Chardonnay fared so well in a now famous tasting in Paris in 1976. Silverado's

Lot 72–73 Cabernet, obviously a blend of the wines of those two years, is another excellent wine buy. It, too, is available in a few of the better shops in the East.

Made from grapes grown farther up the California coast, Fetzer Vineyard's Mendocino Cabernets are good buys, too. Some people prefer the 1973, which is not too easy to find. It is, they claim, a big wine with aging potential not found in the 1974. Actually, the 1974 is softer and at this stage more attractive. Aging might improve it a little, but it can be enjoyed right now.

Alas, we have no equivalent in New York of Ernie's, a liquor-store chain in San Francisco that picks up overproduction wines and sells them under its own label. In California recently, I sampled a 1973 Cabernet under the Ernie's label at $2.50 that was the equal of many bottles at $8. One report said the wine was made by Souverain in Sonoma County when it was owned by Pillsbury.

The 1973's and 1974's may be important wines in California. The 1975's were not rated too highly—although the industry will undoubtedly find hitherto unrecognized qualities when it comes time to sell them—and 1976 was considered to be a generally poor year for California reds. As for this and the next few years to come, everything depends on the drought.

Just Across the River: Bourg and Blaye

WHEN WE TALK of alternatives to the high-priced wines of Bordeaux—the famous wines of the Médoc and St.-Emilion—we tend to think of other countries: Spain, Italy, the United States. For some reason, we usually ignore the fact that some extremely good wines, authentic clarets at that, are produced right in the Bordeaux region and sold at very reasonable prices.

These are the wines of Bourg and Blaye, adjoining wine areas directly across the Gironde River from the Médoc. It is a region almost totally unknown to American wine enthusiasts, and the fact is that even the knowledgeable Bordeaux wine merchants hardly know it. Writing in *The Wines of Bordeaux*, Edmund Penning-Rowsell said that the Bordeaux shippers often had to hire local people to guide them from château to château in Bourg and in Blaye, even though they had spent their lives only a few miles away.

The region is quite large, extending from the border of the Charente-Maritime department to the north to a point east of and slightly south of Margaux on the other side of the Gironde River.

Wines were made in both the Bourg and Blaye areas long before they were made in the Médoc. The best of the wines of both Bourg and Blaye do not compare with the very best of the Médoc, but there are plenty of undistinguished wines produced in the Médoc that can be matched in quality and price by wines from across the river.

Soil is everything in Bordeaux, and it is axiomatic that the poorest soils produce the best wines. Unfortunately for the vineyards of Bourg and Blaye, the soil there is very good—good enough in fact to produce a wide variety of crops that never could be cultivated in the more famous wine-growing parts of the region. Bourg, for instance, has long been known almost as much for its potatoes as for its wine.

Originally, Blaye specialized in dry white wines. When the Institut National des Appellations d'Origine, the governmental agency that controls the wine business in France, granted both areas the right to use their own names in 1972—rather than just Bordeaux or Bordeaux Supérieur—Blaye began to switch to red wines, which had always been preferred in Bourg.

Generally, the Bourg wines have more body and character than the wines of Blaye, possibly because the Bourg area, about one-tenth the size of the Blaye region, is close to the river, where, traditionally, the vines grow best.

A century ago, the Bourg wines were considered better than the average Médoc wines because they were fruitier and had more body. A writer of the time recommended that good Bourg wines be kept at least eight years before drinking and noted that most of them would not begin to decline in the bottle until they were 25 years of age. Alas, those figures do not even apply to some of the finest first growths of Bordeaux anymore. They do indicate, however, that there was—and is—some serious winemaking done on the east bank of the Gironde.

The principal grapes of the region are those of St.-Emilion and Pomerol, where the soil is similar: Merlot, Cabernet Franc and Malbec. The Cabernet Sauvignon grape of the Médoc region is far less in evidence here. Once both Blaye and Bourg were thriving little ports. Blaye, which is just south of St.-Julien across the river, shipped wine north to the sea and south to Bordeaux. The Dutch and Belgians were, and to some extent still are, enthusiastic customers for these wines. The lesser ones went south a few miles to Bordeaux where, because of their good body, they were blended into the lighter wines of the more famous Bordeaux wine regions.

In an excess of generosity, or perhaps of bureaucracy, the I.N.A.O., when it got around to granting *appellations* to the region, came up with five—three for Bourg and two for Blaye, to wit—Bourg, Côtes de Bourg, and Bourgeais; Premiers Côtes de Blaye, and just plain Blaye or Blayais.

For all practical purposes, the American wine drinker need only be concerned with Côtes de Bourg and Premiers Côtes de Blaye, both reds. Côtes de Blaye is exclusively white and is rarely seen here.

There are literally hundreds of châteaus in both the Bourg area and in Blaye and to say that this one is excellent and this one is not would be foolhardy. Outside of the region, very little comparative knowledge of the wines has been gathered. Vintage-wise, they follow the ratings of the rest of Bordeaux with few exceptions. Thus, 1970 and 1975 were excellent years, 1971 fared good, 1973 and 1974 good, and 1972 fair-to-poor. Earlier vintages, except for a rare bottle, are virtually unknown in this country.

Some of the better-known properties in the Bourg area include Châteaus Launay, Guionne, LaCroix Davids, de la Trave, Labarde, and Mille Secousses, which means, by the way, a thousand jolts. The English wine writer Maurice Healy used to take great delight in finding this wine served in the dining cars of the Great Western Railway.

In Blaye, Châteaus Lescadre, Petits Arnauds, and Cazeaux are three of the better-known properties whose wines occasionally find their way to these shores.

Bourg and Blaye are, of course, part of the Bordeaux region, just as are the Médoc and Sauternes and St.-Emilion, and that fact is usually emphasized above all others on the bottles' labels. Unscrupulous wine merchants often use that fact to palm off what should be a relatively inexpensive wine as a high-priced one. A Bordeaux from either the Côtes de Bourg or the Premiers Côtes de Blaye, even in the current inflated market, should not bring much more than $4 (1977). Beyond that, it is a bargain no longer.

Bear in mind that the outside world has begun to discover these wines only in very recent years and the distribution of them is still sporadic. Production at most of the properties is small so that while a shop in Stamford, Connecticut, may have a case or two, there is no reason to expect that shops in Tenafly, New Jersey, and Bronxville, New York, should have the same wine.

Even if you happen to find one you like, there is a good chance that you have purchased the last three bottles in the country. The proprietor in France probably sold the rest of the crop to an importer in Rotterdam.

There are good wines from this part of Bordeaux to be had. But you have to seek them out and make sure not to pay too much for them.

The Company of Vintners

STANDING BEFORE YOU are two pairs of white wines, a pair of *rosés*, and three pairs of reds, all in unlabeled bottles. One wine in each pair is from a recognized French district. The other wine in each pair is not from France.

The idea is to identify each French wine, give its district, and in about 30 words explain why you reached that decision. Then, give the country of origin of all the non-French wines.

You have two hours. If you come through successfully, you may be on your way to the title Master of Wine. The title, which, usually shows up as a discreet "M.W." on a man's calling card in Britain, is bestowed by the Worshipful Company of Vintners, one of the ancient guilds in the City of London. The Company of Vintners maintains closer ties to the wine trade than, say, the Skinners or the Tallow Chandlers, but like all the guilds, much of its function is ceremonial.

The handsome Vintners Hall, off Upper Thames Street, is made available to the wine trade associations for meetings, dinners, and lectures. Its collection of documents and artifacts relating to the wine trade and dating back some 600 years is available to students.

The Company of Vintners

Another contact with the wine trade comes from the Vintners' Privilege granted in a charter dated 1567, during the reign of Elizabeth I. Under the charter, certain "Freemen by Patrimony or Servitude" were granted the right to sell wine without an excise license in the City of London or within three miles of its walls.

To this day, there are still a few "Freemen" who exercise this privilege and who display the ancient title "free vintner" instead of the regular government tax stamps.

The Company of Vintners, along with the Company of Dyers, shares with the Queen a prerogative dating back to the 16th century —the ownership of the swans on the Thames. Each year a census of the Thames swans is taken. To preserve their right to the birds, the Dyers' swans are marked with one nick on the upper bill. The Vintners' swans get two nicks and the Queen's none.

Every so often the Vintners hold a Swan Dinner at which the birds are actually served. "Well, there is some passed around," said Commander Donald Ross, the present Clerk of the Company, "but one pushes it around on the plate."

The origin of the Vintners, like that of most of the guilds, is lost in antiquity. Wine has been imported into England since Roman times and records show that the wine merchants of Rouen actually owned a wharf in London in the year 1042.

The Vintners' Guild was already in existence in the 13th century, records show, but the first Charter was not granted until 1437— during the reign of Henry VI. The Company's records show that even in the Middle Ages, the liquor business worked under tight government controls: in 1311, King Edward II issued a writ fixing the price of a gallon of "the best wine" at five pence, the next best at four pence, and the 14th-century *vin ordinaire* at three pence a gallon.

The City of London is a self-governing domain in the center of the 720 square-mile area that makes up Greater London and even the Queen must ask permission to enter the City. Each year, the City pays to the Queen a rent of six horseshoes, 61 horseshoe nails, a hatchet, and a billhook, a practice that has continued uninterrupted for more than 500 years.

The City of London, presided over by the Lord Mayor, contains all the symbols of British power—or their remnants: the Bank of England, Lloyd's of London, the Stock Exchange, and many shipping concerns and merchants. The City is the home of St. Paul's Cathedral and the Tower of London.

There are some 80 ancient guilds in England but the City recognizes only 12 of them as "Great Companies," in this order of precedence: Mercers, Grocers, Drapers, Fishmongers, Goldsmiths, Skinners, Merchant Taylors, Haberdashers, Salters, Ironmongers, Vintners, and Clothworkers. Since 1270, 25 Vintners have held the office of Lord Mayor.

Perhaps the most interesting of the Vintners' collections, which include wine glasses and silver plate, are their wines, thousands of bottles of which are stored in ancient vaults under Upper Thames Street and about which the Vintners are somewhat reluctant to talk.

"Most people in London don't know the wines are there," said Commander Ross, "and we don't make much of a fuss about it." The wines, some of which were acquired, the Company Clerk said, at "four and five pence a bottle," represent an extraordinary collection used mostly for ceremonial dinners and the like. How extensive is the collection? "Well," said Commander Ross, a bit uncomfortably, "you can say we're into our 1945s."

Dinners and ceremonial affairs have always been part of the Company of Vintners' tradition. One of the earliest on record indicated the prestige of the guild. It also indicated that there were sharpsters in the wine business then as now.

In 1363, Sir Henry Pickard, the Master of the Company, entertained five kings at Vintners Hall: Edward III of England, David, King of Scotland, King John of France, Waldemar III, King of Denmark, and Peter, King of Cyprus.

The ancient manuscripts show that after the dinner, Sir Henry set up a dice game and cleaned out the King of Cyprus. According to one translation, "the King took this ill in part," and Sir Henry gave him back his money. The manuscript indicates that Pickard's wife, Dame Margaret, also had a dice game going after the banquet, but there is no record of how well she fared.

A Bouquet of Rosés

IT ISN'T NECESSARY to be a wine enthusiast to know about the white wine explosion. There isn't a bar in New York where white wine sales haven't approached or passed the sale of gin and vodka. Hard-bitten martini drinkers by the score switch every day to white wine, and many a hostess has saved a fortune on her liquor bills because so many guests now ask for white wine rather than mixed drinks.

But now here is one of the most respected figures in the liquor industry, Louis Gomberg, a California consultant, to tell us a different story. According to him, the fastest-growing wine color in the United States is pink—*rosé*.

Since the early 1970's, according to Mr. Gomberg, the growth rate of *rosé* wines has been half again as fast as that of white wines and twice as fast as that of red wines.

Mr. Gomberg, writing in *The Wine Investor*, noted that if all wine products are considered, chances are better than 50–50 that the predominant wine color today is pink. What's more, he said, the trend to *rosé* started in the late 1940's and continues today, despite the popularity of white wine in the past several years.

Among the reasons he gives is ease of service. Even more so than white wine, *rosé* goes with everything. It bypasses all the off-putting rules of wine service. Also, it is best chilled. Researchers long ago discovered that the majority of American drinkers prefer their wine chilled. *Rosé* apparently is more attractive to the eye than both white and red and, finally, it has an uncomplicated, often sweet taste that newcomers to wine prefer. White wines frequently are too acidy for an uninitiated palate.

Actually there still is a huge market for *rosé* wines in this country as well as Europe. *Rosé* is a major product of the vineyards in the south of France, and although sales have been dropping in recent years, Americans continue to consume millions of gallons of Portuguese *rosé* each year.

In addition to its highly popular Pink Chablis, the huge Gallo Winery offers a Vin Rosé, a separate *rosé* in its varietal wine group, and, most recently, its new Red Rosé. All the large producers, such as Italian Swiss Colony and Almadén, offer *rosés*. In the East, the Taylor Wine Company does well with its Pink Catawba.

Richard Peterson, president of the Monterey Winery in California,

Hargrave Vineyard
North Fork
Long Island   New York
Rosé of Cabernet Sauvignon
Table Wine Produced & Bottled By Hargrave Vineyard Cutchogue, N. Y.

has another view to add. "For the first time in California wine history," he wrote recently, "*rosé* wines are being produced at quality
levels which equal the red and white wines. Wineries now take *rosé*
seriously—something that didn't often happen in past years. We see
some very knowledgeable consumers opting for varietal *rosés* more
and more," he added.

Varietal *rosé* wines are made from premium red wine grapes such
as the Cabernet Sauvignon, Pinot Noir, Petite Sirah, and Zinfandel. In
Europe most *rosé* is made from the Grenache grape. The Grenache is
also used in California, but the bulk of *rosé* wine, the cheap stuff,
both here and in Europe, is a blend of reds and whites sweetened to
hide any defects.

Some wineries have made *rosé* from premium grapes for years.
Others have experimented in recent years because of the surplus of
red wine grapes in California. If people were not drinking red wine,
the theory went, let's make a pink wine with the same grapes and see
if that sells.

Among the wineries making *rosé* from Cabernet Sauvignon are Mr.

THE
FIRESTONE
VINEYARD

Winery Under Construction

Santa Ynez Valley, California

ROSÉ OF
CABERNET SAUVIGNON
1975

PRODUCED AND BOTTLED BY THE FIRESTONE VINEYARD
LOS OLIVOS, CALIFORNIA   ALCOHOL 13.1% BY VOLUME

Peterson's Monterey Vineyards—where, he says, it is the most popular wine—Simi Winery, Firestone Vineyards, Buena Vista, and, here in the East, the brand new Hargrave Vineyards on Long Island. Mirassou Vineyards make a *rosé* from Petite Sirah as does the small Veedercrest Vineyards. Mayacamas, one of the best known of the Napa Valley premium wineries, and several others make a *rosé* from Zinfandel, and the Heitz Cellars has *rosé* made from the Grignolino grape.

If you are one of those who abandoned *rosé* long ago and are inclined to look down on *rosé* drinkers, you may be in for a surprise. These new California wines are well-made, sophisticated wines that add a new dimension to wine drinking.

To find out more about them, we picked up a group at several local shops. The first thing we noticed was that even some of the better shops think nothing of leaving wines such as these on the shelves until they are well past their prime. We avoided a number of *rosés* going back as far as 1969.

WINE TALK

These are the wines we acquired: Mayacamas Zinfandel Rosé, 1972; Firestone Rosé of Cabernet, 1975; Burgess Cellars, Napa Grenache Rosé, 1973; Robert Mondavi, Gamay Rosé, 1976; Sebastiani Vineyards, Grenache Rosé, 1974; Simi Alexander Valley Rosé of Cabernet, 1975; Mirassou Petite Rosé, 1976; Hargrave Vineyards, North Fork Rosé of Cabernet Sauvignon, nonvintage; Almadén Grenache Rosé, nonvintage; Ernest & Julio Gallo Rosé, nonvintage; and, because the Cabernet Sauvignon is also the main grape of Bordeaux, a bottle of Cadet-Rosé, nonvintage, the pink version of Baron Philippe de Rothschild's highly successful Mouton-Cadet.

The Gallo wine was really in a different category than the others in the group. Very light and sweet, it was more of an apéritif wine. The Almadén was harsh and unpleasant and had an acrid, tanky smell. The Cadet-Rosé, surprisingly, was not much better. It was simply a dull uninteresting wine.

The Mayacamas, despite its age, was one of the best of the batch, with a sprightly aroma and a fresh Zinfandel taste. Of the Cabernet *rosés*, the Firestone and the Simi were favorites, although the Simi was a trifle sweet.

The Hargrave *rosé*, which had seemed attractive enough alone in the past, turned out to be stemmy and herbaceous when compared with its California cousins. This is a brand new winery, though, and one suspects there are better things to come.

Of the two *rosés* made from Petite Sirah, the Mirassou was preferred. The Mirassou had fruit and body and freshness. The Veedercrest was flat and uninspired.

Perhaps the most attractive wine in the group was the Mondavi Gamay Rosé. It was light and delicate and actually the only wine in the group to really have a pink color. The rest, as is usually the case with *rosé* wines, were more orange than pink.

Of the Grenache *rosés*, the best was the Burgess, even though it was four years old. It had body. The Sebastiani was a good wine but too soft. A *rosé* needs some tang in it to liven it up.

Wine Gifts

WINE LOVERS come into their own at holiday time. They have the key to the most desirable of all last minute gift giving routines. Anyone else may have fretted for weeks over what to give that grumpy uncle in Boston. The wine enthusiast sends him a bottle of Dom Pérignon. What? He doesn't like Champagne? What difference does that make? There is no finer gift. That's an end to it, grumpy uncle or not.

Not long ago, we discussed wine books. They can be fun, but if you really like wine, why give books about it? Why not give the wine itself?

Few other luxury gifts lend themselves to so many price levels. If you want to spend $150, there are shops around still offering the 1973 Château Mouton Rothschild at $149 a case. This is the wine that Baron Philippe de Rothschild made the year Mouton became a first growth in Bordeaux. It also was the year Picasso died and the label is a reproduction of a Picasso picture in the Mouton Museum.

If ever there was a collector's item in wine, the 1973 Mouton is it. If ever there was a flattering, much-wanted Christmas gift, the 1973 Mouton is it. Of course, there is no need to deal in first growths to provide elegant wine gifts. Any liquor shop worth patronizing has a dozen or more interesting gift packages ready and waiting. Recently, in search of something appropriate for a friend, I came across a wooden case containing six bottles of assorted Bolla Italian wines. The case was attractive, the shop owner was happy to deliver them that same day, and the whole project came in at under $25. Certainly more fun than some tedious coffee table wine book at the same price or higher.

Here is a tip about wine people: Rather than being hard to please, they are actually among the easiest people to satisfy. If you have $10 to spend, ask your dealer for something really good in that price range. He may come up with a fine 1970 Bordeaux. He may suggest a rare Barolo from Italy or three bottles of a lesser known but succulent 1976 Beaujolais. Your respective recipient will be excited by any one of them.

Does someone on your list favor a certain restaurant? Unless that restaurant is a fast food emporium, it will most likely be happy to set aside a bottle or two if you pay in advance. What a pleasant surprise to find a bottle waiting for you at a restaurant you like. The cost would be from $10 up.

My own first choices for holiday gifts are at the opposite ends of the wine scale: Beaujolais and Champagne. Even someone who has never been interested in wine will enjoy a case of Beaujolais. He or she knows the name, and knows that Beaujolais goes with just about everything.

This is the year (1977) to buy Beaujolais for a Christmas gift, too. Not the 1977 Beaujolais Nouveau, a thin, watery product shipped out a few weeks after the harvest, and just now becoming available, but the 1976 regular Beaujolais, one of the really great Beaujolais of recent years. Some of the famous labels, such as Latour and Jadot, cost as much as $6 a bottle for their best—Moulin-à-Vent, for instance— but most good shops have lesser known labels in the $3 to $3.50 range. These make fine gifts.

Champagne is, of course, the ultimate gift. The aforementioned Dom Pérignon, at about $30 a bottle, is the best-known Champagne, but the choice is far wider. Roederer Cristal, a big favorite here in past years, is once again available in some shops, also in the $30 range.

But Bollinger, one of the finest houses, has a full range of Champagnes, including some fine R.D. wines, ranging in price from about $30 down to $10. R.D. refers to a very special step in the Champagne-making process that is too complicated to explain in the midst of this frivolous gift-giving season. Suffice it to say that the wine is extraordinary.

The Veuve Clicquot Gold Label at about $15 is another really fine Champagne at a reasonable price for gift giving. For someone very special you might consider a magnum or a jeroboam of Champagne. Few things are more dramatic at a party or dinner than a really large bottle of Champagne.

Big bottles do not have to be filled with Champagne to be special gifts. A magnum of 1961 Château Lafite-Rothschild will probably cost around $400. It is certainly an impressive gift but if you are not prepared to go that high, there are alternatives. A double magnum of the 1970 Lafite, a very fine year indeed, has been offered this season for around $125. A double magnum holds four regular bottles and the only drawback to the double magnum of 1970 Lafite is that it will mature more slowly than the same wine in a regular 75-centiliter bottle. Warn any friend for whom you buy such a bottle he should not drink it for another 10 years. Then mark the approximate date on your calendar and plan to join him a decade hence.

PRODUCE OF FRANCE

FONDÉE · EN 1859

MONTHELIE

APPELLATION CONTROLÉE

Louis Jadot

NÉGOCIANT A BEAUNE (CÔTE-D'OR)

73 cl

Nor does your large wine bottle gift have to be a legendary Bordeaux such as Lafite. One of the best simple table wines around, Fetzer Vineyards Mendocino Premium Red, is to be had around town for under $5 a magnum. A better everyday wine would be difficult to encounter.

Wine artifacts have never been overly welcome in these precincts, principally because so many of them are overpriced gimmicks meant to capitalize on the wine boom. Vermeil wine bottle baskets, wine racks that cost more than the wine that goes in them, and other silly appurtenances fall into this category.

A few items are nonetheless worth noting. One is the Ah-So corkpuller, a simple device that has two steel prongs which are inserted between the glass and the cork and twisted and wiggled until the cork comes out. It is excellent for old corks and is guaranteed to amaze your friends. It is sold in most places for about $5. Three years ago, it was $1.25; a few places may still have it at around $3. Shop around. It's worth it.

Glasses, of course, are among the most wanted wine gifts, if they are good glasses. Try for something large. Really, a wine glass can't be too large. Ten ounces is really the smallest you should consider and a glass with a 22-ounce bowl is not at all out of line for serious wine drinking.

For Champagne, the only proper glass is the Champagne flute. Baccarat has a couple of lovely models, including one called Dom Pérignon at about $17.50 a glass. But you can buy perfectly acceptable Champagne flutes at stores like The Pottery Barn for $4 or less.

Finally, since we touched on wine books recently, you might be interested in a new wine newsletter that has begun to arrive on the east coast. Robert Finigan's *Private Guide to Wines* has been available on the west coast for several years now and has created something of a stir. Young Mr. Finigan is an iconoclast who says he spends $20,000 a year or more on the wines he tastes. Consequently, he feels free to attack some of the most revered wines and winemakers, both in this country and abroad. You may not always agree with his opinions but you will enjoy reading them.

Avanti Chianti

IT'S FASHIONABLE these days to describe Barolo as Italy's best wine. Certainly, there are some impressive examples around—big, hefty wines, with lots of flavor. They age well and they're not too expensive. No doubt about it, Barolo is a formidable wine and, perhaps, it really is the finest product of the Italian vineyards.

Well, for what it's worth, here's a dissenting opinion. I think Chianti is the best wine of Italy. No, not the stuff they used to sell in straw-covered bottles in pizzerias to neutralize the red peppers. I mean real Chianti from the classic Chianti region—Chianti made

under the strictest controls, by experts, aged and bottled and, sometimes, aged some more.

Everyone spends time and vocal cords arguing over whether
Barolo is more like Burgundy, Bordeaux, Rhône wine, or, sometimes,
even California wine. No one ever tries that with Chianti. It is unique.
It is Chianti.

Italian wine names can be weird. Sometimes they signify the grape,
as with Verdicchio; sometimes they refer to the town where the wine
is made, as in the case of Orvieto or Barolo. Chianti is a place name,
too, but it is the name of both a town and a region. The wine first
came from vineyards around the town. It was too popular. Soon
everyone in Tuscany was making cheap red wine and calling it Chianti. And who could blame them? That went on for a thousand years
or so until the government finally put its foot down. Now there is just
as much Chianti being made—probably more—but the bottles are

supposed to bear a seal showing just which of the handful of Chianti regions—all close to each other—the wine hails from.

Chianti is made all over the dry craggy hills outside of Florence. It is a timeless, ruggedly beautiful land where the cypresses stand tall and still against the cobalt sky just as they must have 3,000 years ago when wine was first made in this part of the world. Once the mountain peasants grew vegetables and fruit in among the vines. Now only olive trees compete with the grapes, and many a vintner in this region is as proud of his olive oil, still stored in huge earthen crocks, as he is of his wine.

Once, too, any and all grapes went into the press to make Chianti. It was wine to be drunk as soon as it was ready; it was wine to be replaced by the next vintage and not to be saved or aged or, for that matter, talked or written about.

In the 1850's, all that was changed. Bettino Ricasoli, one of the founders of modern Italy and the inheritor of almost a thousand years of his own family's winemaking traditions, ended forever the casual approach to Chianti making.

There is a lovely story about how Baron Ricasoli came to spend his time working out the formula for Chianti wine. According to Luigi Barzini in his book, *The Italians*, Bettino Ricasoli, who succeeded Cavour as Prime Minister of the young Italian nation in 1861, was as ugly as he was influential. In fact, he was quite cross-eyed. He was also very jealous.

One evening, soon after his marriage, he escorted his young bride, Anna Bonaccorsi, to a ball in Florence where very briefly she was courted by a young man. Taking her away immediately, Baron Ricasoli instructed his coachman to take them to Brolio, the grim family castle out in the hills south of the city. "They rode in silence through the snow until dawn," Barzini writes, "he in his black evening clothes, she shivering in her ball dress. They lived in Brolio for practically the rest of their lives."

To pass the time, Baron Ricasoli rebuilt Brolio Castle and experimented with vines and blends of wine. His results were so successful that the rest of the growers copied him. "Thus," writes Barzini, "the Baron managed to preserve the sanctity of the family, his wife's name, and his honor unblemished, to amass a fortune and to enrich his neighbors, all at the same time."

The formula he devised is still used today. Chianti is made from four grapes: Sangiovese, Trebbiano, Malvasia, and Canaiolo, with Sangiovese usually making up from 60 to 80 percent of the blend. A little known fact about Chianti is that the Malvasia is a white-wine

grape and that Chianti is actually made of almost 20 percent white wine.

After the blended grapes have finished fermenting, still more grapes are added, in very small quantities. These grapes have been dried a bit in the sun, giving them a greater concentration of sugar and the wine the slightly burned taste that is the characteristic of Chianti. Actually these grapes are added to induce a second fermentation in the wine in order to lower its acid level. Often the youngest of Chiantis are drunk before this fermentation is completely finished, and the little carbon dioxide bubbles that remain give the wine a slightly prickly character.

To the extent that it can be drunk very young, Chianti probably predates Beaujolais Nouveau by a couple of dozen decades or so. But while some Beaujolais can last a decade, some of the greatest Chiantis can go on almost forever, like fine Bordeaux.

These are the famous Chianti Classicos, from the specifically delineated classical region stretching from a few kilometers south of

WINE TALK

Florence to the ocher peaks of Siena, some 35 miles to the south. Of the entire Chianti region's annual production of around 30 million gallons of wine, the Classico area makes about 4 million.

The Chianti League was created in the 14th century to help defend Florence and the Tuscan estates of the rich Florentines from the rapacious Sienese. When they were not slaughtering their neighbors from the south, or being slaughtered in turn, the members of the Chianti League set out some rules about grape planting, harvesting, and winemaking. But it was not until the 1920's that the growers got together to set strict limitations on what is and what is not Chianti and, particularly, Chianti Classico. The current outlines of the region were made legal in 1932.

The organization set up by the growers determines such things as how high up the hill vines can be planted and exactly on what day each year the harvest will begin. Members of the group, which is called the *consorzio*, who follow all the rules, are allowed to affix the group's famous seal, the Gallo Nero, or Black Rooster, to the necks of their bottles.

Some of the bigger producers in the Chianti region ignore the Gallo Nero, contending that their name is more important. For the smaller properties, though, it remains a mark of quality. A Chianti Classico with a silver ring around the Gallo Nero is Chianti Classico Vecchio, which means that it is from the classical area and is guaranteed to have been aged in cask and bottle for at least two years. If the ring is gold, the wine is a Chianti Classico Riserva, which has been aged at least three years.

While Chianti may never have the complexity and elegance of a great French wine, it has a subtlety all its own—a mixture of tastes and aromas that seems to reach its peak after about 10 years in the bottle. By then the harshness of the Sangiovese grape has mellowed out, and the wine is supple and warm.

One of the best features of Chianti is the price. America has yet to discover these wines and, for the present at least, they are among the best bargains in fine wines. Often they cost less than half the price of French wines of similar quality.

Final Bequest

THIS IS a wine story. But only by a vigorous stretch of the imagination. Actually, it is a story about living and dying and the occasionally unexpected nobility of the human spirit.

This story began in Norway in 1889. It came to light in a peculiar way. On February 7, 1975, the International Edition of the *Herald Tribune* in Paris ran a small item. It said that Peder Knutsen of Kindred, North Dakota, had died recently and left a will donating $30,000 to a home for the elderly in the town of his birth, Gol, in the Hallingdal Valley, about 140 miles east of Bergen in Norway. But it was no ordinary bequest. Mr. Knutsen specified that the income from his bequest must be used to buy wine for the old people.

On February 5, the municipal council in Gol agreed to accept Mr. Knutsen's gift. "Even if the donation was odd and put this alcopolitical problem on our neck," said acting Mayor, Ola Storia, in classic political rhetoric that survives the translation.

The councilmen, whose arithmetic should be watched closely, estimated that Mr. Knutsen's bequest would provide about 1,000 good bottles of wine for the 23 old folk in the Gol home, or somewhat less than three bottles a day for the 23 residents. Assuming there are a few teetotallers, it hardly amounts to much more than a glass of wine once a day.

Still, a glass of wine is a treat even if that is all there is. And shared with other old people at the evening meal, it might help to shorten some long Arctic nights.

Mrs. Delice Ebsen lives in Kindred, North Dakota, a farming community of about 600 souls, 30 miles south of Fargo. She remembers Peder Knutsen well. "He was a wonderful old man," she said in a telephone interview. "He died on November 11 at the age of 85. He lived alone in his little house near us on his $78-a-month pension from World War I. He never went to church but he was a religious man. His Bible sustained him."

The Ebsens bought Mr. Knutsen's two acres for $3,000 about four years ago but had no objection to his living on in his small house. "He used to make rhubarb wine," Mrs. Ebsen said, "and he enjoyed a can of beer now and then." As far as she knew he had had little experience with grape wine at all.

Peder Knutsen emigrated from Norway at the age of 19 in 1889. He homesteaded in Canada before drifting down to North Dakota many years ago. He worked as a farm laborer around Kindred until he grew too old to work. He never married but, over the years, he made nine or ten trips back to his native land. His sister still lives in Gol.

"We talked about what he would do with his money," Mrs. Ebsen said, "and he liked the idea of leaving it to a home. But we had no idea he meant to leave it to a home in Norway and, to tell the truth, we had no idea how much money he had. He had the $3,000 from us and he may have made some money selling his land in Canada."

The whole story of Peder Knutsen may have gone unnoticed here had it not been forwarded from Paris by another old-timer, George C. Sumner, to a colleague.

Mr. Sumner, a Yankee of distinguished lineage, sent forth by Harvard in those misty years before the Great War, has made his way as a wine exporter and broker in Paris since the end of the most recent World War, 1947 to be precise.

Appended to the clipping from the Paris *Trib* were a few remarks by Mr. Sumner that, it would seem, bear repeating.

"It is not hard to imagine the drab dullness of life for those whose working days are over and who are confined to the routine of a home and the same old conversation—if any—at meals.

"A few glasses of wine and the fellowship they incite can change the atmosphere of the dining room and make dinner something to look forward to.

"I believe there are some, perhaps many," Mr. Sumner goes on to say, "who would like to leave such an endowment for those who have had their day but still have some time. But before I make a circular of it, I would like to have your reaction and that of a few others of my friends."

Anyone who sees some merit in Mr. Sumner's proposal and who has any suggestions may reach him at 6 Rue Descombes, 75017 Paris. It would be nice to think that somewhere, if anything ever comes of Mr. Sumner's plan, someone now and then raises a glass to old Peder Knutsen. He lived alone with his Bible in North Dakota, but thanks to him, a handful of old people in a little town 5000 miles away from time to time can enjoy a moment of warmth and friendship over a glass of wine.